D0824441

CRIME, PUNISHMENT, and DETERRENCE

CRIME, PUNISHMENT, and DETERRENCE

Jack P. Gibbs
University of Arizona

ELSEVIER

New York/Oxford/Amsterdam

ELSEVIER SCIENTIFIC PUBLISHING COMPANY, INC.
52 Vanderbilt Avenue, New York, N.Y. 10017

ELSEVIER SCIENTIFIC PUBLISHING COMPANY
335 Jan Van Galenstraat, P. O. Box 211
Amsterdam, The Netherlands

© Elsevier Scientific Publishing Co., Inc., 1975

Library of Congress Cataloging in Publication Data

Gibbs, Jack P
  Crime, punishment, and deterrence.

  Includes indexes.
  1. Punishment. 2. Crime prevention. I. Title.
[HV8665.G47]   364.6   75–17662
ISBN O-444-99016-X

Manufactured in the United States of America

To the Kroenleins:
Adele, Ida, Irma, and *Katherine*

Contents

Preface

This book reflects the author's suspicion that many social scientists have dismissed the deterrence doctrine prematurely. The research findings commonly cited as evidence of the doctrine's invalidity are restricted largely to the relation between criminal homicide rates and the death penalty. Since virtually all of those investigations ignored the certainty of actual execution for capital crimes, the findings are questionable; and, in any case, they do not warrant a conclusion about all types of legal punishments and all types of crimes. No less important, the very idea of testing the deterrence doctrine is dubious without first restating the doctrine as a systematic theory. Such a restatement must encompass far more properties of punishment (e.g., the perceived certainty of suffering a penalty) than have been considered in past deterrence research. Still another complexity is that the deterrence doctrine suggests two distinct theories, one having to do with the impact of legal punishment on those who have suffered it (specific deterrence) and the other pertaining to the impact of legal punishment on the public at large (general deterrence). Once those theories are formulated, it may prove that both are valid, only one is valid, or neither is valid.

Unfortunately, this book does not extend to the formulation of a deterence theory, the reason being that it would be premature. Steps toward a theory are taken by identifying several properties of punishment; but the relevance of those properties is disputable, and that will remain the case until certain crucial questions are answered through exploratory research. That line of research would be more defensible than a continuation of purported tests of the deterrence doctrine, which are disputable if only because so many possibly relevant properties of punishment have been ignored.

Since the properties of punishment identified in this book are only possibly relevant, the attention devoted to alternative procedures for the numerical representation of the properties may strike the reader as tedious. However, if a testable theory of deterrence is to be realized, theorists must stipulate research procedures, and in so doing they should make a critical, informed choice among alternatives. Without exploratory work along the lines suggested throughout most of this book, those choices will have to be largely intuitive. Similarly, theorists must recognize that evidence of deterrence is necessarily inferential, and there are all manner of problems when it comes to interpreting statistical relations between properties of punishment and crime rates (even assuming that the rates are absolutely reliable). As one illustration, an inverse relation between the crime rate and the length of prison sentences served may reflect the incapacitation of potential offenders, not deterrence. In addition to incapacitation, several possible preventive consequences of punishment other than deterrence are identified. At present, those other consequences cannot be controlled systematically in testing propositions about deterrence; hence another strategy is proposed. That strategy is to formulate a "preventive" theory of legal punishment, and tests of that theory along with exploratory research may point the way to a methodology for bringing evidence to bear on propositions about deterrence.

The foregoing should make it abundantly clear that the present assessment of the deterrence doctrine is complicated and inconclusive. Those are damning characterizations, but it is an illusion of the first order to suppose that an assessment of the doctrine can be simple and incontrovertible. Yet one may rightly ask: Why devote more attention to an idea that is questionable in light of research findings and one that serves to justify inflicting pain on human beings? The most appropriate answer is that a considerable number of legislators and other officials persist in the belief that punishment does deter crime. It will not do to argue that they persist in the belief despite conclusive evidence to the contrary. Only an incorrigible ideologue would regard the evidence in question as conclusive, one way or the other. At this stage a demand for conclusive evidence is unrealistic, but more sophisticated research may show that the amount of deterrence realized through current penal practices is so negligible that those practices are not worth the cost, however reckoned. In any case, it is idle to assume that officials who shape penal policy will forget the deterrence doctrine or that social scientists have provided them with a defensible alternative. The sad truth is that other theories about crime are no less questionable than the deterrence doctrine, and they are virtually barren when it comes to policy implications.

Five persons contributed to this work. My wife, Sylvia, suffered through "another book" in reasonably good form. Martha Garcia and Karla Neuhauser typed their fingers to the bone. Of those who read the manuscript, Kirk Williams's eye for errors was awesome. Maynard Erickson, my friend and colleague, undertook a critical reading of an early draft and encouraged me in all manner of ways.

Jack P. Gibbs
December, 1974

CRIME,
PUNISHMENT,
and
DETERRENCE

One

Overview

This book is a continuous denial of immediate prospects for satisfactory answers to questions about crime, punishment, and deterrence. Critics may be sorely disappointed by such an inconclusive stance, but horrendous problems preclude a categorical rejection or acceptance of the deterrence doctrine.

After more than two decades (circa 1945–1965), there has been a renewal of interest in deterrence, especially among sociologists.[1] However, recent findings only suggest that some social scientists and correctional experts dismissed the deterrence doctrine prematurely. Those findings stem from a change in research strategy, wherein investigators turned from the traditional preoccupation with the statutory death penalty (see, e.g., Sellin, 1952) to an examination of the relation between *actual* legal punishments (imprisonment in particular) and crime rates. Despite the change, several evidential problems remain unsolved, and

[1]See Chambliss, 1966, 1967; Gibbs, 1968; Tittle, 1969; Gray and Martin, 1969; Chiricos and Waldo, 1970; Bean and Cushing, 1971; Bailey and Smith, 1972; Kobrin et al., 1972; Logan, 1972b; Erickson and Gibbs, 1973; and Bailey et al., 1974. British criminologists (e.g., Walker, 1971; Wilkins, 1969) have been less disposed than their American colleagues to reject the deterrence doctrine, but a few American criminologists (e.g., Tappan, 1960) never rejected it. As for other disciplines, the interest of philosophers in punishment has accelerated in recent decades (e.g., Acton, 1969; Bedau, 1967; Ezorsky, 1972a; Gerber and McAnany, 1972; Madden et al., 1968; Moberly, 1968; Murphy, 1973a; and Pincoffs, 1966), but that literature is largely concerned with the perennial debate over the justification of punishment rather than the empirical validity of the deterrence doctrine. Jurisprudents (e.g., Andenaes, 1952, 1956, 1968, 1970, 1971; Ross, 1970) have defended the deterrence doctrine more persistently than have sociologists. Finally, in recent years, economists have done extensive work on the deterrence question (see Rottenberg, 1973; Silver, 1974; and Tullock, 1974).

consequently recent findings will not silence critics of the deterrence doctrine. So the present work amounts to an appeal for a moratorium on conventional research. Until more attention is devoted to evidential problems, questions about deterrence cannot be answered satisfactorily (assuming they ever can).

Some of the evidential problems cannot be resolved by research alone. The deterrence doctrine is not a systematic theory, and for that reason (if no other) any purported test of it is debatable. So the ultimate goal is the statement of the deterrence doctrine as a systematic theory; but that statement is not an immediate prospect, and it will not somehow emerge of its own accord from research findings.[2] As the first step, someone must identify the *possibly* relevant variables, and that identification is in large part a conceptual problem.

As just suggested, the present work is oriented toward evidential problems and issues. Specific problems and issues are treated throughout, and this chapter introduces them in terms of four major topics: (1) definitions of deterrence, (2) the deterrence doctrine as a theory, (3) evidential problems, and (4) ideological issues and policy implications. The introduction is brief and grossly oversimplified, but it sets the scene for more detailed treatments in subsequent chapters.

Definitions of Deterrence

Several definitions of deterrence are examined in Chapter 2, and momentarily a brief commentary will suffice. *Deterrence* can be thought of as the omission of an act as a response to the perceived risk and fear of punishment for *contrary* behavior. Since the deterrence doctrine focuses on crime, the acts in question are violations of criminal laws[3] and the punishments are "legal." But the term "punishment" is ambiguous in that it may refer to *prescribed* punishments (e.g., statutory penalties) or to *actual* punishments.[4] Hence, subsequently, when the term is used

[2] A theory of deterrence should not be confused with philosophical theories of punishment (e.g., Grupp, 1971). They attempt to justify punishment, meaning that they are not scientific theories (see Hart, 1957:446). However, it would be a mistake to dismiss such philosophical works, for many issues and even questions about punishment cannot be resolved or answered by appealing to science (see Andenaes, 1970; Zimring and Hawkins, 1973:32). The same may be said of studies of punishment by jurisprudents (e.g., Packer, 1968; Hart, 1968).

[3] Henceforth, all references to crimes, violations of laws, criminals, incidence of crimes, perpetrators, etc., should be construed in the sense of "alleged." The point is that in the sphere of criminal justice there are few if any unquestioned facts, as opposed to allegations.

[4] The distinction is crucial in contemplating deterrence, but it is blurred in the writings of Beccaria and Bentham. If it is asserted that punishment deters crime, does the

without qualification, it refers to prescribed and/or actual punishments. The terminology does not speak to the meaning of punishment itself, which is an issue dealt with in a subsequent chapter.

Major Problems

The conceptual problem in treating the term "deterrence" is a typical one in the social sciences. It is not that social scientists have clearly different conceptions of deterrence; rather, they commonly write with an uncritical conception, even to the point of avoiding an explicit definition. The omission is especially true of social scientists in reporting research on deterrence. For example, Caldwell's investigation (1944) of the whipping of Delaware convicts is commonly cited as crucial evidence against the deterrence doctrine. Yet Caldwell did not define deterrence or relate his findings to a definition, and the same may be said of more recent research (e.g., Gibbs, 1968; Tittle, 1969; and Logan, 1972b).

Criticism of Caldwell and others may appear pedantic, the objection being that virtually everyone agrees in their conceptions of deterrence. That argument is disputable,[5] and in any case an explicit definition of deterrence is needed if only to appreciate evidential problems in assessing research findings. More generally, a thoughtful definition of deterrence promotes recognition that the term denotes an *inherently unobservable* phenomenon. Common sense to the contrary, we never *observe* someone omitting an act because of the perceived risk and fear of punishment. Observations in a particular instance may suggest that conclusion, but it would be an inference, hence debatable. The importance of that consideration in contemplating purported evidence of deterrence (or lack of it) cannot be exaggerated.

---

assertion refer to prescribed punishments, to actual punishments, or to both? Granted that there can be no actual punishments (at least in the legal sense) without prescribed punishments, the reverse is not true, and it would be premature to declare that only actual punishments deter. Surely prescribed punishments may represent a threat if known to members of the public. This consideration is only one of several that complicates attempts to state the deterrence doctrine as a systematic theory.

[5]Cooper (1973:164) defines "deterrence" as "any measure designed actively to impede, discourage, or restrain the way in which another might think or act." So conceived, imprisonment and fines are deterrents (by definition) if "designed actively" with those ends in mind. A similar objection extends to one of Zimring and Hawkins's many definitions (1973:7) of deterrence as "principally a matter of the declaration of some harm, loss, or pain that will follow noncompliance; in short, the central concept is that of threat." The definition restricts deterrence to declarations; but surely deterrence is both a declaration (or threat) *and also* a particular kind of response to the declaration. Legislators may issue declarations to no avail, that is, without realizing compliance.

Another related consideration has to do with *types* of deterrence. As argued in Chapter 2, a definition of deterrence should be extended to recognition of types of deterrence. Conventional terminology recognizes two types, *specific* (or individual) and *general,* but the adequacy of that distinction is questioned in Chapter 2.

Since there are distinct types of deterrence, it is not realistic to speak of *the* deterrence doctrine as though it were a unitary argument. Research findings that are commonly construed as evidence for or against the doctrine are actually evidence for or against a particular type of deterrence. Returning to Caldwell's study (1944), it is often cited as refuting the deterrence doctrine, but the findings bear on specific deterrence (the impact of actual punishment on those who have suffered it) and have no bearing on general deterrence (the impact of a threat of punishment on the public at large).

A Major Issue

The present concern with conceptualization is not pedantic, for conceptualizations and evidential problems are inseparable, especially in contemplating the deterrence doctrine. Since deterrence is inherently unobservable, consensus in assessments of purported evidence is precluded unless parties to the debate recognize that deterrence can be known only inferentially.

What has been said of the term "deterrence" applies to numerous terms in the social sciences, of which "causation" is only one. As one more instance, anyone who believes that "class conflict" can be seen or heard is simply naïve. But the identification of deterrence as one of many "inferential" terms in the social sciences does not resolve any problems, for social scientists have quite divergent ideas about those terms. Extreme empiricists seek to drive the devils from science, but their exorcisms have been ineffectual (Watson's "behaviorism" being a case in point); and their failure is hardly surprising, since inferential terms (e.g., "electron," "gene") are firmly entrenched in advanced sciences.

Operationalists in the social sciences tolerate inferential terms, but they demand that the terms be defined by reference to some particular measurement or experimental procedure. They do so without recognizing that an unobservable phenomenon can be "measured" only by reference to a theory (if at all). Stated another way, only in the context of a theory can one make a possibly defensible "epistemic assertion" (see Northrop, 1947), meaning an assertion that a particular unobservable phenomenon is associated (in some stipulated way) with a presumably observable, hence measurable, phenomenon. But a measure of the latter phenomenon (the observable) is not also a measure of the former (the unobservable), and the assertion of a relation between them is neither true by definition nor verifiable by itself. So an epistemic assertion is "theoretical" and testable only indirectly within the context of a particular theory. However, operationalists persist in the idea that the treatment of an inferential term is a measurement or experimental problem removed from theory; hence their preoccupation with techniques.

In another camp we find psychiatrists, interpretive sociologists, and humanists using inferential terms with abandon. They may or may not recognize that the terms designate immensurable phenomena; but they clearly do not link inferential terms with terms designating observable phenomena in such a way that testable predictions can be derived systematically. Without such derivations, the use of inferential terms is logomachy.

The previous observations may seem far removed from the deterrence question, but they introduce the central issue in contemplating evidential problems. In particular, "deterrence" cannot be defined so that the phenomenon denoted is subject to observation or measurement in any direct sense. It is inherently theoretical.

The Deterrence Doctrine as a Theory

Although social scientists use the label "theory" indiscriminately, even that license would not justify identifying the deterrence doctrine as a theory. The doctrine is a congery of vague ideas with no unifying factor other than their being legacies of two major figures in moral philosophy, Cesare Beccaria and Jeremy Bentham. It does not detract from either man to point out that their arguments do not amount to a systematic theory, and criticism of their work is softened by recognition that they (especially Bentham) came as close to a systematic theory as did Marx, Freud, Weber, Durkheim, Pareto, or even major contemporary theorists (e.g., Talcott Parsons), and they did so some 200 years ago. Indeed, they came closer to a systematic theory in that many of their ideas (Beccaria, 1963; Bentham, 1962) can be reduced to one fairly simple statement, identified here as generalization I: The rate for a particular type of crime varies inversely with the celerity, certainty, and severity of punishments of that type of crime.

The generalization is less vague than those commonly found in the social science literature, and it gives rise to a specific prediction about any two populations in the following form: If in population A the celerity, certainty, and severity of punishments of instances of a type of crime, C, are greater than in population B, then the rate for C is greater in B

than in *A*. Even though investigators are not likely to agree completely in choosing formulas and data to compute celerity, certainty, or severity, compared to most generalizations in the social sciences, the present one is much more amenable to tests. However, generalization I is not set forth as the definitive version of the deterrence doctrine; rather, it only serves to introduce some of the problems entailed in attempting to state the doctrine as a theory.

Any statement like generalization I distorts or oversimplifies the ideas of Beccaria and Bentham; but arguments along that line indicate the manner in which those ideas were stated. Like contemporary social scientists, Beccaria and Bentham set forth their theories discursively; hence their major empirical premises are buried in a sea of definitions, rhetoric, exhortations, anecdotes, and digressions. Even if those premises could be identified, it is difficult to see how testable generalizations (theorems) could be derived systematically from the premises. The assertion that the celerity, certainty, and severity of punishment *deters* crime is not directly testable. To repeat, the word "deters" does not denote an observable phenomenon, and any assertion that contains the word is by itself untestable.[6] Such an assertion is testable only when translated into the language of space-time relations or, more specifically, the statistical association between properties of punishment (e.g., certainty) and crime rates.

Generalization I is "incomplete," that is, it excludes several of Beccaria's or Bentham's ideas; but it is inconceivable that all of their ideas can be reduced to testable generalizations. Some of their ideas cannot be stated in a testable form even though their meaning is fairly clear, and others are so vague that they virtually defy interpretation. As one illustration, consider Beccaria's (1963:58) and Bentham's (1962:482) emphasis on the certainty of punishment. They apparently regarded certainty as more important than severity, but they did not express that emphasis in the form of a testable generalization.[7] Nor is their treatment

---

[6]In light of this problem and others subsequently described, Ezorsky's statement (1972:xi) about Bentham's views on deterrence is astonishing: "... this sort of view may be empirically confirmed, or refuted, by a factual investigation. ..."

[7]The relative importance of the two properties can be expressed as follows: The deterrent impact of the severity of a punishment is contingent on its certainty. But the deterrent impact of certainty may be contingent on severity. The problem cannot be resolved by turning to Beccaria or Bentham, even though several of Bentham's observations (e.g., 1962:520) suggest that the effects of certainty and severity are additive or, expressed another way, that the two are substitutable: "The less certain your punishments are, the more severe they must be; the more certain your punishments are, the more you may reduce their severity." As an oversimplified illustration of such "additivity," assume that both the severity and the certainty of punishment for robbery can be any value from 0 to 100. Then

of prescribed (statutory) punishments such that it reduces to a testable generalization. For that matter, in one instance after another it is not clear whether their statements refer to prescribed or actual punishments.

Then observe that generalization I makes no reference to the celerity, certainty, and severity of punishments as *perceived* by the public. Instead, the generalization treats those properties as somehow objectively given; but prescribed or "threatened" punishments (e.g., statutory penalties) do not deter individuals unless they perceive some risk. Critics will argue that Beccaria and Bentham recognized the importance of perception; that they did, but their treatment of perception is ambiguous. It is not clear whether perception of punishment is a *qualifying condition* in the way of an assumption *or* an empirical assertion, and the distinction is crucial. An assertion that public perception of punishment is "sufficiently accurate" for deterrence is one thing, but it is quite another merely to assume such perception. If accurate public perception is only a qualifying assumption, then an increase in the certainty, celerity, and/or severity of punishment would be followed by a decrease in that crime rate only to the extent that the citizenry is aware of the change. Even when the prescribed prison sentence for a type of crime is doubled, predictions about change in the crime rate would *not* follow from the deterrence doctrine without evidence that the qualifying assumption about public perception is met. Alternatively, if it is asserted that in all populations the members are sufficiently aware of the certainty, celerity, and severity of punishment, then the deterrence doctrine can be interpreted as predicting a relation between crime rates and properties of punishment without the prediction being conditional.

The safest strategy would be to treat accurate public perception of punishment as a qualifying assumption, but that strategy would make tests of a deterrence theory very difficult. In any case, when formulating a deterrence theory one must do more than merely make reference to public perception of punishment, and the problem is not just specification of sufficient accuracy of perception.

No one can perceive the severity of a punishment for a type of crime

---

suppose that in jurisdiction *A* the severity value is 20 and the certainty value is 80, while in jurisdiction *B* the two values are reversed (20 for certainty and 80 for severity). If the deterrent effects of certainty and severity are additive, then *(ceteris paribus)* the robbery rate would be approximately the same for the two jurisdictions. Whether they are additive remains debatable (Gibbs, 1968; Tittle, 1969; Gray and Martin, 1969; Bean and Cushing, 1971; Logan, 1972b; Antunes and Hunt, 1973; and Erickson and Gibbs, 1973), and the question should be considered further before attempting to formulate a deterrence theory.

without knowledge of the punishment, which is a largely cognitive consideration; but it does not follow that the severity of the punishment is somehow objectively given. To illustrate, given two jurisdictions in which the maximum statutory penalty for robbery is ten years imprisonment, residents of one jurisdiction may view such incarceration as far more severe than do residents of the other jurisdiction. As another illustration of the *evaluative* quality of perceived severity, contemplate this question: If the punishment for prostitution is a $2,000 fine in one jurisdiction but a jail sentence of 30 days in another jurisdiction, which of the two punishments is the more severe? Considering more exotic forms of reaction to deviance, among some tribes of New Guinea a suspected adultress faced the prospect of being raped by a gang of men in public (see Berndt, 1962). Is such a punishment more severe than, say, one year of imprisonment? Such questions indicate that judgments as to the severity of punishment are bound to be subjective and/or ethnocentric.

Unlike severity, there is a basis for an objective assessment of the certainty of punishments, meaning that an investigator can estimate the incidence of some type of crime in a particular population during a year and then compute the proportion of cases that result in the imposition of the prescribed punishment. However, no objective measure of certainty could provide an answer to two crucial theoretical questions. First, does the deterrence doctrine assume that the public perceives the certainty of punishment accurately? Second, what are the alternative assumptions? To illustrate, Gibbs (1968) estimated the certainty of imprisonment for criminal homicide as 77 percent in Utah but only 23 percent in South Carolina over 1959–1961. It is significant that South Carolina's official criminal homicide rate was some ten times greater than Utah's rate, but how did the residents of either state perceive the certainty of imprisonment? It taxes credulity to suppose that they would have stipulated the number in question (77 or 23) if asked to estimate certainty, and it will not do to argue that public perception need be only approximately accurate. What is "approximately," and do individuals consciously assess the certainty of punishment when contemplating a crime? More generally, what is the most plausible assumption about public perception?

Such questions indicate that Beccaria's and Bentham's works are incomplete; consequently, it is more realistic to speak of a deterrence doctrine rather than a deterrence theory. The point is not just that the doctrine must be restated to arrive at a testable generalization; additionally, it cannot be converted into a theory without assumptions. Those assumptions are not somehow implicit in Beccaria's and Bentham's writings, awaiting exegetical discovery. In formulating a deterrence theory, the theorist must choose among numerous alternative assumptions, some of which are not even suggested by Beccaria or Bentham. For that matter, it might be a mistake to accept their identification of the principal deterrence variables, that is, the celerity, certainty, and severity of punishment. Surely it is not clear why the celerity of punishment is important for general deterrence.[8] If someone reads an account of an execution, why would he or she be deterred more if the crime took place six weeks rather than one year previously?

Beccaria and Bentham used terms that are largely alien to contemporary social science, and even their conception of what punishment *ought to be* is no longer consistent with criminal justice in Anglo-American jurisdictions. Both wrote (though not consistently so) as though there should be *one* type of punishment for a particular type of crime, with its severity exceeding the pleasure or benefit that might be derived from the crime (Beccaria, 1963:43; Bentham, 1962:87–90). That "classical theory of justice" may be vulgar hedonism or uncritical rationalism, but it is outmoded in any case. In many contemporary jurisdictions, including the United States, there is an astonishing range of alternative legal reactions to the same type of crime (e.g., probation, a fine, imprisonment, or both a fine and imprisonment, with the length of the sentence, the terms of probation, and the amount of the fine left partially to the discretion of the judge or jury). So when one speaks of perceived severity or perceived certainty, which of the various alternative punishments are relevant? Do members of the public perceive them all? Is perception of the maximum sentence more important than perception of the minimum? Beccaria and Bentham did not speak to all of those questions, and there are many others that they left unanswered.

Subsequent Developments

It is not surprising that Beccaria and Bentham failed to formulate a systematic theory; but it is remarkable that social scientists, criminologists in particular, have devoted so little attention to restating the deterrence doctrine. Yet there is no particular mystery. Throughout this century the doctrine has been attacked by a multitude of diverse critics, some prompted by humanitarian considerations (especially with regard to the death penalty), others speaking as scientists, and still others advocating nonpunitive reactions to crime. With humanitarians supplying moral ammunition, scientists performing as merchants of facts (virtually all pertaining to the death penalty), and social engineers (e.g., psychia-

---

[8]Maynard Erickson has suggested that a long delay in the prosecution of crimes (especially "business" crimes) could deter such acts, in that the defendant dreads the delay itself.

trists, social workers) offering alternatives to traditional punishments, the deterrence doctrine fell into disrepute decades ago; and today those speaking for the doctrine are largely confined to legislative and law-enforcement circles.

Recently, several writers (e.g., Gibbs, 1968; Tittle and Logan, 1973; and Zimring and Hawkins, 1973) have argued that the deterrence doctrine was dismissed prematurely by social scientists. That argument has been questioned (see Osborne, 1968), but it is something more than the opinion of five writers.[9] Elaborate attacks on the deterrence doctrine by sociologists ceased in the 1950's (the last major salvo having been fired by Barnes and Teeters, 1959), but the ensuing silence only indicated that most social scientists no longer considered the deterrence doctrine as deserving attention. More compelling evidence is found in examining contemporary sociological theories on crime and deviance, none of which emphasizes deterrence (see Wilson's commentary, 1974), and that is particularly true of Merton's theory (1957) of anomie and deviance. As for Sutherland's theory of differential association (Sutherland and Cressey, 1970), the notion of deterrence can be subsumed under the rubric "definitions unfavorable to crime," but Sutherland rejected the deterrence doctrine nonetheless. Finally, as emphasized by Thorsell and Klemke (1972), the deterrence argument is contradicted by the idea of "secondary deviance" (Lemert, 1967); that is, legal reactions to crime lead to even more criminal acts by individuals who have been subjected to those reactions.

Of course, it may prove that the deterrence doctrine was rightly abandoned, but it is difficult to see how the narrow range of evidence warranted a categorical rejection of the doctrine.[10] Yet the real issue is not the narrow range of evidence; rather, it is the very idea of purporting to test the deterrence doctrine without first stating it as a systematic theory. Otherwise, *all* purported tests are inherently debatable. Taking just one consideration, it could be argued that punishments deter crime

[9]See, e.g., Andenaes, 1952, 1968; Ball, 1955: esp. 348; Biddle, 1969: esp. 354; Cohen, 1971; Hood and Sparks, 1970:172–173; Ross, 1970; Tittle and Logan, 1973; Walker, 1969: esp. 56; and Wilson, 1974.

[10]The literature suggests no relation between the death penalty and crime rates (see, e. g., Bedau, 1967; Doleschal, 1969; Dikijian, 1969; Royal Commission, 1953; Sellin, 1967a; and United Nations, 1968); but it is a narrow range of evidence against the deterrence doctrine. Virtually all research has considered only the statutory death penalty and not the certainty of its imposition. Another shortcoming of capital punishment research is that only homicide has been considered without restricting homicide rates to first-degree murder. In any case, it is ironic that so many arguments against the deterrence doctrine have appealed to findings on the death penalty. The originators of the doctrine (Beccaria, 1963:45; Bentham, 1962:441–450, 525–532) had reservations about capital punishment not just for humanitarian reasons but also because they questioned its deterrent efficacy.

only to the extent that the public perceives the punishments as celeritous, certain, and severe. If the deterrence doctrine is expressed that way, then the evidence offered against it is not compelling because *none* of the putative tests pertaining to *official crime rates* took perceptual considerations into account.

The foregoing is, of course, a justification of attempts to restate the deterrence doctrine as a theory, but some critics will regard any attempt as a lost cause.[11] They view the evidence as overwhelmingly contrary to the doctrine, and efforts to marshal supporting evidence (see Zimring and Hawkins, 1973; Tittle and Logan, 1973) will accomplish little. The point is that until the doctrine is stated as a systematic theory none of the purported evidence is crucial one way or the other.

Justification of attempts to formulate a deterrence theory is found not in research evidence but rather in what is little more than a general observation (Zimring and Hawkins, 1973:3): "There is the potent, ubiquitous, seemingly irrefutable thesis that attaching unpleasant consequences to behavior will reduce the tendency of people to engage in that behavior." But if that observation justifies the deterrence doctrine, there are equally irrefutable observations to the contrary, and they are not limited to vague statements about the "false" or "outmoded" psychology of Bentham. One need only point to inmates of prisons as "proof" that punishment does not deter crime: "Unfortunately, as is abundantly clear from anybody's crime statistics, there is no real deterrent known to man" (Cooper, 1973:172–173).

All of the contradictory general observations about deterrence can be reconciled by one empirical assertion: In some situations some individuals are deterred from some crimes by some punishments. The assertion is hardly informative, but it is difficult to imagine anyone dismissing it as patently false. Indeed, the assertion could not be falsified even if deterrence were directly observable. (Bedau, 1970:546, refers to such assertions as "platitudinously true.") The assertion is unfalsifiable because it does not stipulate the "conditions" in which punishment does deter, that is, kinds of situations, individuals, crimes, and punishments. But such stipulations will be realized only in a theory of deterrence, and that theory has yet to be formulated.

[11]As emphasized by Wilson (1974), a lack of concern with deterrence is obvious in the writings of criminologists on policy questions pertaining to the control of crime (e.g., Sellin, 1967d; the President's Commission, 1967). In numerous instances, "deterrence" is not listed in the index of criminology texts (e.g., Quinney, 1970a, 1970b), and a recent edited book on criminological controversies (Knudten, 1968) contains no papers on deterrence. Even books on punishment and corrections (e.g., Johnston et al., 1962) commonly exclude papers on the deterrence question. Finally, until recently only in the musty issues of sociology journals did authors defend the doctrine (e.g., MacDonald, 1910).

Evidential Problems

No deterrence theory can be formulated in such a way that tests of it would avoid evidential problems, and some of the problems may not be peculiar to particular theories. (There can be contending deterrence theories.) In any case, a consideration of those problems is needed to understand the debatable character of putative tests of the deterrence doctrine.

The Fundamental Problem

Consider an individual contemplating an act and assume that the individual (1) views the act as contrary to a law, (2) knows the prescribed punishment, (3) perceives the punishment as severe, and (4) estimates the actual imposition of the punishment as certain. If the individual commits the act, then the threat of punishment clearly did not deter him or her. However, even if the individual refrains, the omission could be attributed to (1) the dictates of personal conscience, (2) the individual's recognition of and respect for the social (extralegal) condemnation of the act, and/or (3) the fear of some extralegal consequence (e.g., stigma). So we have a paradox—regardless of what the individual does (commits or omits the act), it is not evidence of deterrence.

The paradox cannot be circumvented by comparing crime rates, not even if the populations differ sharply as to the character of punishment of the act. Thus, suppose that over some period the robbery rate was much greater in population *A* than in population *B*, even though the celerity, certainty, and severity of punishment for robbery was much greater in *A* than in *B*. The difference would indicate that punishment *does not* deter robbery; but suppose the difference was reversed (i.e., the *A* rate was much less than the *B* rate). That situation would not be incontrovertible evidence of deterrence because it could be argued that (1) the incidence of a criminal act in a population varies *inversely* with the social condemnation of the act; (2) the celerity, certainty, and severity of the punishment of a criminal act varies *directly* with the social condemnation of the cime; (3) hence a statistical relation between properties of punishment and crime rates only reflects the association of both with the social condemnation of crime. So what appears to be evidence for the deterrence doctrine could be dismissed by critics as spurious (even if the crime rates were absolutely reliable).

The foregoing observations may suggest that the cards are stacked against the deterrence doctrine, but its defenders also have evidential rationalizations. Reconsider the possibility of an individual committing a criminal act even though he or she perceives the punishment for it as likely, harsh, and swift. Such a case would not be regarded as conclusive negative evidence by the advocates of the deterrence doctrine, for they never argue that the threat of punishment deters *all* individuals in *all* situations from *all* types of crime (see Ball, 1955:349–350). For that matter, one can argue that a particular criminal act indicates only that the threat of punishment was not sufficiently certain and severe, an argument that Zimring and Hawkins (1973:4) rightly characterize as "irrefutable."

Then consider the first comparison of populations *A* and *B,* where the robbery rate in *A* was much greater than in *B* even though the punishment of the crime was much more celeritous, certain, and severe in *A.* Those differences would not be regarded by advocates of the deterrence doctrine as compelling negative evidence, especially if they were prepared to argue that certain extralegal conditions (e.g., unemployment) are conducive to robbery and that those conditions were much more prevalent in *A* than in *B.* In brief, advocates of the deterrence doctrine could argue that the rate would have been even greater in *A* had it not been for the celeritous, certain, and severe punishment of robbery. The advocates might be embarrassed by their inability to specify the relevant extralegal condition, but their argument is no less conjectural than the attribution of a low crime rate to some other extralegal condition (e.g., social condemnation).

All evidential debates reflect one consideration—deterrence is inherently unobservable and hence immensurable. Suppose it were otherwise, and again consider populations *A* and *B.* As in the second comparison, suppose that the celerity, certainty, and severity of punishment were much greater in *A* and that the robbery rate was far less in *A.* As already indicated, critics of the deterrence doctrine could attribute the difference to a greater social condemnation of robbery in *A.* But suppose an investigator had somehow measured the deterrence of robbery, with the measure expressing the relative frequency during the period with which individuals have contemplated but refrained from robbery because of a perceived risk of punishment. Then suppose that all parties to the debate accepted the measurement procedure and also its application to populations *A* and *B.* Finally, suppose that the measure of deterrence, *Dm,* was much greater for *A* than for *B.* Given that situation, critics of the deterrence doctrine would have to do more than appeal to the social condemnation of robbery. There could be no doubt that a large proportion of members of population *A* contemplated robbery but refrained from it out of fear of punishment, for that would be revealed by *Dm.* The deterrence argument would not be that all members of population *A* were deterred from robbery or even that any member was deterred at all times or in all situations. Indeed, most members of population A may never have contemplated robbery, and most of those who did contemplate it may have refrained because of social condemnation. Nonetheless, the Dm value would reveal the amount of the difference in the robbery rates of A and B that was due to deterrence.

To realize the full implication of the foregoing, suppose that we also have a measure of social condemnation, Sc, which expresses the frequency with which the A and B members have refrained from robbery because it is socially condemned. Assume that Sc was much greater for A than for B and that no one questioned the difference. As such, the lower robbery rate in A could not be attributed to deterrence alone. But advocates of the deterrence doctrine have never claimed that punishment accounts for all differences between crime rates, and in this particular situation *some* of the difference between the two rates would be attributed to deterrence and *some* to social condemnation.

Pushing hypotheticals still further, suppose the robbery rate was greater in A, despite much greater celerity, certainty, and severity of punishment in A. The evidence would appear clearly contrary to the deterrence doctrine; but again, advocates of the doctrine grant that the crime rate reflects extralegal conditions as well as deterrence. Thus, it could be that unemployment is somehow conducive to robbery, and it could be that the unemployment rate was much greater in A. But that situation would only reveal that punishment does not deter regardless of extralegal conditions, meaning that the Dm value for A could be greater than the Dm value for B even though the robbery rate was greater for A.

Suppose that populations A and B are equal in size (number of members) and that 300 members of A contemplated robbery an average of 10 times during a particular year. So there were 3,000 instances in which armed robbery was contemplated in population $A;$ and suppose that in 2,400 such instances the individual was deterred (i.e., he or she refrained out of fear of punishment). So Dm for jurisdiction A would be 0.80 (i.e., 2,400/3,000), with 600 cases of robbery. Then suppose that in population B 30 individuals contemplated armed robbery an average of 5 times, meaning that in 150 instances robbery was contemplated. Now suppose that in 15 instances the individual was deterred; hence Dm for population B would be 0.10 (i.e., 15/150), with 135 cases of robbery. Observe that the number of robberies would be 600 in A, but only 135 in $B;$ however, Dm would be 0.80 for A and 0.10 for B. The difference in the number of actual robberies stems from the greater frequency of contemplation of robbery in A, possibly because of the greater prevalence of some extralegal condition (e.g., unemployment) in A.

Of course, other possible factors have been ignored. It could be that robbery was contemplated less in B than in A because the act was more socially condemned in *B,* and some individuals may not have committed robbery (even if they contemplated it) for reasons unrelated to deterrence. But none of these possibilities would be revelant for the simple reason that the *Dm* values by themselves would be conclusive *direct* evidence that deterrence was more operative in *A* (where the celerity, certainty, and severity of punishment was greater than in *B*).

Note especially that the *Dm* values would be conclusive even though the population with the greater *Dm* value had the *higher* crime rate. Had the *Dm* value been reversed (0.10 for *A* and 0.80 for *B*), the armed robbery rate would have been even greater for *A* than for *B*. Here we see that a difference between two crime rates is not and cannot be conclusive evidence for or against the deterrence doctrine, and the evidential problems created by that recognition are horrendous.

The foregoing does not make the deterrence doctrine unfalsifiable, nor does it reduce the doctrine to the uninformative assertion that *some* individuals refrain from *some* criminal acts in *some* situations because they fear *some* legal punishment. Note again that in the last illustration population *A* had a much greater *Dm* value than did population *B,* and the celerity, certainty, and severity of punishment for robbery was much greater in *A* than in *B*. If the *Dm* values were reversed (0.10 for *A* and 0.80 for *B*), it *would be* compelling evidence against conventional versions of the deterrence doctrine. If there is a deterrence axiom, it is something like this: The greater the celerity, certainty, and severity of punishment for a type of crime, the more are individuals deterred from that type of crime. Direct tests of the axiom would require a direct measure of deterrence, *Dm,* and such a measure would virtually eliminate major evidential problems.

While evidence can be brought to bear on the deterrence axiom though inferences, it is an illusion to suppose that deterrence can be measured directly. Again, we do not observe others refraining from a criminal act because of fear of punishment; and it would be naive to base a purported measure of deterrence on reasons given by individuals for refraining from criminal acts (not to mention practical problems entailed in attempting to gather such data).

Once it is recognized that deterrence can be known only inferentially, then the premises of a deterrence theory are limited to empirical assertions in three forms: $Lp \longleftrightarrow Pp \longleftrightarrow De \succ\!\!\!-\!\!\!\prec Cr$, where *Lp* is some property of punishments (certainty, celerity, or severity), *Pp* is the perception of those properties by individuals, *De* is deterrence, *Cr* is some type of criminal act (or some type of crime rate if the assertions pertain to populations), the symbol "$\longleftrightarrow$" denotes a direct relation, and the symbol "$\succ\!\!\!-\!\!\!\prec$" denotes an inverse relation.

The forms are simplified in that there are no qualifying conditions, such as "if X is absent," "if X is present," "to the degree X is prevalent," or "to the degree X is a constant." Whatever X may be, any one of these qualifications would indicate that some of the asserted relations would hold only in a particular kind of condition.

Of the three forms of assertions, only $Lp \longleftrightarrow Pp$ can be considered as potentially testable in any direct sense.[12] Assertions of the second and third forms, $Pp \longleftrightarrow De$ and $De \gtrdot\!\!\!\!\lessdot Cr$, are forever untestable in any direct sense, since De is not subject to measurement. Nonetheless, given the initial series of three assertions, one can derive two additional assertions, $Lp \gtrdot\!\!\!\!\lessdot Cr$ and $Pp \gtrdot\!\!\!\!\lessdot Cr$, both of which are testable.[13] So a theory about deterrence could comprise three premises, one testable assertion and two derived testable assertions (theorems). Tests of the derived assertions could bring evidence to bear on the theory; and the theory would be a success only to the extent that tests show (1) an inverse relation between Lp values and Cr values and (2) an inverse relation between Pp values and Cr values, with both relations holding for the same type of crime among jurisdictions (e.g., states) and among types of crime in the same jurisdiction (e.g., a particular state).

The foregoing indicates in a general way the form of a testable deterrence theory; but the strategy will have critics. Some will object that such a theory does not assert causal relations, and still others will demand that the tests reveal causation. In reply to that anticipated criticism, causation cannot be demonstrated. As for the idea that causation can be inferred, it ignores ancient and seemingly irresolvable disagreements among scien-

---

[12]Even that assertion would not be testable if the relational or connective symbol ($\longleftrightarrow$) denoted causation. Rather, it denotes a space-time relation that can be described in mathematical or statistical terms, for only assertions of that form are testable. The idea that causation can be demonstrated or justifiably inferred from measures of statistical association (e.g., correlation coefficients, path coefficients) is indefensible unless one abandons conventional conceptions of causation or leaves the conception of causation unspecified. Even if only the premises of a deterrence theory incorporate causal terms, the derived theorems would not be testable unless stated in the language of space-time relations, and the translation of causal terms into that language poses seemingly insoluble problems. For a debate of the issues, see Gibbs, 1972a; Costner and Blalock, 1972; and Gibbs, 1972b.

[13]Unless the relevant properties of punishment (e.g., certainty, celerity) and the method of measurement are specified, the first derived assertion would not be testable. The second derived assertion would not be testable unless the *theorist's instructions* extend to the measurement of perception of punishment, including procedures for gathering requisite data. Tests of either assertion would be further precluded without an identification of the kinds of populations that are to be compared and an indication of the space-time quality of the comparison (e.g., whether or not the asserted relation holds between change in Lp values and change in Pp values; and, if so, the duration of the time lag between the changes). Without such stipulations, tests of the assertion could hardly be other than idiosyncratic; and it is naive to presume that Beccaria, Bentham, or anyone since them has formulated those stipulations.

tists and philosophers as to appropriate evidential criteria (i.e., rules of inference). The issues have been debated for centuries, and it is surprising that some social scientists, sociologists in particular, avoid those issues as though they will go away if ignored.[14] To the contrary, rules of causal inference are likely to be (1) vague, (2) arbitrary, (3) incomplete, (4) divorced from conventional conceptions of causation, and/or (5) alien to the conditions of work in criminology.

Any rule as to causal inferences must pertain to the space-time relation between variables (the postulated causes and effects), as expressed by some conventional measure of statistical association; but in criminological research those relations are never truly close, let alone constantly so. Accordingly, some possible rules of causal inferences are simply alien to the conditions of work in criminology. One can argue that space-time relations need not be uniformly close to justify a causal inference, but any criterion as to "how close" is certain to be arbitrary. As for the idea that "causal models" are somehow rules of inference, those models are causal only in a nominal sense. They do not reveal the temporal quality of the relation between variables, but conventional conceptions of causation emphasize that the cause precedes the effect in time.[15] Of course, one can reject the idea of a necessary temporal sequence in a causal relation; but atemporal rules of causal inference will not be accepted by many philosophers and scientists. So it is folly to suppose that one can demonstrate that certain, celeritous, and severe punishments cause low crime rates or even that we can realize consensus in causal inferences about the relation, as there is not and seemingly cannot be agreement as to exactly what kind of research evidence would refute a causal assertion.

Objections to the proposed form of a deterrence theory are not limited to the question of causation. Evidence can be brought to bear on

[14] For the latest round of debate and references to key items in the literature, see Gibbs, 1972a; Costner and Blalock, 1972; and Gibbs, 1972b.

[15] Advocates of causal models assume that causation can be inferred from synchronic (cross-sectional) statistical relations, that is, where the values of the variables are for the same point in time. As such, the statistical relations do not refer to *change* in values (a crucial element in conventional conceptions of causation), let alone to a time lag between changes. The statistical relation between changes in values (with or without a time lag) can be revealed only by diachronic (longitudinal) correlations. Those correlations are consistent with conventional conceptions of causation; but advocates of causal modeling persist in the belief that causation can be inferred from synchronic relations, and in so doing they ignore a crucial question: What is the appropriate conclusion when the synchronic correlation between variables and the diachronic correlation between the same variables are quite different? It is pointless to argue that a particular causal model must "fit" all kinds of statistical relations among variables (i.e., synchronic and diachronic), as that argument presumes that all kinds of statistical relations are equally indicative of causation.

such a theory only by tests of derived assertions, but those tests never provide conclusive evidence. Suppose that both Lp values and Pp values do vary inversely with Cr values, as predicted. Could such a statistical relation reflect something other than deterrence? It could; and the possibilities are seemingly infinite. Hence, when critics of logicodeductive theory construction demand a demonstration of a unique derivation (a demonstration that the relation in question can be derived from only one set of premises), they are demanding the impossible.

Rather than attempt to invoke causal criteria or demand unique derivations, an assessment of a deterrence theory (or any theory for that matter) should consider only one question: How much *order* in the world of events does the theory *create* or *identify*? To illustrate, suppose a theory asserts that the certainty of executions in a population varies inversely with the capital crime rate in that population. Now suppose it is found that one can make fairly accurate predictions about the capital crime rate in a population from knowledge of actual executions in that population. What would be gained by dismissing the theory because of pious opinions about causation or unique derivations? After all, the theory has created some order in the world of events. Indeed, recognized or not, the most defensible basis for questioning the deterrence doctrine as applied to the statutory death penalty is that it apparently creates no order, meaning that one cannot derive even fairly accurate predictions about crime rates from knowledge of statutory penalties (see especially Schuessler, 1952; Sellin, 1967b, 1967c; and Vold, 1952).

The present argument is simply to make *predictive power* the criterion for assessing deterrence theories. That criterion avoids the seemingly insoluble problems and sterile debates pertaining to causation and unique derivations; but it does not require uniformly correct predictions. Each deterrence theory can be judged by its predictive power relative to that of contending theories.

Extralegal Conditions

All theorists are likely to assume that differences in crime rates reflect not only differential levels of deterrence but also "extralegal conditions," meaning conditions that inhibit or generate crime in a manner independent of punishments. If so, then the predictive accuracy of a deterrence theory that ignores extralegal conditions could be negligible. Predictive accuracy might be enhanced by qualifying the theory (i.e., limiting tests of it to some specified condition). That strategy is preferable to invoking *ceteris paribus*, meaning that a relation between properties of punishment and crime rates holds if the populations being compared do not differ otherwise. The *ceteris paribus* qualification is naive and unrealistic, naive because it suggests that "everything" is relevant, and unrealistic because it is alien to conditions of work in criminology. Since criminology is largely observational rather than experimental, it is seldom possible to select the members of populations randomly and hence justify the assumption of "no differences" among those populations, let alone conduct genuine experiments. Consequently, invoking the *ceteris paribus* qualification only results in an untestable theory.

In attempting to qualify a deterrence theory, extralegal conditions are the foremost problem; but qualification of the premises may be the most immediate concern. For example, the theorist may be unwilling to assume a close relation between "objective" properties of punishment and public perception of those properties. If so, the first premise in the deterrence sequence would be qualified so that one of the derived assertions would take this form: to the extent that $Lp \longleftrightarrow Pp$, then $Lp \succ\!\!\!\!-\!\!\!-\!\!\prec Cr$. That is, to the extent that there is a close relation between Lp values and Pp values, then there will be a close inverse relation between Lp and Cr values.

Defensible qualifications pertaining to extralegal conditions are more difficult, for very little is known about the relation between specific kinds of extralegal conditions and crime rates. Nonetheless, two classes of extralegal conditions, the *inhibitory* and the *generative*, should be recognized. An inhibitory extralegal condition is any condition apart from laws or their enforcement that prevents criminal acts, while a generative extralegal condition contributes to criminality. The distinction is purely logical; it does not give rise to any testable generalizations.[16] Nonetheless, the distinction has heuristic value in that it enables one to classify possibly relevant variables.

Theories on the extralegal etiology (whether inhibitory or generative) of crime bear on the evidential problem in deterrence research. If there is an *inverse* relation between, say, the certainty of imprisonment and the crime rate, it can be attributed to a *postulated direct* relation between (1) some extralegal condition (e.g., social condemnation of crime) that inhibits criminal acts and (2) the certainty of imprisonment. Conversely, if there is no inverse relation, that can be attributed (by defenders of the deterrence doctrine) to differences among the populations in regard to extralegal conditions conducive to crime. Such attempts to "ex-

---

[16]At this time, no particular generative or inhibitory extralegal condition can be justifiably identified. However, if theories and research findings on crime and delinquency suggest anything, it is that some extralegal conditions generate or inhibit crimes (see e.g., Bonger, 1916; Clinard and Quinney, 1973; Cloward and Ohlin, 1960; Eysench, 1964; Merton, 1957; Radzinowicz and Wolfgang, 1971I; Sutherland and Cressey, 1970; and Walker, 1968).

plain away" findings are dubious unless based on evidence that some particular extralegal condition is related both to properties of punishment and to crime rates. Given such evidence, it might be possible to examine the relation between properties of punishment and crime rates among populations while controlling for the extralegal condition in question.

Turning to the inhibitory extralegal conditions, one idea is firmly entrenched in the folklore of sociology—a type of criminal or deviant act is rare in populations where that act is socially condemned.[17] That idea is consistent with two theories on crime or deviance in general. Social condemnation is a class of definitions unfavorable to crime, a key notion in Sutherland's theory (Sutherland and Cressey, 1970); and it enters into LaPiere's assertion (1954) that conformity is promoted primarily by "regard for status."

All theories that emphasize the social condemnation of criminality are defective in at least one respect—they are stated so vaguely that they preclude systematic tests. Accordingly, they do not provide a basis for identifying and subsequently controlling specific inhibitory variables in tests of deterrence theories.

Turning now to the generative notion, several theorists have asserted that one extralegal condition or another is conducive to crime. One such assertion is that particular kinds of economic conditions (e.g., unemployment) are causal factors in the genesis of some criminal acts (e.g., robbery, theft). That assertion is articulated in a theory of criminality commonly identified as "Marxist" (see Bonger, 1916). However, that identification does not extend to Merton's theory of anomie (1957), even though it is in a sense consistent with but more inclusive than economic causation. The general idea is that a *disjunction* between legal means and culturally approved goals is conducive to crime. To illustrate briefly, such factors as unemployment and low income deprive individuals of legal means to culturally approved goals (including material goods), and some types of crimes (robbery) are illegal means to those goals.

---

[17]The "social condemnation" thesis can be stated in various ways. Thus, Toby indirectly questions the deterrence doctrine by arguing that the "socialization process keeps most people law abiding, not the police" (1964:334) and that individuals may refrain from crimes because they have "introjected the moral norms of their society" (1964:333). All such observations tacitly invoke something akin to the social condemnation of crime. However, individuals may refrain from a crime either because they personally condemn it (i.e., as a matter of conscience) or because they recognize social condemnation and fear extralegal sanctions. The evaluation of illegal types of behavior (i.e., approval or disapproval) by those who engage in them is still, especially in the case of juvenile delinquency, a matter of dispute (see Hindelang, 1974).

Theories that deal with the generative conditions of crime are clearly relevant in contemplating the deterrence doctrine, but they cannot be utilized in tests of it, and the reason is somewhat different than that given in the case of inhibitory theories. Certain generalizations concerning economic conditions and criminality have been tested, but the findings are far from impressive (see Vold, 1958:159–182). So the inclusion of economic variables (e.g., the unemployment rate) in deterrence research is a questionable way to control for generative conditions.[18] As for other theories (e.g., Merton's), they defy systematic tests, and hence there is no basis for utilizing them in tests of deterrence assertions.

To summarize, no theory about the inhibitory or generative conditions of criminality can be utilized (justifiably) in tests of deterrence generalizations, especially since the generalizations are likely to be restricted to particular types of crimes. There is no basis for assuming that punishment deters all types of crimes even approximately to the same extent (see Ball, 1955; Chambliss, 1967), and that would be the case even if one type of punishment applied to all crimes with equal celerity, certainty, and severity. Moreover, what is an inhibitory or generative condition for one type of crime may not be so for others; hence, an etiological theory about each type of crime is needed for deterrence research. Such "special" theories could lead to a general theory of criminality; but the latter is not essential for deterrence research. Given *only one* defensible special theory (e.g., the extralegal inhibitory and generative conditions of robbery), investigators could focus on that type of crime and attempt to control for the extralegal conditions identified by the theory in tests of a deterrence generalization. But social scientists have been preoccupied with formulating a general theory of criminality, and there are no defensible special theories. So we reach a painful conclusion—whatever evidential problems are created by inhibitory and generative conditions, they currently defy solution.

Other Preventive Consequences of Legal Punishments

Arguments against the deterrence doctrine commonly extend to a non sequitur: Since punishment does not deter crime, it should be abolished. Even if punishments do not deter crime at all, there are (as shown

---

[18]The conclusion is not that economic factors play no role in the etiology of crime. Their relevance remains a viable question, and investigators (e.g., Fleisher, 1966) occasionally report findings that justify further consideration of economic factors. So the only point is that currently there are no "accepted" theories that would justify controlling for particular economic variables in conducting tests of a deterrence theory.

in Chapter 3) at least nine ways that punishment could conceivably prevent crimes in a manner independent of deterrence *or* rehabilitation.

Only one of the nine possibilities is considered briefly for illustrative purposes. Imagine a metropolitan area in which a few individuals have accounted for virtually all robberies during the preceding year. Should the police intensify their investigation of robberies and prosecute relentlessly, then a large proportion of the offenders might be incarcerated. One likely consequence would be a sharp drop in the robbery rate, but the decline would have nothing to do with deterrence. The opportunities for robbery are diminished in prison, but in this case the diminishment of opportunities would have to do with *incapacitation,* not deterrence.

Incapacitation is commonly ignored even by those who seek to promote "law and order" through harsh punishments. Thus, advocates of the death penalty persistently invoke the deterrence doctrine, but the only unquestioned consequence of the death penalty is incapacitation. However, for present purposes, the importance of incapacitation is that it creates still another evidential problem in deterrence research. Suppose that a fairly close inverse relation holds among populations between (1) the certainty of imprisonment for robbery and (2) the robbery rate. Suppose further that the populations differ *only* in regard to those two variables. Since all extralegal etiological conditions would be "constant," the relation between the certainty of imprisonment and the crime rate might appear to be conclusive evidence in support of the deterrence doctrine. But the relation could reflect incapacitation, not deterrence. This one illustration should be a sobering consideration for those who think that conclusive evidence can be brought to bear on the deterrence doctrine; it is an illusion of the first order.

Value Judgments and Political Issues

The positions taken in debates over the deterrence doctrine commonly reflect not a concern with its empirical validity but rather value judgments pertaining to punishment itself.[19] The value judgments are

[19]The contrasts in value judgments have become intense in Anglo-American countries during recent years (e.g., Cohen, 1970; Miller, 1972, Miller, 1973; Murphy, 1973b; and Sington and Playfair, 1965), perhaps in part because of alleged evidence of rising crime rates. That alleged evidence has made crime a major policy issue at the national level (Harris, 1969). Critics of the American criminal justice system abound (e.g., Frankel, 1972; Menninger, 1966; and Szasz, 1963, 1965), and they are divided into three rather distinct camps: (1) those who consider criminal justice as excessively lenient, (2) those who condemn it as punitive, and (3) those who see it as a political weapon to control dissidents

hardly surprising; indeed, insofar as the citizenry participate in decisions about penal law, they can scarcely participate without making one of two value judgments: (1) criminal acts should be punished or (2) they should not be punished.[20] That dichotomy oversimplifies, since one may approve of punishment but not all kinds (the death penalty in particular). In any case, the variety of rationalizations of either value judgment is seemingly infinite. Some social critics with a theological bent see punishment as the instrument of a vengeful deity, while others think of punishment (especially the death penalty) as blasphemous preemption of divine will. Divergent opinions abound even more among secularists, with some joining Kant and Hegel in arguing that the punishment of crime is a moral duty or at least ethically justifiable (see especially Armstrong, 1971; Lewis, 1971; Mabbott, 1972; and McTaggart, 1972), and others condemning it as ethically indefensible (see Honderich, 1969; Playfair and Sington, 1957; and Weihofen, 1956). In the way of further contrasts, punishment has been described as serving an important social function apart from deterrence (see Durkheim, 1949), while for others it is dysfunctional, if not pathological (see Menninger, 1966).

Hypocrisy is not likely to be a question in debates over penal policy when a protagonist either (1) opposes punishment regardless of the deterrence presumably realized or (2) advocates punishment for the sake of retribution alone. However, a party to the debate may endorse punishment but only *insofar as it deters crime,* meaning that a value judgment at least appears to be contingent on scientific evidence. When that argument is made, hypocrisy does become an issue, and the very notion of scientific evidence becomes disputable. No scientific finding necessarily (i.e., logically) gives rise to a moral conclusion or value judgment, and

---

and the exploited (Balbus, 1973; Lefcourt, 1971). While deterrence is one rationale for criminal sanctions in virtually all legal systems (Morris, 1966:631; Zimring and Hawkins, 1971), it distorts the situation to say, without qualification, that the "treatment of criminal offenders in the United States is based on the concept of punishment" (Brooker, 1972:469). Surely some programs in criminal corrections are not "based" on the concept of punishment. There are "benign" programs in punitive settings and judges with enormous discretion (D'Esposito, 1969:182) but no guidelines to follow (Frankel, 1972; Wootton, 1963). Actually, commentators often fail to recognize the criminal justice system for what it is—a mishmash, complete with conflicting goals and even conflicting means to the same goal. So the miracle is that the system functions at all.

[20]It is pointless for critics of the criminal justice system, such as Menninger (1966:202), to condemn punishments but not "penalties," as though the two can be distinguished. It is no less pointless for Menninger (1966:204) to assume that his opposition to punishment for crime is not a value judgment (or "sentimental conviction," as he puts it) but rather "a logical conclusion drawn from scientific experience." For further commentary on Menninger's position, see Murphy, 1973c:199.

the compunction to bridge the gap readily leads to "personalized" evidential criteria. Thus, one may believe that crimes should be punished for the sake of vengeance alone but conceal that belief by arguing that punishment deters crime and dismiss all manner of research findings as irrelevant or insufficient. At the other extreme, if one views punishment as intrinsically wrong, that value judgment can be covertly defended by invoking rigorous criteria for positive evidence of deterrence.

Still another consideration is that parties to the debate over deterrence commonly have a very broad conception of relevant evidence. Some parties create the impression that systematic research is not needed to assess the deterrence doctrine; rather, they apparently presume that the empirical validity of the doctrine can be judged by observations on human nature. Thus, there are critics who question the deterrence doctrine by arguing that it rests on the unrealistic assumption that human beings have a "free will" and make a rational choice in contemplating a criminal act (e.g., Schuessler, 1952:55). But the assumption is denied by the argument (van den Haag, 1969) that the deterrence doctrine is entirely consistent with a deterministic conception of human behavior.[21] However, the characterization of the deterrence doctrine as deterministic makes it anathema to those who consider a mechanistic interpretation of human behavior as incorrect and an affront to the dignity of man.

No amount of research evidence is likely to resolve the debate over deterrence in the context of penal policy. Those who oppose punishment in principle will devise a rationale for dismissing what others take to be evidence of deterrence, and those who favor punishment will devise a rationale for dismissing what others take to be negative evidence. In brief, both parties fail to divorce evidential criteria from their value judgments.

The Political Issue

Some of the rationalizations for favoring or opposing punishment may appear exotic, but no one should be surprised that the subject of punishment, including the deterrence question, has political overtones (to put it mildly). After all, criminal law is coercive, and no program for the rehabilitation or "treatment" of criminals (Menninger, 1966) will ever make it otherwise. Indeed, it is dangerous to suppose that criminal law can be benevolent. Legal punishment is an instrument of the State

---

[21]The more general point is, of course, that the bearing of the determinism-indeterminism debate on the deterrence question is most debatable (for elaboration, see Andenaes, 1956).

and hence necessarily political. Putting the matter another way, the coercive quality of criminal law alone makes it a central consideration in political philosophy (Murphy, 1973a:3), which is to say that the subject is inherently controversial. One consequence is that the deterrence doctrine and even deterrence research are political issues (see Zimring and Hawkins, 1973:62). To be sure, there is a purely scientific question: How much order in the world of events is created by any particular restatement of the deterrence doctrine as a systematic theory? But not even that question can escape the controversial because (1) deterrence is supposedly a function of punishment, (2) punishment is an instrument of the State, and (3) the State purportedly serves the interests of some classes or groups more than others. That line of argumentation leads some critics to oppose, openly or tacitly, any research on the deterrence question. They see such research as providing a service or tool for members of the "establishment," that is, the research will enable the oppressors to control the oppressed more effectively.[22]

That argument is not refuted by pointing out that the findings of deterrence research are there for all to use, as laborers are not known for reading scientific journals. True, wittingly or not, terrorists subscribe to the deterrence doctrine, hence it may appear that they can use the knowledge just as readily as can the establishment. But the punishments employed by the State and the procedures for imposing them are quite different from measures commonly employed by terrorists. Nor will it do to reply that research may lead to convincing evidence against the deterrence doctrine, and thereby further adoption of less punitive penal policies. If they are not dull-witted, legislators recognize that deterrence is only one possible consequence of punishment, and from their perspective the other possible consequences may be even more important. For that matter, research on the deterrence doctrine might generate knowledge that facilitates "control" of crime and, subsequently, human behavior in general.

In replying to those who would politicize science by proscribing certain lines of research, one may invoke the familiar argument of "knowledge for the sake of knowledge." Still another argument is that those who would politicize science scarcely have "cornered the market" on right-

---

[22]Tapp's observation (1971:2) is relevant: "To many liberal psychologists the study of normal behavior in a legal setting suggests a sellout. Many fear that their findings may be used by the 'enemy,' i.e., the purveyors of an ideology of repression rather than an ideology of expression." Walker (1969:56) is even more direct: "Deterrence has become a dirty word in penological discussion." Finally, contemplate Quinney's statement (1972:317): "Theories of deviance—sometimes enhanced by research—serve a single purpose: they justify the existing order."

eousness. However, neither argument speaks to the most immediate question. If conventional scientific activity provides a service for the establishment, what is the alternative short of doing absolutely nothing? There appears to be only one answer—conduct research with a view to exposing the powers and privileges of the establishment. But one must surely wonder why journalists and popular writers cannot do a more effective job in the way of an expose, especially since they reach a wider audience and need not pretend to scientific objectivity. In any case, those who would politicize science evidently assume that an establishment cannot bear scrutiny. The assumption is curious, for it suggests that public opinion can sway the establishment, which supposedly controls public opinion and/or rules by coercion. In any case, the strategy of so-called radicals of the left is scarcely distinguishable from that of reformers in the past, and for that reason alone one must surely wonder if their goals are fundamentally different.

While scientific work on the deterrence issue is not necessarily indicative of any particular ideology, it is most unlikely that the work is ever entirely divorced from larger philosophical or sociological questions. That is not the case for the present work, as it reflects the author's belief that coercion is the ultimate basis of social control in all societies. The belief does not extend to a declaration that all societies are equally coercive or that all questions about coercion reduce to deterrence. But *social* coercion cannot be studied as a simple, unitary phenomenon; hence a focus on deterrence is merely one way of analyzing the role of coercion in human societies. Of course, individuals with quite different ideological orientations may all agree that coercion is crucial in social control; but what is commonly identified as establishmentarian sociology (functionalism in particular) does not emphasize coercion, and no elite in any contemporary capitalist society is likely to argue that the existing social order rests on coercion.

Policy Implications

Whereas those who would politicize science denounce deterrence research because it could further governmental control, others advocate it for precisely that reason. But the research would have policy implications only insofar as officials are concerned exclusively with deterrence. Even overwhelming evidence of the inefficacy of conventional punishments as deterrents might not lead to any modification of criminal laws or their enforcement, but that outcome would not reveal that officials are dumb or vindictive. Again, deterrence is only one possible preventive consequence of punishment, and officials are naive insofar as they are unaware of those other possibilities.

Nonetheless, the notion of deterrence is invoked to justify harsh penal sanctions; but insofar as penal policies are based on the deterrence doctrine, they are nothing more than articles of faith. Surely the policies are not based on "obvious" evidence, let alone on systematic research. As for the argument that some punishments deter some individuals from some crimes in some situations, it is hardly a basis for policy decisions, especially since any estimate as to how many would be sheer conjecture.

In light of the foregoing, deterrence research may appear essential for rational penal policies, but that view ignores ideological issues and the possibility that officials will ignore research findings that are contrary to the deterrence doctrine. In any case, there is no immediate prospect for the kinds of research findings needed to modify criminal law and its enforcement (as opposed to vague criticisms or justifications of existing policies). The problem is not simply that of applying theories and research findings, which involves the perennial problem of causation,[23] but also that of answering the difficult question that *must* be answered before criminal laws can be modified rationally. The question is not how does deterrence "work" or even how much does a *particular* punishment deter crime. For policy purposes, the question must take this form: How much more does punishment X deter crime Y than does punishment Z? To illustrate, debates over the death penalty have created the impression that the choice is between executions or "nothing."[24] But that was never the choice unless one proposes to decriminalize first-degree murder. The central question always has been: How much does the death penalty deter an individual from committing first-degree murder relative to imprisonment? That is a difficult question because a defensible answer would require a kind of research design that is alien to contemporary social sciences. If there were two jurisdictions (e.g., states) that differed only in that the death penalty applies in one but imprison-

[23]Any attempt to use or apply a theory is a test of it, and theories may be used even though not stated in a causal language. To illustrate, suppose a theory asserts that an inverse relation holds *over time* between the certainty of punishment and the crime rate. Presuming that officials can increase the certainty of punishment, they can both test and apply the theory simultaneously, for according to the theory, an increase in certainty should be followed or accompanied by an absolute decrease in the crime rate or a decline in the amount of increase. Stating the matter more generally, equating scientific theories and the use of a causal language ignores the argument of Toulmin (1960) and others that a causal language is alien to theory construction in a mature science.

[24]The distinction in question is crucial but commonly ignored in assessments of the deterrence doctrine. Zimring and Hawkins (1973:14) are notable exceptions.

ment in the other, then there would be some basis for answering the question. Such jurisdictions do not exist.

Even if one could precisely describe the deterrent efficacy of some punishment, the next question would become: Why is it not more efficacious? That question could lead to consideration of the relative importance of the celerity, certainty, and severity of punishment; but a precise estimate of their relative importance is at present simply not feasible.

To summarize, even if policy implications justify research on the deterrence question, there is no immediate prospect for the kind of findings needed by policy makers. At best, research can provide only a basis for a general assessment of existing penal policies.

Two

Deterrence,
Types of Deterrence,
and Crime Rates

Although deterrence theories may differ as to the properties of punishment emphasized, all of them will include assertions about crime rates and at least one type of deterrence. Even theories pertaining to specific deterrence will make reference to differences among *categories* of individuals (e.g., those imprisoned and those fined) as to some kind of crime rate. So, in addition to properties of punishment (treated in Chapter 4), there are three central notions—deterrence, types of deterrence, and crime rates.

Some Definitions of Deterrence

No possible consequence of punishment is more difficult to define than "deterrence." Consider Ball's statement (1955:347): "Deterrence is usually defined as the preventive effect which actual or threatened punishment of offenders has upon potential offenders." As Bedau (1970:540) has correctly argued, Ball's definition blurs the distinction between the deterrent effects of punishment and its more inclusive "preventive" effects (e.g., incarceration of felons may prevent crimes through incapacitation). As alternatives, Bedau offers two ostensible definitions.

Definition 1. ". . . a given punishment *(P)* is a deterrent for a given person *(A)* with respect to a given crime *(C)* at a given time *(t)* only

29

if A does not commit C at t because he believes he runs some risk of P if he commits C and A prefers, *ceteris paribus*, not to suffer P for committing C." (Bedau, 1970:540).

Definition 2.   ". . . a given punishment P deters a given population H from a crime C to the degree D that the members of H do not commit C because they believe that they run the risk of P if they commit C and, *ceteris paribus*, they prefer not to suffer P for committing C." (Bedau, 1970:541).

Even though both statements are commendably systematic, they are subject to objections, one of which is formal. Neither statement identifies the *definiendum* and if it is "deters" or "deterrent," those words should not appear in the *definiens*.

Moving to substantive criticism, Bedau's definitions are incomplete and ambiguous in five respects. First, it is not clear if the belief of a "risk of P" is necessary, sufficient, or both for omission of C. Second, the rationale for and implications of *ceteris paribus* are not clear. Third, definition 2 does not speak to the following difference between two hypothetical populations: (1) each of the 200 members of population H_1 commits C during some year but only one time, and (2) 10 of the 200 members of population H_2 commit C 20 times during a year. Presuming that all members of both populations believe that they run some risk of P for committing C, in which population, H_1 or H_2, is D the greatest? The question is not answered by Bedau's definitions, but it is important because investigators seldom have more information than figures on the incidence of C (i.e., they do not have knowledge of the *proportion* of the population who have committed the act). Fourth, Bedau's definitions exclude the possibility of deterrence through "vicarious punishment," that is, instances where an individual refrains from a criminal act in the fear that another person (e.g., a kinsman or a fellow villager) will be punished as a response to the act.[1] Vicarious punishment is not an anachronism when it comes to social control by military authorities or in totalitarian

---

[1]"Vicarious punishment" has become an ambiguous term. Psychologists use it to denote the experience of witnessing (or otherwise having knowledge of) the punishment of another (Morris, 1973); but some jurisprudents use it to denote instances where someone who stands in a special legal or social relation to the perpetrator of a criminal act (e.g., the perpetrator's spouse) is punished as a response to that act. The latter usage is particularly important in contemplating an ethical objection to the deterrence doctrine—it seemingly condones the punishment of the innocent. Be that as it may, vicarious punishment (as known in jurisprudence) could deter crime. As for individuals witnessing or otherwise having knowledge of the punishment of others, that phenomenon can be designated "indirect experience of punishment."

states, and the idea is relevant in contemplating the possible deterrent effect of a fine imposed on a corporation. Fifth, Bedau's definitions do not introduce considerations that are necessary to clearly distinguish types of deterrence.

The Fundamental Problem

The foregoing criticisms are unfair to Bedau in that similar ones can be made of any definition of deterrence. Since deterrence is inherently unobservable, no definition of it can be complete (i.e., answer all possible questions about the "nature" of deterrence *or* evidence of it), nor can it ensure agreement among investigators in identifying instances.

Given an unobservable phenomenon, X, that can be known only inferentially, one can formulate rules of inference in various forms: (1) X is present if Y and Z (observable phenomena) are present, (2) X is present if Y or Z is present, (3) X is present if Y and/or Z are present, (4) X is present if and only if Y and Z are present, and (5) X is present if Y is present. Bedau's definitions are not criticized because they fail to stipulate such rules, for any rule of inference apart from a theory about deterrence is arbitrary and debatable. Contemplate this statement: If at any time an individual is not committing a crime, then deterrence is operative at that time. Even advocates of the deterrence doctrine would regard that rule of inference as absurd. True, one could persist in the rule (it is hardly *logically* false), but the theory in which it is used would be unfalsifiable or uninformative.

Since deterrence is inherently unobservable, rules of inference pertaining to it are unfalsifiable unless stated in the context of a theory. In turn, any deterrence theory necessarily makes assertions in which "deterrence," "deters," or "deterred" is a constituent term. Consider two illustrative assertions: (1) The greater the certainty of punishment for a type of crime, the more that crime is deterred; (2) the more a type of crime is deterred, the less the incidence of that crime. Neither assertion is testable (at least directly) because the word "deterred" denotes an unobservable phenomenon, but the two considered together imply a third assertion that is testable: The greater the certainty of punishment for a type of crime, the less the incidence of that crime.

There could be a variety of deterrence theories, each of them asserting a relation between one or more properties of punishment and deterrence, and the possibly relevant properties are seemingly infinite. Thus, the first of the two foregoing assertions refers to the certainty of punishment; yet other assertions could be made about the association between the severity of punishment and deterrence, between the celerity of punishment and deterrence, etc. All such assertions could be empirically valid to some degree, only some could be valid, or none could be valid. The point is that different assertions (or even different theories) about deterrence need not be contradictory.

Whatever the theory, evidence that punishment deters crime is necessarily inferential. A deterrence theory would be discredited when the predictions that follow from it are not substantiated; but not even consistently correct predictions would *demonstrate* deterrence. One may predict differences in the crime rates of populations or contrasts in the criminal activities of individuals; but one cannot predict *deterrence*.

The foregoing may appear irrelevant for conceptual purposes, but a definition of deterrence is difficult primarily because the term denotes an unobservable phenomenon. No definition of deterrence can make it observable nor resolve the evidential problems (i.e., stipulate evidence of deterrence). What is relevant evidence depends entirely on theories about deterrence.

Absolute Deterrence

As previously suggested, no one can improve substantially on Bedau's definitions of deterrence. However, alternative definitions can avoid some of the objections to Bedau's conceptualization, and to that end it is necessary to define three types of deterrence.

The term "absolute deterrence" denotes instances where an individual has refrained throughout life from a particular type of criminal act because in whole or in part he or she perceived some risk of someone suffering a punishment as a response to the crime. Here, as in subsequent definitions, the term "someone" denotes (1) the individual, (2) another person who stands in some special social relation to the individual, and/or (3) a group of other such persons.[2] Finally, the phrase "in whole or in part" means that the threat of punishment was a necessary and/or sufficient condition for the individual's having refrained from the act each instance when contemplated.

Appearances to the contrary, if an individual has never committed the crime in question, it does not follow that he or she has been deterred absolutely.[3] Some individuals may never contemplate committing certain types of crimes; if so, they have not been deterred by the threat of punishment.

---

[2] The terminology is a recognition of the possibility that vicarious punishments (actual or threatened) may deter.

[3] Zimring and Hawkins (1973:13, 72) also speak of absolute deterrence, but they are concerned with (1) the frequency with which an act would be committed if there were no punishment *at all* and (2) the difference in frequency if there were some punishment other than that presently prescribed. The first consideration has to do with the *absolute deterrence* realized by a presently prescribed punishment, and the second consideration pertains to

The rationale for the definition will become evident as other types of deterrence are considered and evidential problems are examined in detail. For the moment, one general observation will suffice. The notion of absolute deterrence is a way of recognizing that some individuals may be totally deterred by the threat of punishment, others only partially deterred, and still others not deterred at all. However, the definition does not make absolute deterrence an observable phenomenon, nor does it stipulate substantiating evidence.

Restrictive Deterrence

When motorists perceive a fine for speeding as improbable, absolute deterrence is most unlikely, meaning that all motorists exceed the vehicular speed limit occasionally. But they may have some sense (however dim) of a cumulative risk of punishment, and for that reason they do not violate speed regulations regularly, flagrantly (e.g., driving 60 miles per hour in a zone posted for 30), or uncritically (without regard to avoiding detection). Stating the idea briefly, some individuals curtail their violations of law in the belief that repetition is likely to result eventually in their suffering a punishment, and such curtailment is a manifestation of restrictive deterrence.

Defined explicitly, "restrictive deterrence" is the curtailment of a certain type of criminal activity by an individual during some period because in whole or in part the curtailment is perceived by the individual as reducing the risk that someone will be punished as a response to the activity, even though no one has suffered a punishment as a consequence of that individual's criminal activity. The period in question commences after the individual's first offense of that type; but that qualification does not make restrictive deterrence an observable phenomenon, and for that reason alone the definition is not regarded as complete.[4]

---

marginal deterrence (which is always relative to some other punishment). The distinction is crucial but commonly overlooked in assessments of the deterrence doctrine. However, if only to indicate that both terms pertain to a quantitative phenomenon and not to types of deterrence, the appropriate labels should be "absolute deterrent efficacy" and "marginal deterrent efficacy."

[4]In particular, the notion of restrictive deterrence is not clearly distinct from Morris and Zimring's "channeling effect" (1969:140), which they illustrate by describing the case of a motorist who comes to a 50 miles per hour speed zone and slows from 75 to 60. Yet Zimring and Hawkins (1973:72) use virtually the same example to illustrate "partial deterrence," and it appears that the term refers to reductions in the magnitude of offenses. By contrast, "restrictive deterrence" refers to a reduction in the frequency of offenses, including any strategies or tactics employed by individuals to evade detection, identification, or apprehension that have the effect of reducing the frequency of offenses. Of course, it could be argued that the notion should not be construed so narrowly, but the present conceptualization does not purport to identify all conceivable facets of deterrence.

However, restrictive deterrence can be distinguished (analytically) from absolute deterrence.

Whereas restrictive deterrence pertains only to individuals who have committed the crime in question at least once, absolute deterrence pertains to individuals who have never committed it. The distinction does not deny that individuals limit their offenses for reasons unrelated to the perceived risk of punishment, but it is of significance in contemplating putative evidence against the deterrence doctrine. Critics of the doctrine never tire of alluding to prison inmates and the crime rate as proof that punishment does not deter, but the alleged proof has little bearing on restrictive deterrence. At present, there is no systematic knowledge as to how much individuals curtail their criminal activities to *reduce* the risk of punishment, but the possibility of substantial curtailment is scarcely purely theoretical; evidence of it is conspicuous in statements made by individuals who have had a long career in crime (see, e.g., Sutherland, 1937; Irwin, 1970). Indeed, it could be that the deterrent effect of punishment is largely restrictive, and restrictive deterrence is especially important in contemplating the following question: How much more crime would occur if there were no basis whatever for perceiving a cumulative risk of punishment for criminal acts?

Specific Deterrence

The deterrence doctrine is likely to be misunderstood and rejected unless critics recognize two categories of individuals: (1) those who have suffered a punishment for having committed a crime and (2) those who have not. The distinction is relevant because the deterrence doctrine can be construed as asserting *(inter alia)* that individuals who have suffered a punishment for a type of crime are deterred from further offenses.

So we arrive at the notion of "specific deterrence," defined as the omission or curtailment of some type of criminal activity by an individual throughout a period because in whole or part he or she has been accused of a crime for which someone was punished, and he or she is therefore unwilling to risk someone being punished again. The period in question commences after the punishment of someone, as a response to the criminal acts of the individual in question.

One alternative is to confine specific deterrence to instances where individuals have refrained *entirely* from the type of crime in question.[5] That alternative is suggested by other definitions of specific deterrence, but that is so only because those definitions speak of the effects of punish-

[5]The distinction in question can be recognized by speaking of absolute specific deterrence and restrictive specific deterrence.

ment on those punished without stipulating what those postulated effects are.

Some Complexities

The foregoing definitions may appear unnecessarily complex, but past attempts to assess the deterrence doctrine have been defective partly because they relied on an implicit or at best an oversimplified conceptualization of deterrence.[6] It would greatly simplify conceptualization to speak of deterrence as the omission of a criminal act because of the fear of *the* prescribed punishment for that *type of crime*. However, that narrow conceptualization ignores the possibility of alternative prescribed punishments (e.g., a fine and/or imprisonment, with varying magnitudes of each) for crimes of the same type,[7] and it precludes the possibility of an individual being deterred from a crime even though he or she does not know or misperceives the prescribed punishments for that crime. Further, when the narrow conceptualization is extended to specific deterrence, it precludes the possibility of an individual being deterred from a particular type of crime (e.g., burglary) because he or she has been punished previously for another type of crime (e.g., robbery), perhaps a type with different prescribed punishments. Stating the matter more generally, a narrow conceptualization of specific deterrence admits no more than the possibility of an individual being deterred by an actual punishment *only* from further offenses of the same type and even in those cases only if the prescribed punishments for that type of offense have not changed.

By contrast, the present definitions speak only of "a punishment," thereby admitting all of the *possibilities* that are precluded by a narrow conceptualization of deterrence. It may be that some of the possibilities are never realized, but such an inclusive conception of deterrence permits a greater range of empirical questions (e.g., to what extent are individuals deterred from one type of crime as a consequence of previous punishment for another type).

A more specific rationale is that the present conceptualization does not preclude the possibility that the "system of punishments as a whole" deters and perhaps more so than do the prescribed or actual punish-

---

[6]In a survey of evidence, problems, and issues, Tittle and Logan (1973) scarcely recognize the conceptual problem.

[7]Hence the present preference to speak of prescribed punishments for a type of crime rather than *the* prescribed punishment. That terminology may appear peculiar, but there may be two or more alternative prescribed punishments (e.g., a fine of $1,000 and/ or six months in jail) for a type of crime.

ments for *particular types of crimes.* Individuals will not perceive a risk of *legal* punishment if there is no penal system; and despite ignorance or misperception of prescribed punishments, one may be deterred by the belief that the contemplated act is a crime, hence subject to some kind of punishment. That possibility has received little attention in systematic research, and it is often tacitly denied: ". . . if a deterrent is to be effective, a potential criminal must *know* which penalties apply to which crime" (Biddle, 1969:355). A similar line of reasoning was followed by investigators when interpreting the survey finding that California residents were largely ignorant of statutory penalties for various crimes (California Assembly Committee on Criminal Procedure, 1968). The interpretation created the impression that such ignorance precludes deterrence, but surely individuals may be deterred if they believe that the statutory penalty for, say, burglary is five years imprisonment when it is really only three. Such beliefs are most improbable in the absence of any system of punishments.

It will be difficult to bring evidence to bear on the possibility of deterrence through the system of punishments, but the findings of one investigation (Erickson and Gibbs, 1974a) indicate that the possibility is not farfetched. In a comparison of states, it was found that the rate for a particular type of felony is more inversely related to the *average* certainty and/or severity of imprisonment for all major felonies *combined* than to the certainty and/or severity of imprisonment for that type of felony alone.

The present conceptualization ignores some of the complexities introduced by Table 2-1. Each of the 16 conditions in the table could be identified as a type of deterrence,[8] and those distinctions could be justified on the grounds that the empirical validity of the assertion "punishment deters crime" is relative to particular types of conditions. However, that strategy is not followed here because it would be extremely cumbersome to formulate a separate theory for each of 16 types of deterrence. Nonetheless, Table 2-1 furthers understanding of the present conceptualization, the rationale for it, and related problems.

A narrow conceptualization would admit the possibility of specific deterrence only in conditions IA, IC, IIA, and IIC, for only in those conditions has the individual previously suffered a punishment for the type of crime in question.[9] Note particularly that a narrow conceptualiza-

---

[8]Vicarious punishments are excluded from the conditions described in the table only because reference to them would be extremely cumbersome.

[9]"Specific deterrence" could be defined even more narrowly, such that it is limited to condition IC in Table 2-1. That narrow definition would eliminate possibly confounding factors (other punishments for other crimes), but narrowing the meaning of one type of deterrence (e.g., specific) requires an expansion of the meaning of another type (e.g.,

Table 2-1.　*Some Conditions in Which an Individual May Contemplate Commission of a Particular Type of Crime*

		Individual Has Previously Committed the Type of Crime and Also Other Types of Crime	*Individual Has Previously Committed Crimes but Not This Type*	*Individual Has Previously Committed Only This Type of Crime*	*Individual Has Never Committed Any Type of Crime*
Individual Has Suffered One of the Presently Prescribed Punishments for the Type of Crime	*Individual Has Suffered No Other Kind of Punishment*	IA Potential Specific Deterrence	IB Potential Specific Deterrence	IC Potential Specific Deterrence	ID Potential Specific Deterrence
	Individual Has Also Suffered Some Other Kind of Punishment	IIA Potential Specific Deterrence	IIB Potential Specific Deterrence	IIC Potential Specific Deterrence	IID Potential Specific Deterrence
Individual Has Never Suffered One of the Presently Prescribed Punishments for the Type of Crime	*Individual Has Suffered Some Other Prescribed Punishment*	IIIA Potential Specific Deterrence	IIIB Potential Specific Deterrence	IIIC Potential Specific Deterrence	IIID Potential Specific Deterrence
	Individual Has Never Suffered Any Prescribed Punishment	IVA Potential Restrictive Deterrence	IVB Potential Absolute Deterrence	IVC Potential Restrictive Deterrence	IVD Potential Absolute Deterrence

tion would exclude conditions IIIA and IIIC only because (1) the pre-scribed punishments for the type of crime have changed since the individual was punished or (2) the individual was punished in some other jurisdiction (one with different prescribed punishments for the crime).

---

absolute or restrictive), and that consideration complicates matters more than it may appear. Nonetheless, a strategy of reconceptualization is suggested by the conditions identified in Table 2-1. Whenever feasible, crime rates should be computed separately for each condition in Table 2-1, meaning that each condition is treated as a subtype, and the major types are subject to reconceptualization in light of research findings. For example, if the average incidence of crimes in condition IC appears to be substantially lower *or* higher than the average in condition IIIA, then it is questionable to subsume both conditions under the same rubric ("potential specific deterrence").

Conditions ID, IID, and IIID indicate why a truly critical conceptualization of deterrence cannot avoid complexities. While the punishment of the innocent may be rare, a question remains: To what extent does their punishment deter them from actually committing a crime? There is no purely "logical" answer; and the only way to identify that kind of deterrence is to extend the meaning of "specific deterrence."

The present conceptualization should not be construed as complete or final. One merit of the scheme is that it permits a wide range of empirical questions about deterrence, and answers could lead to a reconceptualization. For example, given evidence of no relation whatever between the punishment for one type of crime and the commission of other types of offenses, then specific deterrence should be reconceptualized to exclude conditions IB, IIB, and IIIB in Table 2-1. Such a strategy may appear to be "unscientific," but research and reconceptualization should go hand in hand. In any case, the present conceptualization forces recognition of issues and problems that have been slighted in previous definitions of deterrence and related distinctions.

Related Terminology: General Deterrence

Andenaes rightly distinguishes between specific deterrence and general deterrence, but his related definitions (1971:17–18) are vague and seemingly far too inclusive. "Insofar as this threat of punishment has a restraining effect with regard to criminal conduct, we speak of *general deterrence*." "If he is now deterred by the actual experience of punishment, we speak of specific deterrence."

The conceptualization fails to emphasize the element of fear in deterrence, and the notion of a "restraining effect" hardly distinguishes the deterrent effects of punishment from its more general preventive effects.[10] As shown in the next chapter, there are several ways that some types of punishment may prevent crimes or have a restraining effect apart from inculcation of fear.

To conclude, the best way to limit the meaning of "general deterrence" is to equate it with absolute *and* restrictive deterrence.[11] Similarly, deterrence comprises three classes of phenomena, those delimited by

[10]Andenaes (1966) has made observations on the general preventive effects of punishment, but his conceptualizations are all too general.

[11]By contrast, consider Schrag's definition (1971:23): "*General deterrence* refers to the enforcement of normative codes and regulations in such a manner as to prevent their violation by members of the community, criminals and noncriminals alike." Enforcement would surely include imprisonment, which through incapacitation alone may prevent violations, that is, without any deterrent effect.

the definitions of absolute, restrictive, and specific deterrence. If a simpler definition is desirable, then it will suffice to define "deterrence" as the omission or curtailment of criminal activity by an individual in whole or in part because the individual perceives the omission or curtailment as reducing the risk that someone will be punished as a response to the activity.

Related Terminology: General Prevention

Purely theoretical though it is, one can think of the difference between (1) the actual rate of some type of crime and (2) the rate that *would obtain* if there were no actual or prescribed punishments. Some writers would attribute that difference to deterrence. "It is impossible to define the term deterrence as anything other than the counter-force which makes some sort of balance in a situation which would otherwise be out of balance" (European Committee on Crime Problems, 1967:97). The notion of deterrence (even ignoring distinctions as to types) is not as vague as the statement suggests. Again, the central notion should be fear of punishment; but actual or prescribed punishments have consequences other than the inculcation of fear, some of which may reduce the crime rate (i.e., below the level that would obtain without any punishment). Accordingly, if all such consequences are considered in addition to deterrence, the appropriate term is "general preventive effects of punishment."

Although the term "general preventive effects of punishment" has been used by writers (e.g., Andenaes, 1966), it is of questionable utility. It cannot be equated with "general prevention" of crime, as one can imagine the prevention of crimes by measures that are not perceived as punitive (e.g., strengthening coin boxes in public telephones).[12] Moreover, "general preventive effects of punishment" cannot be defined clearly; hence, the term is likely to be confused with "general deterrence" (a less inclusive notion).

Implications for Theory, Research, and Penal Policy

Recognition of types of deterrence precludes a statement of the deterrence doctrine as a unitary theory; rather, it must be stated as three theories, one pertaining to absolute deterrence, another pertaining to restrictive deterrence, and still another pertaining to specific deterrence. Whatever form those theories assume, test findings could indicate that

[12]The notion extends even to "city planning" (Jeffery, 1971).

all of them are empirically valid, that only some are, or that none are.[13] Moreover, the design for research on one type of deterrence will not be appropriate for other types, and that is especially so in regard to the kind of crime rates considered.

The present conceptualization does not preclude the possibility of individuals being deterred from a crime even though they misperceive the prescribed punishments, and that "cognitive" consideration has policy implications. When legislators seek to deter crimes by increasing statutory penalties, they clearly assume that the public will come to know of such changes. Yet if deterrence is realized largely through the system of punishments as a whole, then legislative concern with particular punishments for particular types of crimes is misguided. Briefly, to the extent that the public is ignorant of prescribed punishments, then the amount of deterrence from any particular crime is a function of the overall character of punishments, including certainty. The counterargument is that a gradation of severity is justified with a view to specific deterrence (i.e., to punish no more severely than is necessary to prevent repetition of the particular offense in question). But if that is so, distinctions as to types of deterrence have real policy implications, even though legislators are seldom sensitive to those distinctions. In particular, when legislators increase statutory penalties, it is commonly not clear what type of deterrence they are contemplating. If the answer is "all of them," then the strategy would be subject to question. Even supposing that long prison sentences do achieve some specific deterrence, they are costly; and the reluctance of judges or jurors to inflict severe punishments could reduce the certainty of imposition (see Bailey and Smith, 1972) to the point that absolute and/or restrictive deterrence declines.

Crime Rates

Described briefly, a conventional crime rate expresses the number of legal offenses during a period (e.g., a year) as a ratio to the size of the population. The incidence figures are typically "official" (e.g., crimes reported by the police), and the perennial question is the reliability of

[13]It is difficult to understand Zimring and Hawkins's refusal (1973:72, 224) to attribute any significance to types of deterrence, especially since they themselves use the conventional terminology. True, as they point out, those who have advanced such distinctions (e.g., specific versus general) commonly make no real use of them, but that is so because there are no truly systematic theories of deterrence. Given such theories, assertions about one type of deterrence (e.g., specific) may be rejected by tests, while assertions about other types of deterrence (e.g., restrictive) may be supported. As such, it is surely difficult to see how distinctions as to types of deterrence are of no consequence.

those figures (see Beattie, 1960; Sellin and Wolfgang, 1964; Wilkins, 1963; and Wolfgang, 1963). However, even if conventional crime rates were absolutely reliable, they would not be satisfactory for deterrence research.

Most deterrence investigators have used crime rates in one of two ways: (1) comparing the rates of jurisdictions that differ as to punishments or (2) comparing the rate in a jurisdiction before and after a change in prescribed punishments or enforcement procedures. Even if all the statistics in such comparisons were absolutely reliable, the findings could not refute the deterrence doctrine in toto, if only because no one particular kind of crime rate is suitable for tests of all deterrence assertions.

Conventional and Unconventional Rates

There are at least seven kinds of rates for any particular type of crime in any territorial unit (e.g., a city, a state, or a country), six of which are unconventional in that they are seldom used.

Conventional rate = C/R,
where C is the number of crimes in the unit during a period (e.g., 1970–1972), and R is the number of residents at some point (preferably the midpoint) during the period.

Crude de facto rate = $C/\Sigma X$,
where X is any individual who has been within the boundary of the unit at any time during this period.

Refined de facto rate = $C/\Sigma T$,
where T is the total amount of time (e.g., hours, days) that any individual (resident or otherwise) has been within the boundaries of the unit.

Residential rate = Cr/Rt,
where Cr is the total number of crimes committed within the unit by residents during the period, and Rt is the total number of individuals who resided in the unit at any time in the period.

Refined residential rate = $Cr/\Sigma Tr$,
where Tr is the total amount of time (e.g., hours, days) that any individual has been within the boundaries of the unit as a *resident.*

Nativity rate = Cn/Rn,
where Cn is the number of crimes committed in the unit during the period by individuals who have resided in the unit since birth, and

Rn is the total number of native-born residents at the midpoint of the period.

Refined nativity rate = Cn/ΣTn,
where *Tn* is the total amount of time that each native-born resident was within the boundary of the unit during the period.

Conventional crime rates are used extensively in criminological research because investigators have little choice other than to use official data. Those data are compiled largely by place and time of crime, and they do not reveal the identity of suspected perpetrators, let alone their residential history. Indeed, since many perpetrators are not even identified, place and time are the only systematic bases for compiling figures on crime. Nonetheless, one is hard pressed to justify using conventional crime rates.

The denominator of the conventional rate does not represent all individuals who had an opportunity to commit a crime in the territorial unit. Opportunity is not restricted to residents, and a territorial unit (especially the central city of a much larger metropolitan area) may have a very high crime rate primarily because ΣX is much greater than R. Accordingly, investigators would prefer to work with crude de facto crime rates or refined de facto crime rates (especially the latter) rather than conventional rates. They do not do so (and scarcely contemplate it) if only because astronomical resources would be required to gather data for the computation of Cr, ΣX, or ΣT. Census statistics and official crime figures cannot be used, and it is not feasible to obtain the requisite data by other means.

The situation is further complicated by recognition that neither of the two de facto rates is entirely adequate for deterrence research. The deterrence doctrine ostensibly assumes that individuals know something about punishments and the certainty of their imposition. Of course, the assumption is most debatable, especially when extended to individuals who are not even residents of the territorial unit in question. Accordingly, with a view to the putative cognitive assumptions of the deterrence doctrine and the opportunity factor, investigators should use a residential or nativity crime rate (preferably the refined versions), but they cannot do so.

Special Crime Rates for Deterrence Research

Although any of the six alternatives would be more defensible than the conventional rate, not even the refined nativity rate would be entirely satisfactory for deterrence research. Suppose that rate is very high for some type of crime in a jurisdiction where the prescribed punishments are ostensibly severe and regularly imposed. That finding would cast doubts on the deterrence doctrine; but it would not be known whether the high rate was due to infrequent absolute deterrence, infrequent restrictive deterrence, or infrequent specific deterrence. Granted that it may never be possible to attribute a certain proportion of crimes to any of the three types of deterrence, there can be no truly defensible inferences without the use of special crime rates that correspond to the types of deterrence.

The *categorical crime rate* is the proportion of members of the population who have committed the type of crime in question at least once during some designated period.[14] Such a rate corresponds (in an inverse sense) to the idea of absolute deterrence.

A *repetitive crime rate* is the average number of times that the members of a population have committed the type of crime in question during the designated period, excluding (from the denominator) members who have not committed it and excluding (from the numerator) crimes committed by members of the population after being punished for some previous crime. The repetitive rate corresponds to the idea of restrictive deterrence.

Finally, the *recidival crime rate* is the average number of times that members of the population have committed the crime in question during the designated period *after* being punished for some type of offense. That type of rate corresponds to the idea of specific deterrence. Of course, if one chooses to speak of absolute specific deterrence and restrictive specific deterrence, those two notions can be extended to recognition of a categorial recidival rate and a repetitive recidival rate. Those distinctions are not really treated or utilized here, but only because they might be more than the reader can tolerate.

The correspondence between special crime rates and types of deterrence should be thought of as only "approximate," and the approximation may be less in some investigations than in others. For one thing, to simplify matters, the definitions of repetitive and special rates make no reference to the possibility of vicarious punishment, whereas that notion is incorporated in the definitions of absolute, restrictive, and specific de-

---

[14]Here, as elsewhere in explicating kinds of rates, the "period" is a relative consideration. In one study, the period may be a particular year (e.g., 1973) or range of years (e.g., 1970–1974), while in another it could be an interval relative to each individual (e.g., since birth, since age seventeen). The "appropriate" period is that one which maximizes the correspondence between the special type of crime rate and the type of deterrence in question; but practical considerations (the availability of data in particular) may force investigators to base special crime rates on data for some arbitrary and brief period.

terrence.[15] Moreover, if the period in question is a particular year or range of years (e.g., 1974 or 1970–1974), then distinctions pertaining to special rates ignore the "criminal history" (offenses and punishments) of all individuals prior to that period. However, obviously, punishments prior to that period may partially determine both the amount and the type of deterrence during the period. Thus, speaking generally, the longer is the period, the greater is the correspondence between special crime rates and types of deterrence; but the special rates could be computed for any period, and practical considerations may force investigators to consider a brief period.

While the special rates can be described readily, computational instructions are difficult to formulate, largely because there can be several versions of each rate. All of them are relative to designated conditions, and those conditions entail more than different criteria for a "member of a population." Even if a member is simply any resident at any time during the period (e.g., 1973), there are several distinctions as to the place and time of offenses and the punishments. As one possibility, all offenses committed by residents outside the territorial unit and/or prior to the period could be ignored, with the same being true of punishments. Another possibility is to consider crimes and punishments prior to or during the period but to ignore those outside the territorial unit (regardless of time or occurrence). Still another possibility is to consider all crimes and punishments regardless of time and place.

The choice among alternative versions of a special crime rate may be dictated by circumstances (the availability of data in particular), even though some versions more nearly correspond to a type of deterrence than do other versions. However, for illustrative purposes, only one version of each special rate will be considered in explicating computational procedures.

Categorical crime rate = Rc/Nr,
where Nr is the total number of individuals who resided in the territorial unit at any time during the period (e.g., 1970–1973), and Rc is the number of such individuals who while residents committed the type of crime in question at least once in the unit during the period.

Repetitive crime rate = ΣXc/Rc,
where ΣXc is the total number of crimes (of the type in question) committed by Rc individuals in the territorial unit during the period

[15]Investigators should take vicarious punishments into account when computing special crime rates, but practical considerations are likely to preclude it.

but (1) excluding crimes committed by individuals after they have been punished for some offense (regardless of the time and place of the offense or the punishment) and (2) excluding all Rc individuals who have been punished.

Recidival crime rate $= \Sigma Xpc/Rp$,
where Rp is the total number of individuals who resided in the territorial unit at any time during the period and who have been punished for some offense (regardless of the time and place of the offense or the punishment), and ΣXpc is the total number of crimes of the type in question committed by Rp individuals in the unit during the period but after the first punishment.

The Significance of Special Rates

Contemplate a territorial unit with a high nativity crime rate for a particular type of crime (e.g., robbery), despite very celeritous, certain, and severe punishment for that offense. Would that unit be a truly defensible basis for rejecting the deterrence doctrine in toto? By no means, for the deterrence doctrine can be construed as comprising three distinct arguments, one about absolute deterrence, another about restrictive deterrence, and still another about specific deterrence. Only by using special crime rates can the empirical validity of the three arguments be assessed independently.

The foregoing does not mean that special crime rates would provide answers to all questions about deterrence. Even if a categorical or repetitive rate is zero, it cannot be attributed solely to deterrence. Similarly, even if no individual commits an offense after being punished (i.e., the recidival rate is zero), that in itself would not be conclusive evidence of specific deterrence. Nonetheless, to the extent that any of the three special cial rates exceeds zero, the kind of deterrence in question (absolute, restrictive, or specific) *was not operative*. So a zero categorical crime rate is *necessary* to infer maximum absolute deterrence, a repetitive rate of 1.0 is *necessary* to infer maximum restrictive deterrrence, and a zero recidival rate is *necessary* to infer maximum specific deterrence.

Of course, a zero conventional crime rate in itself is necessary to infer maximum absolute, restrictive, *and* specific deterrence; but what is the appropriate conclusion if the conventional rate is not zero? It would not follow that punishment had no deterrent impact on the residents, for all the crimes could have been committed by nonresidents. Even if the refined nativity rate exceeds zero, the excess could be attributed to infrequent absolute deterrence, infrequent restrictive deterrence, *and/or* infrequent specific deterrence. Only special crime rates would provide a defensible basis for inferences as to the relative importance of the three types of deterrence.

Problems in Computing Special Rates

Crimes reported to the police or other similar official figures cannot be used to compute special rates, for those statistics pertain *only to incidence*. Official statistics on arrests are more relevant; but as subsequent comments on Table 2-2 indicate, such data provide at best only a basis for inferring special rates, and some kinds of arrest statistics are irrelevant.

The figures create the impression that murderers commonly repeat the crime, but that impression is contrary to other findings, which *indicate* that the typical murderer kills only once (see, e.g., Waldo, 1970). The apparent contradiction is resolved by recognizing that the figures in Table 2-2 refer to all offenses, not just the type for which the individual was arrested in 1971. It is likely the murderers have a record of more frequent arrests and convictions than do other offenders because they are older on the average.

For reasons just alluded to, statistics like those in Table 2-2 are not suited for inferences about categorical, repetitive, or recidival rates; but other kinds of arrest or apprehension data can be used.[16] Even the *Uniform Crime Reports* for certain years prior to 1971 contain more relevant data. Table 2-3 shows 1968 figures on previous arrests for the *same type of crime,* and those figures indicate that the repetitive rate for murder is very low (less than 2 percent of those arrested for murder had been arrested three or more times for that offense). Extending the inferences, of the six types of offenses, the repetitive rate would seem to be greatest for burglary; but the repetitive rate may actually be greatest for auto theft, a type of crime that seldom results in arrest. Figures are not reported for larceny, and the repetitive rate for that crime may be greater than that for burglary or auto theft.

It is questionable to assume a close relation between number of arrests and number of crimes among individuals. Police esprit de corps to the contrary, an arrest does not demonstrate guilt. In any case, less than 20 percent of the crimes known to the police in the United States are "cleared by an arrest," and the percentages are far less for some offenses (about 10 percent for larceny). But even if all arrests actually made by the police were reported accurately to the Federal Bureau of Investiga-

---

[16]This is especially true if the investigators have access to police and judicial records, that is, the study is not limited to published data. As illustrations of the innovative use of such records, see Forslund (1970) and Wolfgang et al. (1972).

Table 2-2. *Arrests of a Special Group of Individuals in the United States during 1971 for Seven Types of Offenses and Statistics Pertaining to Previous Arrests and Convictions**

Previous History	Frequency	Percentage Figures by Type of Crime						
		Murder	Assault	Rape	Robbery	Burglary	Larceny	Auto Theft
Frequency of Charges, Including Present One	One	22.8	29.2	34.7	25.1	27.3	33.7	25.3
	Two	21.1	23.1	21.8	17.2	18.7	21.4	17.4
	Three	12.0	12.3	9.9	12.3	11.4	10.4	11.6
	Four or More	44.1	35.4	33.6	45.4	42.6	34.5	45.7
	TOTAL	100.0	100.0	100.0	100.0	100.0	100.0	100.0
Frequency of Convictions	One	18.3	19.4	13.5	17.8	16.6	22.4	17.9
	Two	9.9	8.5	7.3	9.8	8.2	8.5	9.4
	Three	6.1	5.2	3.0	6.2	5.3	4.1	7.1
	Four or More	11.3	8.6	8.1	10.0	10.0	9.6	14.9
	TOTAL	45.6	41.7	31.9	43.8	40.1	44.6	49.3

*Data from the Federal Bureau of Investigation (1972:38).

Table 2-3. Arrests of a Special Group of Individuals with a History of Previous Arrests, by Type of Offense, United States, 1968*

Frequency of Arrests for Same Type of Crime	Percentage Figures by Type of Crime					
	Murder	Assault	Rape	Robbery	Burglary	Auto Theft
One†	86.0	59.1	78.9	61.5	42.2	55.7
Two†	12.6	23.6	14.8	24.7	26.0	24.0
Three or More†	1.3	17.3	6.3	13.7	31.8	20.2
TOTAL	100.0	100.0	100.0	100.0	100.0	100.0

*Data from the Federal Bureau of Investigation (1969:37).
†Ostensibly including the present (1968) arrest.

tion and even if all "arrestees" were guilty of the offense charged, the relation between frequency of arrest and frequency of offenses would still be largely conjectural. For example, the ratio of arrests for burglary to actual offenses could be about 0.33 for individuals arrested the first time, 0.10 for those with a history of two arrests, and 0.05 for those with a history of more than two arrests. Those ratios could also vary a great deal from one type of crime to the next. Finally, the arrest figures in Table 2-3 are questionable in themselves. They pertain to a group of arrestees selected by the Federal Bureau of Investigation for special study. That group is only a fraction of some 6 million arrests each year, and it is not clear how the group was selected, let alone how representative it is of individuals arrested during a year (for further critical commentary, see Ward, 1970).

The only distinct alternative to arrest statistics is "self-reported" crime. A sample of residents can be asked to report their past criminal acts and residential history by answering several questions for each type of crime: (1) whether or not the individual has ever committed the offense and, if so, where and when; (2) whether or not the individual has ever suffered a punishment and, if so, when, where, and for what offense.

Self-reported offenses after punishment could be strategic in computing recidival rates, because the only other relevant data are limited largely to records on reimprisonment. Those records are defective in many respects (see Glaser, 1964), especially with regard to using them to estimate recidival rates. Former inmates may be reimprisoned for technical violations of parole, and even in the case of new offenses they may be reimprisoned for a different type of crime (e.g., the first sentence for burglary and the second for robbery). In any case, reimprisonment records do not reveal the frequency of criminal offenses between release and reimprisonment, and it is pointless to assume that only former inmates who have been reimprisoned are recidivists.

Although data on self-reported crimes could be used to compute special crime rates, the strategy would be haunted by problems, even assuming unlimited resources for survey research (see Doleschal, 1970; Reiss, 1973). The most obvious difficulty is to secure the cooperation of prospective respondents, some of whom would surely resent such intimate questions and/or fear the consequences of answering truthfully.[17] Resentment and fear might be allayed by a procedure that promises anonymity; but not even that promise would ensure valid responses to questions. Faulty memory is a problem; and respondents have to judge the criminality of their past acts, which is questionable even if the respondents are provided with legal definitions of the crimes under consideration.

Although numerous surveys of self-reported crimes have been conducted (see Doleschal, 1970; Reiss, 1973), they have been limited largely to juveniles (one often-cited exception being Wallerstein and Wyle, 1947). In any case, there is very little evidence as to the reliability of data on self-reported crimes, and the relation between self-reported crimes or delinquencies and official crime data is far more complicated than it appears (see, e.g., Erickson, 1972; Gould, 1969). Whatever the relation, there are several reasons for questioning the reliability of self-reported crimes (Doleschal, 1970; Hood and Sparks, 1970:13–14, 64–70; and Reiss, 1973). So the use of self-reported crimes to compute special rates would be not only costly but also disputable.

Reconsideration of Official Data on Crime

There is a widespread belief among social scientists that official crime rates are grossly unreliable. That belief ignores the distinction between absolute reliability and relative reliability; in the latter case, the question hinges on the *correlation* among populations between the "true" rate and the official rate. In either case, however, there can be no incontrovertible evidence for the simple reason that the true incidence of

[17]Victimization surveys are more feasible and perhaps more defensible than are surveys of self-reported crimes, primarily because the alleged victims are likely to be more cooperative and have less reason for concealing knowledge of a crime. Nonetheless, the veracity and accuracy of reports of alleged victims is debatable (see, e.g., Conklin, 1972:14), and there remains the problem of the divergence of the alleged victims' conceptions of crime and legal definitions. In any case, victimization data cannot be used to compute any of the special crime rates because the victims often cannot identify the perpetrator, let alone provide information on the perpetrator's previous criminal history, including punishments.

crime is unknowable. Nonetheless, the subject is relevant in contemplating the eventual restatement of the deterrence doctrine as a systematic theory. To realize a testable theory, the theorist must stipulate the requisite kinds of data for tests, and such a stipulation is a tacit assertion that the data are in *general* at least sufficiently reliable. The tacit assertion is not a claim that all data of the kind stipulated are absolutely reliable, and hence one cannot possibly falsify the assertion directly. So in formulating a deterrence theory, the theorist *could* stipulate that test data are to be gathered through surveys of self-reported crime, but systematic tests would be precluded unless the theorist also stipulates a survey procedure.

When it comes to the stipulation of data for tests of a deterrence theory, the theorist's choice is not limited to self-reported crimes. Despite widespread doubts about the reliability of official crime statistics, a theorist could stipulate that they be used in tests. The subject takes on a quite different character in contemplating a theory, and that is the rationale for introducing unconventional and special crime rates. However, since data are not available to compute those rates, one may wonder: Why bother with such notions at all?

The preceding notions were introduced to indicate the shortcomings of past deterrence studies, virtually all of which were based on conventional crime rates; and those notions indicate the necessary kinds of data for more satisfactory answers to questions about deterrence. But there is another rationale, one less obvious, yet no less important. While practical reasons preclude the use of unconventional or special rates in deterrence research, the notions themselves can be incorporated in a deterrence theory without precluding tests of it.

The conventional crime rate does not distinguish between crimes committed by residents and nonresidents. However, the proportion of crimes committed by nonresidents may be relative to the characteristics of the territorial unit, spatial extent in particular. For the central cities of metropolitan areas the proportion may be appreciable, but it is probably minimal for large states and countries. With that possibility in mind, a theorist may state the following assertion: Among large territorial units, the residential crime rate varies directly with the conventional crime rate.

The assertion is not presently testable, for it is not feasible to gather the data needed to compute the residential rate.[18] Nonetheless, the conventional crime rate can be computed for numerous large territorial

---

[18]Of course, the assertion would not be testable unless the theorist defines a "large territorial unit," but that is not the problem in question.

units, and hence the assertion links an immensurable phenomenon with a mensurable phenomenon. However, the assertion is not *true by definition,* nor does it mean that the residential crime rate *is* the conventional crime rate. To the contrary, the statement is an assertion, one that may or may not be true. It asserts that *were it possible* to compute a residential crime rate and a conventional crime rate for each of several large territorial units, there would be a close direct relation between the two. Since the assertion is not testable, it merely reflects the theorist's belief, one that other theorists may reject.

To all of the foregoing one may say: But what would be gained by the assertion? Consider it in conjunction with two others. First, among large territorial units, the certainty of punishment for a type of crime varies directly with the deterrence of that type of crime. Second, among large territorial units, the deterrence of a type of crime varies inversely with the residential crime rate for that type of crime. Those two assertions along with the initial one imply a fourth assertion: Among large territorial units, the certainty of punishment for a type of crime varies inversely with the conventional rate for that type of crime. Given a definition of a "large territorial unit," the derived assertion is testable, but its predictive accuracy may be substantially less than still another derived assertion: Among large territorial units, the certainty of punishment for a type of crime varies inversely with the residential crime rate for that type of crime. Indeed, the theorist would prefer to derive that assertion, but it would not be testable.

As an extension of the proposed strategy, a theorist could make assertions about special rates (categorical, repetitive, and/or recidival). However, data on arrests cannot be used to compute special rates, if only because those rates refer to offenses, *not* arrests for alleged offenses. Nonetheless, some kinds of arrest data provide a basis for inferences about special rates, but the inference must be stated as an assertion of an empirical relation between a type of special rate and some kind of arrest figure. The assertion would not be logically true or logically false, but it *could be* empirically false. However, since special rates cannot be computed, the assertion is untestable and hence meaningless outside a theory. As previously shown, even when the premises of a theory are all untestable, it may be possible to derive testable assertions. As an oversimplified illustration, suppose a theorist commences a theory with two assertions.

Assertion I.   Among types of crimes in a territorial unit, the greater the certainty of arrest for a type of crime, the greater the restrictive deterrence of that type of crime.

Assertion II.   Among types of crimes in a territorial unit, the greater the restrictive deterrence of a type of crime, the less the repetitive rate for that type of crime.

The two assertions taken together imply a third, one that asserts an inverse relation (among types of crimes in a territorial unit) between the certainty of arrest and the repetitive crime rate; but since that rate cannot be computed (at least from official statistics), the derived assertion is not testable. So the theorist would have to add at least one more assertion to arrive at a testable theory, and to that end the theorist may be willing to assume an inverse relation between the repetitive rate and the "multiple-arrest rate" (the proportion of indiviudals arrested for a type of crime during a period who have a record of at least one previous arrest for that type of crime). If so, the third assertion would be stated as follows:

Assertion III.   Among types of crimes in a territorial unit, the greater the repetitive rate for a type of crime, the greater the multiple-arrest rate for that type of crime.

Given assertions I, II, and III, one can derive a fourth and testable assertion.

Assertion IV.   Among types of crimes in a territorial unit, the greater the certainty of arrest for a type of crime, the less the multiple-arrest rate for that type of crime.

Up to this point, the focus has been on the theorist's effort to arrive at a testable assertion, but other features of the theory deserve attention. Observe that the theorist has considered only one property of punishment, certainty of arrest, but that limitation is only for illustrative simplicity. The theorist may have refrained from making any assertion about categorical or recidival rates, being unwilling to assume that either special rate is closely related to any kind of arrest figure. As for the asserted relation between repetitive rates and multiple-arrest rates (as stated in assertion III), it is restricted to types of crimes in a territorial unit, which suggests that the theorist is unwilling to assume that the same relation holds for any type of crime *among* territorial units. Granted that the theory is incomplete, a testable theory is better than none at all.

Tests of assertion IV would be limited to territorial units where official statistics can be used to compute the certainty of arrest (the proportion of crimes reported by the police that result in an arrest) and the multiple-arrest rate for each of several types of crimes. Requisite statistics are regularly compiled in only a few countries, and the United States is not one of them. However, the Federal Bureau of Investigation's *Uniform Crime Reports* do include the requisite statistics for certain years (e.g., 1968). So to complete the illustration (it is nothing more), data for the United States have been arranged in Table 2-4 to test assertion IV.

The assertion anticipates an inverse relation between the values in column 1 of Table 2-4 (certainty of arrest) and the values in column 2 (the multiple-arrest rate). The rank-order coefficient of correlation between the values in column 1 and the values in column 2 is −.88, which is consistent with assertion IV.

Since the test and the assertions themselves are illustrations, they are of no great significance. However, consider two likely objections, one being that the test does not demonstrate causation or justify a causal inference, and the other being that assertion IV might be derived from other premises. Those objections only introduce insoluble problems and irresolvable issues. It is far more constructive to grant that, at least in this case, thinking in terms of deterrence variables and special rates has created order.

Table 2-4. The Certainty of Arrest, 1968, and the Multiple-Arrest Rate, 1967–1968, for Seven Types of Crime in the United States*

Types of Crime	Certainty of Arrest†	Multiple-Arrest Rate‡
	Col. 1	Col. 2
Murder	.86	.058
Assault	.66	.302
Rape	.55	.156
Robbery	.27	.320
Burglary	.19	.507
Larceny	.18	.421
Auto Theft	.19	.373

*Data from the Federal Bureau of Investigation, (1969:31, 36).
†Proportion of crimes reported by the police as cleared by an arrest.
‡Proportion of individuals arrested for the crime during 1967–1968 who had a record of one or more previous arrests for that type of crime.

Conventional Crime Rates

A truly sophisticated deterrence theory will make assertions about unconventional and/or special crime rates; but if it is limited to those rates, it cannot be tested readily (if at all). Enormous resources would be required to gather the requisite data, and regardless of available resources the only viable alternatives to official crime data are victim-reported crimes and self-reported crimes, both of which are questionable.

As already indicated, one alternative is for theorists to assert a relation between special crime rates (categorical, repetitive, or recidival) and *some kind* of official arrest figure. A theorist does have an advantage in that a wide variety of arrest figures can be considered especially in the case of certain European countries (see Lunden, 1961). However, some theorists may consider arrest statistics in general so unreliable that they are unwilling to stipulate their use in testing a theory. That is a matter of judgment, and it is complicated by recognition that the reliability of arrest statistics is only one problem. Even if arrest statistics are absolutely reliable, there may be no close relation between the frequency of arrest and the frequency of actual offenses. That is still another matter which the theorist must judge.

The only practical alternative to the arrest rate is the conventional crime rate, and a theorist may conclude that at least for some types of crimes (e.g., robbery) there is a fairly close direct relation between a particular special rate (e.g., the repetitive) and the conventional rate. The immediate problem is the widespread belief that conventional crime rates are grossly unreliable. As indicated previously, that belief ignores the distinction between absolute and relative reliability, and the data in Table 2-5 justify the distinction.

Three types of rates are shown in the table for each of seven major classes of crime in the United States. The first type of rate (column 1) is based on statements made by individuals in a "victimization survey" of a sample of the national population, and those statements are independent of official statistics. The rates in column 2 are based on crimes reported by the police, and they are conventional. That is also true of the rates in column 3, but they pertain to reports of crimes against individuals *or* organizations.

The idea is not that any value in Table 2-5 represents the true crime rate, which is unknowable. So each rate is at best only an estimate of the true rate, and a close relation between any two sets of rates would be evidence that both *could be* fairly reliable (i.e., both vary directly and closely with the true rates). For certain types of crimes there is an enormous discrepancy between the unofficial victimization rate and the offi-

Table 2-5. *A Comparison of Three Types of Crime Rates by Type of Offense in the United States, Circa 1965**

Type of Crime	Rates Based on Frequency of Crimes Reported in a National Survey	Rates Based on Crimes Reported by Police for Individuals	Rates Based on Crimes Reported by Police for Individuals and Organizations
	Col. 1	Col. 2	Col. 3
Homicide	3.0	5.1	5.1
Forcible Rape	42.5	11.6	11.6
Robbery	94.0	61.4	61.4
Aggravated Assault	218.3	106.6	106.6
Burglary	949.1	299.6	605.3
Larceny ($50 or more)	606.5	267.4	393.3
Motor Vehicle Theft	206.2	226.0	251.0
Rank-order Coefficient of Correlation with Col. 1	----	+.96	+.96

*Rates (per 100,000 population) from Biderman (1967:17).

cial rate; but the rank-order coefficient of correlation between the rates in column 1 and those in column 2 is +.96, and it is also +.96 between column 1 and column 3. Accordingly, insofar as a theory deals with *ordinal differences in rates by type of crime,* test results would be much the same for official and unofficial data. Putting the matter more generally, the finding is not consistent with the belief that all official crime rates are grossly unreliable in both an absolute and relative sense.[19] However, the reliability (absolute or relative) of official crime rates can never be known with certainty, and for that reason alone their use in tests is a decision that only the theorist should make.

To conclude, the kind of crime rate considered in deterrence research depends on the theory in question. Accordingly, even though the crime rate will be a principal variable in any deterrence theory, the kind of rate may not be the same in all theories.

[19] For other findings along the same line, see Skogan (1974). However, the relation between official and unofficial rates is undoubtedly contingent on the unit of comparison (e.g., types of crime, as in the present case, or jurisdictions) and the kind of offense in question. The general point is that the findings question the belief that all official rates are grossly unreliable in both an absolute and a relative sense.

Three

Other Possible Preventive Consequences of Punishment

Deterrence is only one of ten possible ways that punishment may prevent crimes, and henceforth all of these ways are referred to as *preventive consequences of punishment* or, more simply, *preventive mechanisms.* The other nine preventive mechanisms are important not only in the contemplation of evidential problems in deterrence research but also in debates over penal policy.[1] In particular, it is misleading to base an argument for a rehabilitative penal policy on the allegation that punishment does not deter an individual. Since deterrence is only one of several preventive mechanisms, the debate over penal policy cannot be limited realistically to "deterrence versus rehabilitation."[2] Unfortunately, expansion of the debate cannot be enlightened by research findings, for social scientsts have done very little research on preventive mechanisms other than deterrence.

Even the vocabulary of criminology, penology in particular, is ill-suited for an analysis of preventive mechanisms. For example, Walker (1969) has described several "aims" of punishment at length, but that

[1]Though hardly compelling evidence of their importance, most of the other nine preventive mechanisms have been recognized in the literature; but there is no conventional terminology to identify them. Zimring and Hawkins (1973) recognize several of the mechanisms that are described in this chapter, but they persistently blur the distinction between those mechanisms and deterrence. Andenaes (1966) attempts to maintain the distinction but fails to recognize several of the mechanisms.

[2]It is even more questionable to create the impression that the only arguments in defense of punishment pertain to deterrence or retribution (see, e.g., Bittner and Platt, 1966:89).

terminology can be misleading. When one speaks of such aims (or objectives), it is commonly not clear whether the statements are *prescriptive* (i.e., what the consequences of punishment should be) or *descriptive* (i.e., pertaining either to the intention of punishment or to the actual consequences). Moreover, in some countries, the United States in particular, the rationale for penal practices is so obscure that it is questionable to speak of "intention," and the paucity of research on the subject precludes defensible assertions about actual consequences. So the present analysis is little more than speculation about the possible consequences of punishment other than deterrence, whether intended or unintended.

Speculative or not, the analysis is in no sense a "functional explanation" of punishment. The idea is not that the consequences of a type of prescribed punishment explain that punishment. Rather, the subject is taken up because it is most unlikely that defensible answers to questions about deterrence can be realized without devoting more attention to other preventive mechanisms.

Incapacitation

Virtually all crimes require opportunities (i.e., they cannot be committed in all situations), and some punishments diminish opportunities for certain types of crimes. No imagination is required to recognize that imprisonment diminishes opportunities for (*inter alia*) passing worthless checks and auto theft. Accordingly, one preventive mechanism of actual punishments is designated as *incapacitation.*

The general meaning of "incapacitation" is fairly clear, but there are several complexities, the most obvious being that only execution incapacitates absolutely. All manner of crimes against persons occur in prisons, and few crimes against property are literally impossible in prison; so incapacitation is largely a matter of degree. Further, again excluding the death penalty, it is unlikely that each kind of punishment diminishes opportunities for all crimes equally, and opportunities for each type of crime are diminished more by some punishments than by others. But it is not feasible to measure incapacitation for each kind of punishment and each type of crime; indeed, it is doubtful that one can formulate a truly defensible measure of the incapacitating effect of any kind of punishment for any type of crime. So incapacitation must be treated as virtually a purely theoretical notion, but that is also true of deterrence. If critics object to the distinction between incapacitation and deterrence because it is largely conjectural, they will not find any deterrence theory to their liking (or any theory in nuclear physics for that matter).

Despite the theoretical character of the incapacitation notion, no one is likely to doubt that particular kinds of punishment (e.g., imprison-ment) are incapacitating to some extent with regard to particular types of crimes.[3] Moreover, general observations can be made about trends in the incapacitating character of punishments. In Western countries, there have been two major shifts in penal sanctions since about 1800: first, a decline in the number of statutory capital offenses along with an increase in imprisonment; and, second, a subsequent decline in imprison-ment along with an increase in fines and probation. Those shifts were in the direction of less punitiveness, but legal reactions to crime became less incapacitating.

The Evidential Problem

The notion of incapacitation creates a difficult evidential problem in attempting to assess the deterrence doctrine. Consider two jurisdic-tions, A and B, with approximately the same population size. Suppose that in A during a particular year there were 100 cases of robbery, with 20 individuals accounting for 40 cases before being imprisoned. Now suppose that another 20 individuals committed robbery at least once without ever being imprisoned so that they accounted for the remaining 60 cases, or 3 per individual. Turning to jurisdiction B, suppose that there were also 40 individuals who committed robbery at least once dur-ing a year, but that only 5 were imprisoned, having committed 10 robber-ies prior to arrest. So the remaining 35 committed 105 robberies (3 on the average) without being imprisoned.

Thus, B's robbery rate (115 cases) would be greater than A's (the two having the same population size), and the certainty of imprisonment would be greater in A. Those differences are consistent with the deter-rence doctrine, but the contrasts in the robbery rates could be attributed entirely to incapacitation. Had 15 more B individuals been imprisoned before repeating the offense, the robbery rates of A and B would have been equal, and the certainty of imprisonment would have been equal. Hence, it would be a mistake to infer that the certainty of imprisonment generated more absolute deterrence in A; indeed, the categorical rob-bery rate was the same for the two metropolitan areas. For that matter, the lesser incidence of robbery in A could not be properly attributed to greater restrictive deterrence. The repetitive robbery rate (for the year) would be 3.0 for A (i.e., 60/20) and also 3.0 for B (i.e., 105/35). Specific

---

[3]An emphasis on incapacitation is one way that "social defense" can be differentiated from the older classical theory of justice and its preoccupation with deterrence. However, after several decades the distinctive features of social defense (as a penal policy) have yet to be clearly identified (see Ancel, 1965, for a recent attempt).

deterrence would not have been a factor, since the incarcerated offenders would not have been released until after the year.[4] So the difference in the conventional robbery rates of the two jurisdictions could be due solely to incapacitation, not deterrence of any kind.

Observe particularly that incapacitation may be reflected in statistical relations between properties of punishment and crime rates that are consistent with the deterrence doctrine. Generally speaking, the greater the certainty of imprisonment, the greater the incapacitation, and the less the crime rate. Moreover, an inverse relation between crime rates and severity of imprisonment (length of sentences served) may partially or wholly reflect incapacitation.[5] For example, if the repetitive robbery rate is 3.0 per year, then the imprisonment of an offender for 5 years *might* prevent some 15 robberies.

The nature of the evidential problem at hand can be best understood by considering statements as possible components of a deterrence theory. In the five asserted relations below, Cs denotes the certainty-severity of imprisonment,[6] De denotes deterrence, Ic denotes incapacitation, and Cr denotes the conventional rate for a particular type of crime (e.g., for robbery).

    I.   Among populations, the greater Cs, the greater Ic.
   II.   Among populations, the greater Ic, the less Cr.
 III.   Among populations, the greater Cs, the greater De.
 IV.   Among populations, the greater De, the less Cr.
   V.   Among populations, the greater Cs, the less Cr.

Assertion V (or some version of it) has been tested several times in deterrence research (e.g., Logan, 1972b), but positive test results cannot be interpreted readily. The evidential problem is that assertion V cannot be considered as a unique derivation, meaning that it can be derived either from I and II *or* from III and IV.

---

[4]In actual instances, some of the robberies in a jurisdiction are likely to have been committed by individuals who have been punished previously for some offense, meaning that recidival rates are components of conventional crime rates. To simplify the illustration, recidival rates are ignored; but observe that two jurisdictions could have the same recidival robbery rate and yet differ in regard to the conventional rate.

[5]Even surveys of purported evidence on the deterrence question (see Doleschal, 1969; Tittle and Logan, 1973; and Zimring and Hawkins, 1973) do not emphasize this kind of evidential problem, largely because they have employed an uncritical or incomplete conception of deterrence, one that does not distinguish it from other possible preventive consequences of punishment.

[6]Here, as elsewhere, certainty and severity are taken only as illustrative properties of punishment, and the intent is not to formulate even a partial theory of deterrence.

One possible solution of the problem may appear obvious—examining the relation between Cs and Cr after eliminating the influence of Ic on Cr. But that solution is simply not feasible. Reconsider the robbery figures for jurisdictions A and B. Only a difference between two versions of the repetitive rate would suggest a greater incapacitating effect in A than in B. Figures for one of these versions (3.0 for both A and B) have been given; and in the other version those individuals punished during the period also enter into the denominator of the repetitive rate, while crimes committed by those individuals prior to punishment also enter into the numerator. As such, the alternative repetitive rate is 2.9 for jurisdiction B (i.e., 115/40) but only 2.5 for A (i.e., 100/40). Since the repetitive rates of the two jurisdictions differ only when figures pertaining to those punished enter into the computation of the rates, the contrast indicates that the two conventional robbery rates differ only because a greater proportion of A robbers were imprisoned prior to what otherwise *might have been* a repetition of the offense.

Unfortunately, inferences about incapacitation are not as feasible or defensible as the illustration indicates. In actual research there is rarely a basis for even a crude estimate of special crime rates. Certain kinds of police or judicial statistics (e.g., the proportion of individuals who have been arrested or convicted more than once for the same type of offense) can be used to infer special rates; but those statistics are rarely published, and, as indicated in Chapter 2, their use to that end is debatable.

Still another complication lies in the recognition that special crime rates are in no sense direct measures of the amount that punishment prevents crime through incapacitation. Even imprisonment may not incapacitate absolutely, and there is the horrendous problem of "selectivity." Suppose the annual repetitive robbery rate in a particular state is 3.0, and suppose that during a particular year 200 individuals were imprisoned for robbery. It might appear that incapacitation prevented some 300 robberies (assuming that the 200 individuals were imprisoned an average of 6 months during the year). However, suppose that those individuals who were skilled in avoiding imprisonment committed the most robberies. That possibility is scarcely implausible, and it virtually precludes "subtracting" some postulated constant effect of incapacitation from the conventional crime rate.

Import for Deterrence Research

One is surely inclined to ask: Given such problems in deterrence research, why bother? However, awareness of the problems is the first step toward their solution. As for the idea that social scientists can avoid problems by analyzing simple phenomena, it is fallacious. Regardless of the seeming simplicity of the phenomenon in question (e.g., the relation between social class and fertility), the problems and complexities are "there," but investigators are blissfully unaware of them.

The evidential problem at hand is complicated but not as insurmountable as it might appear. Although there is no one effective strategy for taking incapacitation into account when testing deterrence theories, the evidential problem can be diminished by focusing research on (1) particular kinds of punishment and/or (2) particular types of crimes.

As for punishments in contemporary Western countries, fines appear to incapacitate the least, even though they may diminish opportunities for a few types of crimes. Lovald and Stub (1968) found that the time between court appearances for consecutive charges of public drunkenness in Milwaukee was slightly less on the average for those fined. Their interpretation is that fines temporarily reduce access to alcoholic beverages. Be that as it may, it is difficult to imagine a fine having more than a negligible incapacitating effect for most types of crimes, and it definitely appears negligible even for drunkenness.

A wide range of crimes are subject to a fine, but typically a fine is only one of several alternative prescribed punishments for an offense (imprisonment or probation being the other major alternatives), and that consideration complicates matters. However, whatever the alternatives, for all practical purposes a fine is the only punishment for numerous kinds of traffic violations, and the incapacitating effect in such cases may well be negligible. Accordingly, traffic offenses take on special significance in deterrence research if only because a relation between the certainty-severity of punishment and the offense rate cannot be attributed readily to incapacitation.

A preoccupation with fines would be questionable because that punishment is seldom if ever imposed for various kinds of felonies (e.g., robbery). Deterrence theories should apply to various types of crimes; accordingly there is a need to identify a type of crime that is subject to imprisonment but has minimal incapacitating effects.

Consider a type of crime for which the repetitive rate approaches 1.0, meaning that individuals seldom commit it more than once (before or after punishment). As such, it is most unlikely that an incapacitating punishment could have an influence on the conventional rate. Homicide appears to be such a crime, at least in some countries. It is possible even in prison, and apart from that consideration research findings indicate a very low repetitive rate.[7] So homicide is strategic for deterrence re-

---

[7]See again Table 2-3 (Chapter 2) and the commentary on it. See also Waldo, 1970. The problem with all such investigations is that they do not consider the number of homi-

search in that imprisonment for that crime evidently does not substantially reduce the conventional rate through incapacitation.

Critics may object to the present attempt to distinguish deterrence from other possible preventive mechanisms, such as incapacitation, and that is especially so if their conception of deterrence is so broad that it does not recognize the distinction between omission of criminal acts out of fear of punishment and omission because of limited opportunities.[8] But the present rejection of such a broad conception does not stem from a pedantic concern with semantics. If deterrence is not distinguished from incapacitation, then numerous research findings may be anomalies. To illustrate, Logan has reported (1972b) that there is a much more inverse relation (among states) between certainty of imprisonment and robbery rates than between certainty of imprisonment and homicide rates. That difference could be interpreted in various ways, but the distinction between deterrence and incapacitation is surely relevant. Specifically, if imprisonment reduces the robbery rate through both incapacitation and deterrence but only reduces the homicide rate through deterrence, then a closer inverse relation between the certainty of imprisonment and the robbery rates would be expected. Then consider still another possible anomaly. Suppose it were found that the relation between the maximum prescribed term of imprisonment for a type of crime and the crime rate is much less inverse than the relation between the average prison sentences actually served and the crime rate. Suppose further that the differential relation holds even when the certainty of imprisonment is somehow controlled. One interpretation would be that prescribed punishments deter individuals but do not incapacitate them, whereas actual punishments both deter and incapacitate individuals.

Such interpretations do not amount to a tacit admission that causation is, after all, the central consideration. Specifically, here and elsewhere, the concern with controlling for or taking into account variables other than deterrence (e.g., other possible preventive mechanisms, extralegal conditions) is not inconsistent with the emphasis on predictive power as *the* criterion for judging deterrence theories. It is pointless to presume that correct predictions can be derived from any theory regardless of conditions, and in the case of deterrence theories those conditions include, *inter alia,* types of punishment and types of crimes. So entertaining the idea of incapacitation simply promotes recognition of the possibil-

---

cides committed by individuals *prior to* a first arrest or conviction, and only those numbers should be used to compute a repetitive rate. However, given the large proportion of homicides reported as cleared by an arrest, it is difficult to imagine that police or judicial statistics somehow conceal a high repetitive rate for criminal homicide.

[8]Virtually all extensive treatments of the possible preventive consequences of punishment (e.g., Andenaes, 1966) recognize incapacitation.

ity that the empirical relation between some property of punishment and the crime rate is contingent on the type of punishment and the type of crime. One may insist that such reasoning entails the notion of causation, but that is simply not the point. Making causation the central consideration in assessing deterrence theories (or any theory, for that matter) creates insoluble problems and issues that defy resolution. The primary reason is that causation cannot be demonstrated, and dissensus as to appropriate criteria for judging causal assertions is inevitable. However, it does not follow that theories have no policy implications. All policy questions ultimately reduce to the following form: If such-and-such is done, what will happen? An answer to such a question *is a prediction*; hence any theory that generates predictions is relevant in contemplating policies.

Policy Issues

The long debate over deterrence versus rehabilitation has diverted attention from other preventive mechanisms; and given compelling evidence that incapacitation rather than rehabilitation is the only preventive consequence of imprisonment, policy makers would be confronted with a dilemma. There is an understandable reluctance to abandon attempts at rehabilitating even the most "hardened" criminals in a prison setting; but once the primary function of imprisonment is taken to be incapacitation, rehabilitation programs in prisons will receive even less support than is now the case. Granted that the support is now largely lip service, even that might cease.

It is an illusion to suppose that the incapacitating effect of imprisonment can be taken as given. The effect may be very slight for, say, criminal homicide but marked for larceny, burglary, robbery, and auto theft. Yet a defensible policy would require careful estimates of repetitive rates for each type of crime; generally, imprisonment reduces the incidence of a type of crime only to the extent that the type is characterized by a high repetitive rate. The relation becomes more complicated when considering the "locus" of a reduction in crimes. For some crimes (e.g., sex offenses), imprisonment may merely shift the location to a prison. Advocates of "law and order" may not be bothered by relocating crime, but policy makers should confront the issue.

Still another issue stems from the long trend away from classical justice (a specific and mandatory punishment for each type of crime) toward "individualization" (making the sentence "fit" the criminal). Judges and correctional officials now have discretion as to how long the incarcerated should be denied liberty; but the issue is not just the abuse of discretionary power or the inevitable disparities in sentences for the same offense.[9] Additionally, the power of discretion has been given without defensible guidelines (see Davis, 1969), and some candid judges have become perplexed (see, e.g., Frankel, 1972). It might appear that admonishing judges to consider incapacitation as well as deterrence and rehabilitation would only complicate matters. However, insofar as judges are concerned with the impact of sentences on the crime rate, an emphasis on incapacitation would be more defensible than one based on conjectures about deterrence or rehabilitation. To be sure, such a policy would be partial return (retreat, if you will) to the classical theory of justice; but who is prepared to argue that the alternative, the individualization of justice, effectively prevents crimes through rehabilitation?

It might appear that a concern with incapacitation would lead to longer prison sentences for all crimes, but that would be contrary to the incapacitation principle. For example, homicide sentences would become shorter not only because those convicted would be "good parole risks" (see Waldo, 1970) but also because of the supposition that long sentences do not reduce the homicide rate through incapacitation.

Punitive Surveillance

As argued in the next chapter, any authorized action taken by legal officials is a legal punishment when it is perceived by some members of the population in question as a cause of pain or discomfort. So conceived, probation or parole is punishment when it is perceived by the probationer or parolee as discomforting. The question is not whether one welcomes probation or parole but whether the conditions are viewed as discomforting, which is probably so in the vast majority of cases.

The conditions of parole or probation are set up so that parolees and probationers are subject to some kind of surveillance. The surveillance is commonly negligible (see Conrad, 1965: 24–25), but probationers and parolees are undoubtedly aware of it and view it as punitive. Insofar as that awarness prompts individuals to curtail their criminal activity, probation or parole may prevent crimes to some extent. The phenomenon is not specific deterrence, for the individuals do not refrain from criminal acts out of fear of probation or parole. Moreover, the phenom-

[9]See Carter and Wilkins, 1967; Chiricos et al., 1972; Davis, 1969; D'Esposito, 1969; Frankel, 1972; Green, 1961; and Hood, 1962. The literature clearly shows that two individuals found guilty of violating the same law may receive quite different sentences. However, the extent to which those disparities reflect only idiosyncratic inclinations or racial-ethnic prejudices on the part of judges is still very much a debatable question (see esp. Green, 1961; Zeisel, 1969).

enon is not limited to probation or parole. Surveillance is a feature of any punishment insofar as the conditions of the punishment make an offender's behavior more visible, either to officials or to potential informers; and the term "punitive surveillance" is used here in that sense.

Import for Deterrence Research

No claim is made that all forms of punitive surveillance prevent crimes effectively, and that is especially true of the surveillance inherent in probation or parole.[10] Even if that form of punitive surveillance does prevent some crimes, there is no evidence to indicate that the volume prevented is substantial. Another relevant consideration is that the character of parole and probation practices probably does not vary enough among all territorial divisions (e.g., metropolitan areas) of a jurisdiction (e.g., a state) for differing amounts of surveillance to produce substantial differences in the conventional crime rates of those divisions. In any case, the preventive consequences (if any) would be reflected only in the recidival rate; hence it is not relevant in contemplating absolute or restrictive deterrence. So there is more than one rationale for ignoring punitive surveillance in deterrence research, at least in contemporary Western countries.

Since the present assessment of the preventive consequence of punitive surveillance is largely impressionistic, it would be desirable to control for or take into account the possibility of that consequence in conducting deterrence research. However, there are practical limits as to the number of variables that investigators can consider when testing deterrence theories.

Policy Issues

The real significance of punitive surveillance may lie in the distant future, meaning that eventually it could create anomalies (e.g., a population with a low recidival rate despite mild punishments). Yet that possibility is not likely without major changes in penal policies, especially the development of surveillance techniques that are alien to contemporary parole and probation practices; but policy changes in that direction would be most controversial.

At present, there is no basis for estimating how much surveillance

[10]The concern is not with surveillance in the form of routine patrols by police officers or the use of radar equipment in traffic control. Those activities are not construed as punishments; and their preventive consequences have to do with deterrence largely through increasing the perceived certainty of punishment.

prevents criminal acts *relative* to its emphasis in the activities of probation and parole officers. A defensible estimate could have considerable impact on penal policy because (1) probation and parole as components of correctional programs are likely to continue to expand, (2) it is not clear what probation or parole presently accomplishes, and (3) there are doubts as to the feasibility of certain roles for probation and parole officers.[11]

Probation and parole officers attempt to play various roles—those of therapist, policeman, counselor, supervisor, and clerk—and for that reason alone their case loads are excessive. The questions as to appropriate or feasible roles is debatable; but insofar as crime prevention is a goal of probation and parole, the preventive efficacy of punitive surveillance becomes a crucial question. The question is not only how much surveillance in current probation and parole reduces crime but also how much crime prevention could be increased by a greater emphasis on surveillance.[12] The latter question is all the more important since specialization of function may be the only feasible alternative if the case loads of probation and parole officers increase even more (see Czajkoski, 1969).

Punitive surveillance as practiced today poses no policy issues, largely because its role in the penal system is scarcely noticed. However, technological innovations may create opportunities for kinds of punitive surveillance that heretofore were not feasible. Thus, as Ingraham and Smith (1972) have suggested, transmitters could be attached to the bodies of probationers and parolees with a view to increasing surveillance. The use of electronic equipment to that end could increase punitive surveillance enormously, not only because it would enable officials to locate an individual at any time but also because the signals transmitted could be such as to indicate the emotional state of the individual and therefore the kinds of activities he or she was engaged in or contemplating. However, such a use of technology would be construed, perhaps even by some advocates of law and order, not only as a violation of an individual's constitutional rights but also as an offensive concept apart from legal considerations (Shapiro, 1972).

---

[11]See esp. Carter and Wilkins, 1970; Conrad, 1965; Czajkoski, 1969; England, 1957, 1962; Hauge, 1968; Silverman, 1956; and Sparks, 1971.

[12]Probation and parole officers devote little time to surveillance as it is known in police work (e.g., "tailing" a subject). See Conrad, 1965; Czajkoski, 1969; and Silverman, 1956. Further, it would be a mistake to assume that reducing the case loads of probation and parole officers would lead to more surveillance. The literature clearly reveals divergent opinions as to the appropriate roles of probation and parole officers. In any event, it is doubtful that there is a consistently close inverse relation between probation-parole case loads and recidivism or failure rates (see Adams and Vetter, 1971).

Enculturation

As suggested in Chapter 2, deterrence cannot take place unless the individual in question believes that a contemplated act is illegal and therefore punishable, but ignorance of a law is neither necessary nor sufficient for violations of that law. For example, there is no reason to suppose that infrequent marriages of widowed grandmothers and grandsons reflect their knowledge that such unions are illegal, nor is the point that knowledge of a law ensures conformity to it (an argument that no one would defend). Nonetheless, for *some* individuals knowledge of a law may be a sufficient condition in itself for conformity. Indeed, some individuals apparently accept the precept "obedience to law" even to the point of conforming to laws that they regard as unjust, and numerous jurisprudents or philosophers have argued that obedience is a duty independent of the particular law in question or a citizen's sense of morality and ethics (see Gerstein, 1970). That principle is incompatible with certain versions of the "natural law theory" and is often an acute social issue, as in the cases of Nazi Germany and the United States in the 1960's (especially for minorities and war protestors). Moreover, an ethical principle is one thing, but actual behavior is another. Yet it is pointless to deny that in all countries a substantial proportion of the citizenry at least gives lip service to "respect for the law," but it is no less obvious that such respect has no bearing on the incidence of crime if the citizens *have no knowledge of particular laws.*

Whatever the association between conformity and knowledge of the law, the latter is relevant in contemplating consequences of punishment other than deterrence. One line of reasoning goes something like this: On coming to believe that a particular type of act is illegal, individuals anticipate punishment for committing it and refrain out of fear. That line of reasoning may well apply to some individuals; but even so, it does not follow that punishment prevents crime only through deterrence. On the contrary, an individual's knowledge of criminal law may derive in part from witnessing, reading of, or being told of instances where a type of act has been punished; and it is conceivable that the individual may subsequently refrain from that act not out of fear but because of an uncritical obedience to law. If so, punishment may have prevented a criminal act but not through deterrence.

The process by which individuals acquire knowledge of and respect for norms, legal or extralegal, is commonly referred to as *enculturation* or *socialization*. Accordingly, all of the foregoing observations reduce to one assertion: Enculturation of a law is furthered by instances where violators of it are punished. The assertion is not that all individuals acquire knowledge of laws only through experiences pertaining to punishment or that knowledge of a law is a necessary or sufficient condition for conforming to it. Rather, the assertion is nothing more than a claim that public knowledge of laws is furthered by punishment.

Whereas some kinds of enculturation are entirely cognitive (e.g., learning to distinguish stars from planets), others are evaluative in that the novice comes to adopt standards as to what is good or bad, right or wrong. The evaluative quality may be minimized in the training of law students (i.e., one may acquire "technical" knowledge of laws), and some laws are instructions to a particular end (e.g., changing a will) rather than proscriptions. For that matter, cognitive and evaluative enculturation are by no means distinct when it comes to criminal laws, not even when knowledge of those laws is acquired through experience of punishment.

Knowledge of laws can be communicated to children by simple statements, such as: "That is against the law." However, the statement may contribute only to cognitive enculturation (depending on the tone of voice or context), and statements take on a definite evaluative quality only when voiced something like this: "Don't do that; it is against the law." Then consider another statement: "If you do that, the police will put you in jail." Presuming a child connects the police with "the law" and perceives "jail" as punitive, the statement furthers the child's knowledge of the law by reference to punishment. Moreover, a reference to the kind of punishment (e.g., the death penalty) may convey the intensity of condemnation (see Ewing, 1929; Rashdall, 1948).

The notion of enculturation of law through punishment is not limited to acquiring knowledge by being punished. Although one can acquire knowledge of a law (both in a cognitive and in an evaluative sense) through being punished, enculturation may take place through various experiences. Thus, informing a child (or any individual for that matter) that some type of act is subject to ten years imprisonment furthers enculturation of the law by reference to punishment.

We now arrive at a central question: To what extent do experiences pertaining to punishment further knowledge of the law? Research on the question cannot be confined to the young. Whereas some kinds of enculturation (e.g., toilet training) are limited to the very young, acquisition of legal knowledge commonly occurs throughout life. However, even if the question is limited to children, we know very little about the connection between punishment and knowledge of the law. There has been extensive research on the acquisition of normative standards by children, and some investigations have focused on "law" (see Tapp and Kohlberg, 1971, for a survey). The findings indicate that very early in life children develop a conception of law, one in which punishment looms very large. Unfortunately, however, the findings do not reveal to what extent children acquire knowledge of laws from experiences pertaining to punishment; nor do we know how much children judge the intensity of evaluations of conduct by reference to the severity of punishment.

Even if it were known that punishment is *the* major source of public knowledge about laws (illegal acts in particular), it would not follow that punishment prevents crimes through enculturation. Insofar as knowledge of a law extends to the prescribed punishments for violations of it, then that knowledge may prevent crimes through deterrence; but for some individuals knowledge that a type of act is illegal may be sufficient to refrain from it in a manner *independent* of fear of punishment (i.e., not through deterrence). However, there is simply no way even to estimate the proportion of such individuals in any population,[13] and the proportion may well vary substantially from one law and/or population to the next.

Import for Deterrence Research

Regardless of how much punishments further knowledge of laws and how much such knowledge promotes conformity, there is no method to control for that possibility in testing deterrence theories. But one consideration justifies tests without controls. Even if knowledge of the law itself promotes conformity, it may well be that the frequency of actual punishments plays a minor role at most in furthering knowledge of laws pertaining to certain types of crimes. Thus, the vast majority of adult Americans are probably aware that threatening a store owner with a gun to obtain money is "against the law," and their awareness is probably independent (at least within very broad limits) of the frequency with which instances of armed robbery have been punished. In any case,

---

[13]Even judging the relevance of evidence is difficult (see Zimring and Hawkins, 1973:143–149). There have been a few studies of the relation between knowledge of a law or changes in a law and the social evaluation (i.e., approval or disapproval) of the related type of act. The findings of those studies (e.g., Berkowitz and Walker, 1967; Walker and Argyle, 1964) certainly cast doubt on the idea that knowledge of a law alters social evaluations of the type of act in question. For example, individuals may not disapprove of attempted suicide even though they know it is against the law, and for many individuals knowledge that an act has been decriminalized does not alter their disapproval of it. However, it would be questionable to generalize from those findings to all laws and all types of acts. No less important, the studies have considered adults; and knowledge of the law may have an appreciable impact on social evaluations of conduct only among children. In any case, the findings do not contradict the two central assertions: (1) for some individuals knowledge that a particular type of act is illegal is a sufficient reason for refraining from that act and (2) actual legal punishments further the dissemination of such knowledge.

there is no reason to suppose that public knowledge of the legal proscription of that act varies substantially among territorial divisions (e.g., metropolitan areas) of a jurisdiction.

The foregoing provides a rationale for focusing deterrence research on what are loosely identified as major types of crime (e.g., forcible rape, criminal homicide, and robbery). That has been the focus in past research, but it has been accepted uncritically (i.e., without justification). The focus is unfortunate in that business crimes, political crimes, and misdemeanors are ignored; but it does provide some assurance that knowledge of the law is not a major uncontrolled factor in tests of deterrence propositions.

Policy Issues

Legislators commonly appear to presume either that the public knows which types of acts are illegal or that an increase in the serverity of prescribed punishments will promote that knowledge. Either presumption is most debatable, and the lack of concern on the part of legislators with publicizing laws (including prescribed punishments) is contrary to the deterrence doctrine and ethically indefensible.[14] Even if ignorance of the law does not mitigate the situation, a strange mentality is required to argue that the citizenry should be informed of laws by punishing them for violations.

Advocates of the deterrence doctrine commonly do not grasp the full implications of the doctrine, or they grasp the implications but fail to act accordingly. Specifically, a truly complete and consistent policy to deter crimes would extend to the systematic dissemination through mass media (e.g., newspapers) of accounts of legislative action on matters pertaining to criminal law, including (1) definitions of types of acts that have been declared illegal and (2) stipulations of prescribed punishments. It would be pointless for legislators who advocate the deterrence doctrine to argue against a dissemination policy on the grounds that it is not needed, for all findings to date clearly indicate that public ignorance of criminal laws and prescribed punishments is substantial (see, e.g., California Assembly Committee on Criminal Procedure, 1968). Alternatively, publicizing criminal laws may be rejected by some legislators because it is "threatening"; but defenders of the deterrence doctrine cannot make that argument without being inconsistent, for the doctrine is based on the notion of threats.

---

[14]The issue is only one of several in which a concern with the possible preventive consequences of punishment cannot be divorced from the "morality of law," a notion ably explicated by Fuller (1964).

Reformation

Critics of the classical theory of justice have argued that the appropriate legal reaction to a crime should depend on the offender rather than on the crime. That argument does not amount to a categorical rejection of punishments (insofar as the punishment depends on the offender, not the crime); but an antipunitive or nonpunitive orientation is suggested when the argument is extended to a plea for the rehabilitation of offenders through counseling, clinical therapy, vocational training, group therapy, etc.

The goal of those practices may encompass more than preventing recidivism. In any case, two terms, "rehabilitation" and "reformation," are commonly used as though they are alternative identifications of the same goal, that is, as though the terms are interchangeable. The present argument is that the meanings of the terms should be distinguished. Criminal rehabilitation is the alteration of an offender's behavior by nonpunitive means, so that he or she no longer violates laws. Criminal reformation is the alteration of an offender's behavior *through punishment,* so that he or she no longer violates laws, yet for reasons *independent of fear of punishment.*

The distinction is subject to several objections, and they are not limited to the exclusion of reference to covert behavior (e.g., attitudes, values). For one thing, the empirical applicability of either definition is dubious at best, meaning that independent investigators are not likely to agree in applying the definitions to particular offenders.[15] Then there is the problem of distinguishing reformation and specific deterrence.

In the case of reformation, an individual refrains from criminal acts after punishment but not because of the fear of suffering punishment again, whereas the fear of suffering punishment again is the central consideration in specific deterrence. (The distinction is ignored in Zimring and Hawkins, 1973:75.) Describing the distinction another way, in the case of specific deterrence, individuals do contemplate crimes but refrain from them, whereas the reformed individual no longer contemplates criminal acts.

The notion of reformation cannot be explicated further without re-

[15]The problem in making such judgments is the efforts at rehabilitation are virtually always made in a punitive context; and since punishment and nonpunitive programs are coextensive, it is difficult to distinguish the effects of the two. Nonetheless, at the purely conceptual level, one can distinguish, as Hawkins does (1971:15), between "reformation procured *through* punishment and reformation procured *in association* with punishment." Given the proposed distinction, an instance of Hawkins's second type of reformation would be designated as "rehabilitation," even though it need not be procured in association with punishment.

course to antiquated expressions: Punishment may lead the perpetrator to recognize the "moral enormity of his deed." Yet it is not that the perpetrator may have been unaware that the type of act was illegal. If an individual violates a law in ignorance of it and subsequently conforms solely because his or her knowledge has been altered by punishment, it is an instance of enculturation, not reformation. However, if an individual knowingly violates a law, the experience of being punished may generate feelings of shame and remorse, which in turn promote subsequent conformity. To illustrate, consider observations on a common reaction of adults (mostly women) in Chicago on their being apprehended the first time for shoplifting: ". . . once arrested, interrogated, and in their own perspective, perhaps humiliated, pilferers apparently stop pilfering. The reward of shoplifting, whatever it is, is not worth the cost of reputation and self-esteem" (Cameron, 1964:151).

The postulated "moral jolt" of punishment and its possible reformative effect (see Andenaes, 1968:89) does not mean that reformation is accomplished only through a long sentence, during which the offender supposedly contemplates the "evil of his ways" in silence and solitude (a much favored idea in early nineteenth century penology). Even an arrest may produce the moral jolt, and the shock of short-term incarceration could have a reformative effect equal to that of a long sentence (see Friday and Petersen, 1973).

Opposing Theories

It may appear that reformation poses an evidential problem only in tests of propositions about specific deterrence (i.e., a low recidival rate could be attributed either to specific deterrence or to reformation). However, when conventional crime rates are employed to test deterrence propositions, reformation is still another possible consequence of punishment that could reduce the crime rate in a manner independent of deterrence.

There is no defensible basis for even a crude estimate of the frequency of reformation in any population. Widespread doubts about the efficacy of rehabilitative programs in "criminal corrections" may suggest that reformation is rare, but observe again that rehabilitation and reformation are distinct phenomena, at least analytically.

The most compelling evidence of infrequent reformation is found in statistics on reimprisonment, which are indicative of the minimum proportion of convicts who commit an offense after release. At one time there was a widespread belief that at least one-half of the individuals who serve a prison sentence are subsequently reimprisoned, but Glaser's systematic analysis of the evidence (1964) led him to conclude that the figure is more nearly about 35 percent. Such divergence in estimates is not surprising, for statistics on reimprisonment are difficult to interpret. (One of the several problems has to do with the distinction between reimprisonment on parole violation and reimprisonment on conviction for a new offense.) It is even more difficult to make inferences about the reformative influence of imprisonment. Even if parole violations are excluded, reimprisonment figures only indicate the minimum proportion of former convicts who commit felonies after release from prison. Of course, there is no way to arrive at even a gross estimate of the proportion of prison inmates who commit felonies after release, and the proportion may vary a great deal from one population (e.g., state) to the next. Nonetheless, it is unlikely that any criminologist would be surprised by an estimate of, say, 80 percent. Moreover, the remaining 20 percent could not be attributed to reformation, for specific deterrence and extralegal inhibitory conditions are relevant considerations. So, all in all, there is no basis for assuming that the reformative consequences of imprisonment are other than negligible.

Since the reformation of an offender is evidently very rare, at least as it relates to contemplating the possible consequences of imprisonment, there is some justification for ignoring the phenomenon in tests of deterrence theories. However, another evidential problem emerges when it is recognized that punishment may result in the very opposite of reformation. At least two theories suggest that possibility.

According to Sutherland's theory of differential association (Sutherland and Cressey, 1970), criminal behavior is learned in much the same way as other behavior. Whether one learns and commits a criminal act depends on the ratio of "favorable definitions" to "unfavorable definitions," with both definitions acquired through association with others. That brief summary grossly oversimplifies Sutherland's theory, but even an elaborate statement would not remedy one of its defects—after nearly four decades it is seemingly untestable. Nonetheless, the theory does suggest how certain punishments, imprisonment in particular, could generate crimes.

While imprisonment in itself is undoubtedly a definition unfavorable to crime, favorable definitions evidently flourish in prisons. Far from being condemned, the past criminal activities of convicts may enhance their prestige, and that enhancement is surely a definition favorable to crime. Moreover, the prison offers opportunities to learn techniques for committing crimes, and the knowledge acquired (however indifferently) surely qualifies as definitions favorable to criminal acts. So imprisonment may well generate definitions that are far more favorable than unfavorable to crime.

Still another theory suggests that a punishment "labels" the individual as a criminal and thereby creates a condition conducive to further criminal acts by that individual. The key notion is "secondary deviance" (see Lemert, 1967), and the mechanism by which labeling generates subsequent criminal acts is both social and psychological. The central idea seems to be that once labeled the individual is reacted to by others in such a way that the individual comes to identify himself or herself as a criminal and conforms to beliefs as to how criminals should and will behave. The ensuing subsequent criminal acts are "secondary deviance," meaning that they stem from reactions to "primary deviance" (the act or acts that initiated the legal reaction).

The labeling theory (more accurately, the theory of secondary deviance) is unusual in two respects. First, it ignores the possibility of specific deterrence or reformation (see Thorsell and Klemke, 1972, for a criticism of that omission). And, second, it is doubtful that the theory is falsifiable even in principle. As for the idea of secondary deviance, it can be construed as nothing more than a definition (e.g., any deviance caused by reaction to prior deviance *is* secondary deviance). Further, insofar as there is a theory of secondary deviance, it asserts no more than (1) that *some* deviant acts are secondary deviance or (2) that *some* reactions to deviance cause subsequent deviance. Like all existential assertions, neither of the two alternative expressions can be falsified. Even if extensive research fails to identify one instance of secondary deviance, the argument could be that the research did not consider all cases (past and future). For that matter, the discovery of one unquestioned case of secondary deviance would scarcely be informative.[16] Nonetheless, the idea of secondary deviance is one rationale for recognizing the possibility that punishments generate more crimes than they prevent (presuming they prevent any at all).

The postulated cause of secondary deviance is not an instance of "extralegal conditions conducive to crime"; rather, it is one of the few instances of "legal conditions conducive to crime." So the idea of secondary deviance is considered here not only because it is the exact opposite of reformation but also because the ideal research design for tests of deterrence propositions would take both possibilities into account.

The amount of secondary crime is unknowable, and the same is true

---

[16]In light of various methodological problems in assessing the theory of secondary deviance, it is hardly surprising that surveys of purportedly relevant evidence are inconclusive, even when the survey is conducted by someone who appears to see merit in the theory (e.g., Hagan, 1973; Schur, 1969, 1971). However, the belief that legal reactions to crime generate more crime is not confined to advocates of the "labeling perspective" in the study of deviance (see Schrag, 1971:1).

of the amount of criminality reduced by reformation.[17] So investigators can only take into account the possibility that secondary deviance and reformation are relevant to some unknown extent. There is no effective means to that end at present, but an effort can be made by focusing deterrence research on categorical or repetitive rates, neither of which could be influenced by reformation or secondary deviance. If such a focus is not feasible and only conventional crime rates can be used, then the alternative is to consider a type of crime that is supposedly characterized by a very low recidival rate. If the crime is such that individuals seldom commit it again after punishment, then reformation or secondary deviance could not have an appreciable impact on the conventional rate. Homicide evidently approximates the type of crime in question,[18] and so we have still another reason to regard it as strategic for deterrence research. However, should research be limited to criminal homicide, tests of deterrence propositions would be limited largely to absolute deterrence.

Policy Issues

As indicated in Chapter 5, a penal policy predicated on specific deterrence is dubious, and that is perhaps the principal reason for the emergence of a rehabilitative orientation in criminal corrections. That movement has a long history, but in recent years doubts about the feasibility, effectiveness, and even the "legality" of rehabilitative programs in criminal corrections have grown (see, e.g., Allen, 1964; Bailey, 1971; Cohen, 1971; Cressey, 1962; Gibbons, 1965; Gould and Namenwirth, 1971; Hood, 1971; Hood and Sparks, 1970; Kassebaum et al., 1971; Martinson, 1974; Morris, 1966; Morris and Hawkins, 1970; Murphy, 1973c; Radzinowicz and Wolfgang, 1971III; Szasz, 1963, 1965; Uusitalo, 1972; and Wilkins, 1969).

Rehabilitation is difficult in a punitive context, and custody is perceived by offenders as punitive under the best of conditions. Moreover, rehabilitative programs are expensive, and legislators are unwilling to allocate the resources needed for truly extensive programs. Their reluctance reflects budgetary concerns, a lingering adherence to the deterrence doctrine, and justifiable doubts about the efficacy of rehabilitative

---

[17]Unfortunately, the term "secondary crime" is conceptually ambiguous. Some writers do not use the term to denote instances of "secondary deviance" but rather use it to denote instances in which individuals engage in one kind of criminal activity (e.g., burglaries) to make possible or facilitate what is another kind of criminal activity (e.g., illegal purchase of narcotics). See Hills, 1971:53.

[18]See footnote 7, supra.

programs in reducing recidivism. Of course, a rehabilitation program may fail because of limited scope, the punitive context, and/or extralegal conditions (see Reitzes, 1955); nonetheless, legislators will not abandon custodial institutions or provide funds for expanding rehabilitative programs without evidence of success.

As an alternative to rehabilitation, a penal policy could be based entirely on deterrence and incapacitation. However, indifference to prisoners (in effect, locking them up and forgetting them) would be difficult to defend, especially if it is shown that recidivism accounts for a substantial proportion of crimes.[19] But that demonstration would be further evidence against specific deterrence; and, assuming no rehabilitative innovations, the only alternative way to check recidivism (short of relying on specific deterrence or incapacitation) is through reformation.

As already indicated, all evidence suggests that conventional punishments rarely reform. Yet, eventually, it may be possible to schedule certain kinds of punishments so that those punished react aversively to opportunities for committing a criminal act or even to contemplating a criminal act. Even though there are no perfected techniques for inducing such aversive reactions, attempts to develop and use them will pose the most controversial issue in the long history of debates over penal policy; and that issue is already emerging (Kittrie, 1971; Lewis, 1971; and Mitford, 1973).

One need not look to Orwell's *1984* for "new means" to reformation. Research on aversive conditioning may lead to effective techniques of "behavioral modification," and systematic attempts already have been made to repress drinking, psychotic behavior, the use of drugs, and sexual aberration through scheduled punishments.[20] Experimentation with

[19]Gould and Namenwirth (1971) have argued that it is impossible for convicts to contribute a great deal to the total crime rate on release from prison because there are so few of them relative to the total population. Although their argument has been endorsed by others (Tittle, 1974:391; Tittle and Logan, 1973:374), investigators cannot determine how much recidivism contributes to the total crime rate without computing recidival rates, and there is no defensible way at present to compute those special rates. Furthermore, what recidivism contributes to the total *general* crime rate is one thing, but what it contributes to the rates for particular types of crime (e.g., robbery, burglary) is quite another.

[20]The term "aversive conditioning" does not extend to all experimental or clinical methods of behavioral modification, and some of those methods are not based on punishments. In particular, punishment is not the central notion in "operant conditioning" (it cannot be equated with negative reinforcement), and the distinction takes on special significance because the idea of aversive conditioning is much more in keeping with conventional penal practices than is operant conditioning. For a survey of experimental or clinical methods of behavioral modification (through aversive conditioning or otherwise), see Bandura, 1969; Bucher and Lovaas, 1968; and Campbell and Church, 1969.

a view to modifying the behavior of felons through aversive conditioning has not been extensive, but it is underway.[21] A perfected technique might well reduce the recidival rate without custodial institutions; and, if so, the monetary cost would be less than conventional rehabilitative programs. Those programs commonly require custodial institutions, and they are costly for that reason alone (see Zimring and Hawkins, 1973:57).

Reformation through aversive conditioning will not want for advocates, especially among those who see no political implications in the control of crime. But, just as surely, reformation through aversive conditioning will be opposed, and objections to it will transcend the constitutional proscription of cruel and unusual punishment.[22] Indeed, aversive conditioning could be less painful than a long prison sentence.

The most basic objection to reformation through aversive conditioning is that it would "dehumanize" offenders, perhaps permanently. That objection reflects two things: first, an emphasis on "choice" in human conduct; and, second, recognition that aversive conditioning could eliminate the experience of making choices. Whether offenders would be fundamentally different after aversive conditioning is not the point; they would be viewed as less than human (i.e., not as responsible moral beings).

Apart from philosophical considerations, reformation through aversive conditioning could have a crippling effect on "normal" behavior (e.g., a rapist subjected to such "treatment" might find the presence of women intolerable).

Critics of aversive conditioning in a penal system would not overlook the political implications. Reformation through aversive conditioning could be a step toward the control of all manner of conduct, for nothing encourages the control of human beings more than recognition that it can be done. In that connection, the control of one human being over another through the threat of a punishment is effective only if the threatened party is unwilling to risk that punishment; but the inability to commit an act eliminates that choice.

[21]See Kittrie, 1971; Mitford, 1973. The experimentation in question is not limited to aversive conditioning; it also extends to "organic therapy," including psychosurgery (see esp. Shapiro, 1973).

[22]See Kittrie, 1971; Mitford, 1973; and Shapiro, 1973. Opposition to the modification of the behavior of felons through experimental or clinical methods is not limited to aversive conditioning; it also extends to organic therapy, including psychosurgery and what is called (euphemistically or not) "electro-chemical treatment." However, the opposition reflects not so much reservations about the cruelty or even the effectiveness of the techniques of behavioral modification; rather, it reflects a concern with legality and philosophical considerations that touch on the moral and political character of social life (see Allen, 1964).

All of the foregoing may appear far removed from the deterrence doctrine, but debates over penal policy will not end with the question: How much does punishment deter crime? Regardless of the answer, there always will be another question: What are the alternatives?

Normative Validation

The notion of a norm is difficult to define even though it can be related to immediate experience. Rare is the individual who has never experienced disgust or indignation as a reaction to the conduct of others; and few if any individuals have never experienced feelings of guilt or shame as a reaction to their own conduct. Disgust, indignation, guilt, and shame are all indicative of evaluations of conduct (i.e., right or wrong, good or bad), and such evaluations are "normative" to the extent that they are socially shared. Stated more abstractly, a norm is something more than an isolated evaluation of conduct by a particular individual; it is a collective phenomenon in that members of the same social unit *tend* to agree in their evaluations of conduct. Evidence of such agreement is found in responses of members to normative questions, such as: Should children smoke cigarettes? The argument is not that the responses necessarily reveal the true evaluation of conduct; rather, it is that members commonly agree in their responses.

Saints and divines notwithstanding, everyone has lashed out verbally or physically in an indignant response to the conduct of others. Such reactions tend to be institutionalized, in that for each type of criminal or deviant act there is a common or typical reaction. Institutionalization also extends to the development of shared beliefs as to the appropriate reaction, including not only what should be done but also who should do it. Such beliefs are reactive norms, and they assume their most explicit form in criminal law (though particular laws may not have popular support).

So there are two major classes of normative phenomena: (1) evaluations of conduct (i.e., shared beliefs as to what conduct *ought* to be) and (2) evaluative reactions (shared beliefs as to what ought to be done given undesirable conduct). Just as we learn to evaluate acts (i.e., to consider some acts as right and others as wrong), so do we learn the appropriate reactions to acts, including punitive reactions. Accordingly, while we may react to an act in a certain way because we regard it as wrong, we have learned that the *type* of act in question is wrong by observing that others react punitively to instances of it.

The foregoing is not another allusion to enculturative consequences of punishment, but the distinction must be clarified. Consider an individual who (1) knows that some type of act is contrary to a norm and subject to punishment and (2) condemns the act. The condemnation may reflect experience pertaining to punishment, but further punishments would have no strictly enculturative consequences, for the individual is already aware of the proscription of the act and the prescribed punitive reaction to it. But what maintains the individual's condemnation of the act? One argument contends that it is further experiences of instances where the act is punished.

If an individual condemns a type of act but observes in one instance after another that the act is not punished, the severity of the individual's condemnation is likely to decline. Conversely, on observing that the act is punished regularly and severely, the individual's condemnation is likely to be maintained or enhanced. All such arguments are summarized by the notion of "normative validation," meaning the maintenance or intensification of an evaluation of conduct through experience of punitive reactions to contrary acts.

The notion of normative validation is relevant in assessing the deterrence doctrine, for law is a type of norm and legal punishments are reactions to contrary acts. One well-known argument is that punishment of a type of act has little or no influence on the incidence of that act; rather, incidence is largely a matter of the extent to which the public disapproves of the act. The argument implies that legal punishments are ineffective means of social control, and it rests either (1) on the assumption that there is no relation between purely social evaluations of conduct and legal evaluations or (2) on the assumption that the severity of the legal punishment for a type of act merely reflects the degree of negative social evaluation of the act. What the argument ignores, or tacitly denies, is that legal punishment may give rise to or at least reinforce social condemnations of an act.[23] Stated more abstractly, one possible consequence of legal punishment is normative validation, and the indirect consequence is greater conformity to laws in a manner *independent of deterrence*. Individuals refrain from illegal acts not because they fear punishment but because they evaluate the acts negatively, and legal punishments maintain or intensify those negative evaluations. Stated another way, individuals have internalized the norm (see Campbell, 1964) that the law expresses, and legal punishments contribute to that internalization. However, no

[23]The argument is not that acquiring knowledge of a law or change in a law *alters* the individual's evaluation of conduct (e.g., an individual may continue to disapprove of attempted suicide after learning that the act has been decriminalized). Some research findings (Berkowitz and Walker, 1967; Walker and Argyle, 1964) are contrary to that argument; but those findings are of questionable relevance in contemplating normative validation for reasons not previously mentioned (see footnote 13, supra). The argument in the case of normative validation is that actual punishments of types of acts *reinforce* social condemnation of those types of acts.

claim is made that punishment is necessary for the internalization of norms, legal or extralegal.

Recognition of normative validation creates an evidential problem in deterrence research, especially in the case of absolute deterrence. Individuals who never commit the type of crime in question are likely to evaluate it negatively; hence it may appear that their conformity has nothing to do with punishment. But their negative evaluation may be maintained (at least in part) by punishments of the act.

The foregoing is relevant only to the extent that punishments do "validate" norms, and any judgment of the extent would be sheer conjecture. The notion of normative validation rests not on systematic evidence but rather on argumentation. Durkheim's version of the argument (1949) is the most forcible one ever made; but he did not use a systematic terminology to describe what is here designated as "normative validation," nor did he offer more than general observations on the subject.[24] Nonetheless, Durkheim's argument is especially relevant here because he viewed the primary function of punishment as normative validation, not deterrence. However, it appears that Durkheim made two arguments about punishment: First, the severity of punishment *reflects* the intensity of social condemnation; and, second, severe punishments *reinforce* social condemnation. The two arguments are not really inconsistent, but they are more complicated than it might appear.

Import for Deterrence Research

For various reasons, it is not feasible to attempt the measurement of normative validation and then to use those measures as controls (e.g., through partial correlation) when examining the relation between the crime rate and properties of punishment. The only alternative is to focus deterrence research on those types of crime for which punishment has negligible consequences in the way of normative validation. Criminal homicide is not such a type because it is severely condemned in most social units, and that intensity could be maintained (in part) by punishment. Alternatively, deterrence research can focus on crimes that scarcely appear to be subject to social condemnation, one being parking violations. Since the social condemnation of parking violations is negligible, punish-

---

[24]Like Durkheim, numerous writers on deterrence or the preventive effects of punishment have recognized the notion of normative validation without using the term. They commonly speak of the "educative-moralizing effect" or simply observe that punishment "expresses social disapproval." The major terminological problem is that writers commonly do not distinguish the *enculturative* and the *validating* effects of punishment (see Zimring and Hawkins, 1973:77), and those two notions are not distinguished in what is known as the "declaratory theory" of law. For an introduction to the literature on such matters, see Andenaes, 1952, 1968, 1971; Berkowitz and Walker, 1967; Cohen, 1971; Feinberg, 1972; and Zimring and Hawkins, 1973.

ments (fines) of them are not likely to further normative validation, for there is nothing to validate. Nonetheless, the certainty and severity of punishment for parking violations may vary appreciably from one city to the next.

Policy Issues

Those who emphasize sanctions to reduce crime have been so preoccupied with deterrence that they seldom invoke notions akin to normative validation (Devlin, 1965, being a notable exception). Nonetheless, there is a policy issue, one that pertains to publicizing actual punishments.[25] If punishments validate laws and thereby reduce the crime rate, they do so only to the extent that they are publicized. But in the United States and many other countries, actual punishments are not publicized systematically, and the citizenry is informed only at the whim of news media. The situation is all the more remarkable because publicizing punishments might further both normative validation and deterrence.

Any proposal to publicize punishments systematically would raise the specter of public executions, floggings, etc. Those spectacles were abandoned in response to humanitarian protests, and today they are virtually precluded by the nature of criminal sanctions. Imprisonment cannot be made public, and paying a fine is not likely to draw a crowd. Accounts of actual punishments could be publicized systematically, but critics would regard the proposal as suggesting a "police state." Yet virtually everyone knows that there are police, that arrests are made, and that people are punished. As for the argument that public identification of the individuals who have been punished would generate more crime in the form of a secondary deviance, accounts of punishments can be publicized without identifying particular individuals. So arguments against publicizing punishments reduce to a plea for maintaining appearances, meaning a tacit denial of organized coercion in social control.

Retribution

Critics of legal punishment (e.g., Menninger, 1966; Barnes and Teeters, 1959) typically pay little attention to the demands of victims of crimes for retribution. To the extent that victims demand retribution, punishment of crimes is something more than vengeance; it is at the same time a means of controlling vengeance. Even in contemporary societies, there are isolated instances where the victim of a crime or the

---

[25]There is a prior and much more general issue, that being whether criminal law should be employed to create or reinforce moral standards (see Devlin, 1965; Hart, 1963; Sartorius, 1972; and Schur, 1965).

victim's surrogate assaults the suspected perpetrator, and not just in self-defense. Hence the question: How many more crimes would be privately avenged if there were no prospects of legal punishment? Those who respond "none" should read accounts of reactions to deviance among the Eskimo and the Comanche prior to their subjugation by Europeans (see Hoebel, 1954). A *distinct* system of criminal law was not present in those two populations, and the victims of wrongful acts or their surrogates commonly sought vengeance by violence.

Even in societies with "law," the certainty and severity of punishment could become so negligible that the citizens would seek personal retribution; and what the injured party would take to be justifiable vengeance could be criminal assault, criminal homicide, robbery, extortion, kidnapping, or theft. So no imagination is required to see that retribution "outside the law" generates crimes. Hence, retribution through legal punishments may prevent crimes, and it is another preventive consequence distinct from deterrence.

Critics of "legal vengeance" are likely to dismiss the postulated preventive consequence by pointing out that personal retribution is extremely rare. But that argument is misplaced; the rarity of personal retribution may be attributed to the citizenry believing that there is some prospect of legal punishment for acts that they are inclined to avenge personally.

Import for Deterrence Research

Assume that the celerity, certainty, and severity of punishment decline to the point that they are negligible, and consequently that citizens resort to private vengeance of crimes. Since private vengeance commonly takes the form of violence, the rate for certain types of crime (e.g., assault) would then increase; but, if so, it would be erroneous to attribute the increase to a decline in deterrence.

The evidential problem just alluded to is hypothetical, but it is so only because the private vengeance of crimes is rare. Whether it will remain rare if the celerity, certainty, and severity of punishment reach even lower levels is another question. The immediate consideration is that the prevention of crime through retribution can be justifiably ignored in deterrence research.

Policy Issues

The preventive consequence of legal retribution is not likely to enter into debates over penal policy even if critics of criminal justice commence arguing for the elimination of all punitive measures. Legislators seldom look beyond public demand for retribution of crimes, and at least in the United States their shortsightedness is most understandable, for next to being "soft on communism" the quickest route to political retirement is being "soft on crime." Nonetheless, legislative sensitivity to public demand for retribution contributes an irrational element to debates over penal policy, insofar as the goal of policy is the prevention of crimes. The point is not that legislators habitually overestimate public demand for retribution, which would be a most debatable assertion. Rather, attempts on the part of legislators to satisfy the real or imagined yearning of the public for retribution would directly prevent crimes only if an increase in private vengeance of crimes were an immediate prospect. But the public has bemoaned "excessively lenient treatment of criminals" for decades without an obvious upward trend in the private vengeance of crimes.

The obvious counterargument is that the public demand for retribution furthers deterrence indirectly, with legislators reacting to the demand by resisting proposals to decrease the severity of punishments for crimes. Yet, as indicated in Chapter 5, the severity of punishment appears to play a minor role in deterrence. Moreover, the preoccupation of legislators with the severity of punishment diverts attention from promoting deterrence by increasing the certainty of punishment. In any case, we have a paradox. The foremost consideration in penal policy—real or imagined public demand for retribution of crime—has no direct bearing on crime prevention.

Stigmatization

Whatever the punishment for a particular felony, punishment publicly and dramatically identifies the perpetrator as "criminal" and thereby becomes a *criterion* for subsequent social condemnation (see Schwartz and Skolnick, 1962). The punished individual faces the prospects of incontestable divorce, loss of job, denial of alternative employment opportunities, exclusion from voluntary associations, and termination of all manner of other social relations (e.g., friendships, romantic attachments, kinship ties).

Even experienced felons are sensitive to the stigma of punishment (see Irwin, 1970), and the anticipation of stigma may deter the typical citizen more than the punishment itself.[26] Indeed, even if individuals do

[26]In a British study, only 10 percent of a sample of youths (15–20 years old) attributed the most important consequence of being arrested to legal punishment; by contrast, 49 percent attributed the greatest importance to "what my family would think about it" (see Zimring and Hawkins, 1973:192).

not know the prescribed punishments for particular types of crimes, their ignorance does not prevent them from perceiving all punishments as stigmatizing.

Stigmatization is perhaps the most complex consequence of legal punishment. Even if the typical citizen has an awesome dread of stigmatization *through* punishment, it does not follow that he or she refrains from criminal acts because of that dread. For that matter, stigmatization may not be perceived in all divisions of a social unit (especially classes or castes) as a consequence of punishment. In the United States, for example, it does not tax credulity to suggest that blacks, Chicanos, and low-income individuals are less prone to view punishment as a stigma than are upper-class Anglos. Indeed, it is a testimonial to the solidarity of exploited and repressed peoples when they ignore legal considerations as a criterion for moral judgments.

The hypothesized difference along racial, ethnic, or class lines takes on added significance in contemplating another contrast. Arrest rates for nonbusiness crimes in general are much greater among blacks and low-income divisions of the American population, which suggests that punishment prevents crimes only insofar as stigmatization is a correlate of punishment. Generalizing, punishment prevents crime through stigmatization in an inverse ratio to the degree of social stratification. Given a society with rigid class or caste lines and marked poverty in some classes or castes, the prevention of crime through stigmatization could be negligible. The more general point is that the preventive consequences of punishment through stigmatization may well be extremely relative.

Here, as elsewhere, one may object to or choose to ignore the distinction between deterrence and other possible preventive mechanisms (see Zimring and Hawkins 1973:190). The objection in this case is that if punishment prevents crimes through dread of stigmatization, then the prevention is deterrence. Yet the fear of stigmatization is analytically distinct from and in addition to whatever fear one may have of legal punishment itself. Moreover, stigmatization is a *problematical* consequence of punishment; whether it is a consequence depends on extralegal conditions.

Finally, we have the possibility of a paradox. Even if numerous individuals refrain from crime to avoid stigmatization, those who are punished may commit even more crimes because of stigmatization. Stated more analytically, at the same time that stigmatization reduces the categorical crime rate, it raises the recidival rate. The argument parallels that considered in contemplating reformation; specifically, stigmatization may generate secondary deviance or result in definitions favorable to crime through differential association. In the case of secondary deviance, the offender identifies himself as a criminal not only because of punishment but also because of subsequent stigmatization. As for differential association, when normal social relations are terminated because of stigmatization, the offender may turn to those who attach no stigma to punishment, and they are likely to be sources of definitions favorable to crime.

Import for Deterrence Research

Even with unlimited research resources, it is difficult to imagine a procedure that would enable investigators to measure stigmatization through punishment, let alone assess its impact on the incidence of crime apart from deterrence. However, the impact of stigmatization on the incidence of crime may well be minimal for certain types of offenses, parking violations in particular. The argument is, of course, that punishments of those offenses scarcely stigmatize.

The focus of deterrence research on "minor" offenses would not provide a basis for inferences about the magnitude of either the preventive consequences or the generative consequences of stigmatization. Inferences along that line would require comparisons of different types of crimes, but there is no obvious rationale for reaching a conclusion. To illustrate, although punishment for criminal homicide undoubtedly stigmatizes far more than punishment for parking violations, it would be most questionable to argue that the much lower rate for criminal homicide reflects the preventive consequences of stigmatization. After all, the ostensibly greater certainty of punishment for criminal homicide is in itself sufficient to anticipate a differential rate.

Policy Issues

Attempts to justify severe punishments by appealing to stigmatization are most questionable. One may be stigmatized more if imprisoned rather than fined or placed on probation, but it is difficult to see how stigmatization is greater for imprisonment of, say, ten years rather than five. The public is unlikely to draw such fine distinctions (see Zimring and Hawkins, 1973:193). Whatever the relation between the severity of punishment and stigmatization, the preventive consequences of stigmatization are purely conjectural. Opponents of punitive penal policies should welcome research on the subject, as the findings might indicate that stigmatization through punishment generates more crime than it prevents.

Normative Insulation

Theories of criminality solve no evidential problems in deterrence research, but they are useful in identifying possible preventive consequences of punishment other than deterrence. Sutherland's theory of differential association is especially useful, largely because (1) it emphasizes social relations in the etiology of crime and (2) some kinds of punishment have an obvious impact on social relations.

One of the many ostensible theorems of Sutherland's theory can be stated as a simple assertion: The crime rate among sons of felons is higher than the crime rate among sons of nonfelons. There are various problems with the assertions: (1) because of the discursive way Sutherland stated his theory, the assertion cannot be derived from it systematically; (2) the wording of the assertion is subject to question, especially limiting it to sons of felons and nonfelons; and (3) the same assertion could be derived from contending theories, e.g., one that attributes criminality to heredity. Nonetheless, the assertion is consistent with the idea that crime is a product of favorable definitions, the assumption in this case being that sons of felons are exposed to more favorable definitions.

To the extent that Sutherland's theory and the present correlative assertion are valid, then at least three punishments—death, imprisonment, and banishment—may prevent crimes independently of their efficacy as deterrents. Those punishments terminate or reduce the interaction between a possible source of definitions favorable to crime (the offender) and those who might otherwise be exposed to that source, e.g., the offender's children, other kindred, colleagues, and friends (see Gibbs, 1971).

When an offender is executed, imprisoned, or banished, the consequence is normative insulation, meaning that the offender has less opportunity to influence the attitudes and values of his or her associates. Assuming that the influence in some cases would have involved more definitions favorable to crime, then normative insulation reduces crimes through means other than deterrence.

Import for Deterrence Research

The problem in attempting to deal with normative insulation in deterrence research is not just one of measurement. Additionally, its preventive consequences (if any) are probably limited to categorical crime rates. As for recidival rates, the imprisonment of offenders places them in a condition where (so the argument goes) they are exposed to definitions favorable to crime.

With a view to controlling for or otherwise taking normative insulation into account, the only solution is to focus deterrence research on certain types of punishments.[27] Fines are especially strategic in that connection. They probably have negligible consequences in the way of normative insulation, and they are prescribed (as an alternative to imprisonment) for a wide range of crimes.

Policy Issues

Policy issues are commonly adversarial, meaning that contending parties are engaged in an argument. However, in some instances a policy issue is more nearly a dilemma, and that is the case in contemplating normative insulation.

Judges and probation officers are aware of the normative insulation notion (though not the term) when the convicted defendant is the father, mother, brother, or sister of young children. If they subscribe to the principle articulated in Sutherland's theory and are concerned with crime prevention, they are inclined to imprison the convicted defendant; but other and more compelling considerations are likely to enter into their deliberations.

There is no explicit policy in United States jurisdictions that promotes imprisonment to realize normative insulation, and such a policy would be (1) contrary to the ideal of "family unit" and (2) far more costly in strictly economic terms than it might appear. When a parent is incarcerated for even a few months, the family may be forced to live off welfare payments.

Habituation

Parties to the debate over deterrence often lose sight of a crucial consideration—what is relevant evidence depends on the definitions of deterrence. A definition should speak to this question: Can punishment deter an individual who is not even contemplating a criminal act? The definition set forth in Chapter 2 implies a negative answer; that is, one cannot refrain from an act without having contemplated it. Since a multitude of citizens seldom if ever contemplate a criminal act, it may appear that the threat of punishment scarcely touches on everyday life and hence could not possibly prevent a substantial amount of crime. The

---

[27]There are far more alternatives in the way of experimental work on punishment; but here, as elsewhere, possible control strategies are limited to nonexperimental studies.

point is not that the typical citizen continually refrains from criminal acts because of the dictates of conscience or in recognition that those acts are socially condemned. Those factors are distinct from the threat of legal punishment, but it is questionable to assume that even they loom large in conformity to laws. The most remarkable feature of that conformity is its unreflective, uncritical quality. It is even misleading to speak of the typical citizen as refraining from criminal acts in everyday activities, for that phrase suggests a conscious contemplation of violations. Indeed, the typical citizen is seldom aware of conforming to the law, let alone that conformity avoids punishments, social condemnation, stigmatization, etc.

Imprecise though it may be, "habitual" is the appropriate characterization of conformity to the law by the typical citizen, and habitual conformity is not the same as refraining from a criminal act out of fear of punishment. However, critics of the idea of the prevention of crime through punishment are prone to overlook an important possibility— that threatened punishments may create or contribute to what is later habitual conformity. Andenaes (1952) has stressed that possibility, and Zimring and Hawkins (1973:85) have clarified the idea by this illustration: "The threat of punishment may cause a man to refrain from speeding on his way to work. After a while, however, more than the simple deterrant effect may be at work, for he may have developed the habit of driving at a certain speed, and this habit provides additional insulation against future law violation."

The central issue in identifying "habituation" as a possible preventive consequence of punishment distinct from deterrence is strictly conceptual. If one accepts the definition of deterrence proposed in Chapter 2, then what is here called an "habituative consequence of punishment" is clearly not deterrence, because one who habitually conforms to a law does not contemplate violation of it, let alone contemplate the prescribed punishments. Of course, one can prefer another definition of deterrence; but once a definition of deterrence admits more than "compliance in response to the fear of punishment," it extends to virtually anything that could prevent crimes one way or another. The problem is not resolved by speaking of a "simple deterrent effect" (Zimring and Hawkins, 1973), for that terminology does not limit deterrence as a class of phenomena.

Import for Deterrence Research

The habituative consequences of punishments cannot be assessed systematically in any social unit, for it is not possible to estimate the amount of habitual conformity to any law, let alone to what degree threatened punishments contribute to the establishment of those habits. Described in terms that are relevant in contemplating tests of deterrence propositions, investigators cannot distinguish readily between habitual conformity to a law and conformity that is prompted by fear of punishment.

Unlike some of the other preventive mechanisms (e.g., normative validation), there are several bases for inferences about punishment, habituation, and crime. One approach is to consider decriminalization, that is, instances where some type of act has ceased to be legally proscribed. To the extent that conformity to the law is habitual, decriminalization will not be followed by an increase in the incidence of the formerly proscribed act. The end of Prohibition in the United States is illustrative, and it also illustrates the major interpretive problems. Any major change other than decriminalization casts doubt on the proposed interpretation; that is, stability in the incidence of the act is indicative of habituation. Since Prohibition ended when the country was in the midst of a major depression, the proportion of the population who recommenced drinking may have been lessened by purely economic factors.

Another and perhaps more feasible approach is to intensify law enforcement so that members of a population are likely to perceive an increase in the certainty of punishment. If that change reduces violations to a negligible level, then stability in the frequency of violations after an abrupt termination of intense enforcement would indicate habituation (the smaller the increase in violations, the greater the habituation).

The proposed strategy is feasible for only a few types of crimes, one being speeding. A marked increase in the number of patrols on a road, along with rigorous imposition of penalties for speeding, could reduce violations by regular drivers to a negligible rate; and intense enforcement activity could continue for several months after a negligible violation rate is realized. After abrupt termination of such intense enforcement, the frequency of violations by regular drivers at the end of another period (with no patrols) would indicate the amount of habituation established by intense enforcement. Of course, such experimentation would provide only a basis for inferences about habituation, and those inferences would be debatable.

If there were a marked increase in violations immediately after cessation of intense enforcement, then there would be no habituation (at least for most drivers), but it would not follow that no punishment could induce habitual conformity. Should violations increase immediately, it could be attributed to a short period of intense enforcement or to mild punishments. Then suppose that the violations remained negligible after intense enforcement ended. Even though patrols had ceased altogether, motorists could be driving with a view to their resumption, which is to say that their conformity might be reflective. Of course, a comparison of the speeding violations of the same regular drivers on other roads might be informative, but it is most unlikely that any experimental design would yield incontrovertible evidence of habituation.

In attempting to assess preventive mechanisms other than deterrence, investigators have only one advantage—the strategies are seemingly infinite. As just suggested, the "experimental" approach is limited to a few types of crimes, but there is a "control" strategy that is not limited. Habitual conformity to a law is especially difficult to distinguish from deterrence proper in considering categorical crime rates. By contrast, changes in the repetitive rate are much less likely to reflect habituation resulting from punishment. The individuals in question are not "conformers," habitual or otherwise, and that is especially true when the repetitive rate is computed for a brief period. Stated more generally, insofar as there is a relation between the repetitive rate for some type of crime and properties of punishment, the relation cannot be attributed to the habituative effect of punishment.

Policy Issues

The distinction between deterrence and habituation is a slim one, and it may appear inconsequential, for either way punishment prevents crime. But a policy issue is posed indirectly, and considerable significance would attach to a research strategy that purportedly distinguishes the deterrent and the habituative prevention of crime. The punitive prevention of crime is most efficient through habituation, and it could be that different properties of punishment (e.g., low certainty–high severity versus high certainty–low severity) result in approximately the same amount of deterrence but quite different levels of habituation.

In light of the foregoing, it might appear that research should be directed toward identifying conditions of punishments that are especially conducive to habituation. But any attempt to control crime has political implications, and the very idea of habituative effects gives rise to an issue. While one may condemn laws that are contrary to extralegal norms, that principle is questionable when extended to a pluralistic or complex society. Given marked conflict in interests, divergent beliefs, inconsistent values, etc., punishment may be the only way that certain forms of behavior can be controlled. However, the idea of citizens conforming to laws only out of fear of punishment is distasteful; hence the argument that punishment should aim for habituation. But with a view to maintaining political liberties, deterrence is preferable to habituation. Whatever the risk, one can violate a law at his or her peril; but if punishment has an habituative effect, it promotes uncritical conformity. Of course, if one views laws as equitable and criminals as sick or maladjusted, then the idea of habituative effects poses no issue; but in recent decades those views of law and criminals have been rejected by a multitude of social critics (see Quinney, 1970a, 1970b, 1972, 1973; Turk, 1969). They see law as a tool by which an establishment controls the exploited, and from that perspective a criminal is a dissident, one who is neither sick nor maladjusted. Reservations about law are not peculiar to the young or so-called radicals. Except when they periodically succumb to a craving for law and order, conservatives voice reservations about the beneficence of the law; and their idols, the "liberals" of the eighteenth and nineteenth centuries, clearly viewed law as a necessary evil. In any case, whatever the reasons for reservations about law, those who hold them will see a danger in the idea that punishment should engender habitual conformity.

Summary

Chapter 1 introduced the possibility that crime rates reflect extralegal conditions as well as preventive consequences of legal punishments. We have now considered still another possibility—that preventive mechanisms are not limited to deterrence. So at this point it is appropriate to simply outline all seemingly relevant conditions.

I.   Extralegal generative conditions
II. Extralegal inhibitory conditions
III. Possible preventive consequences of legal reactions to crime
    A. Preventive consequences independent of punishment (e.g., rehabilitation)
    B. Preventive consequences resulting from the fear of punishment
       1. Absolute deterrence
       2. Restrictive deterrence
       3. Specific deterrence
    C. Preventive consequences of punishment independent of the fear of legal punishment
       1. Incapacitation
       2. Surveillance
       3. Enculturation
       4. Reformation

5. Normative validation
6. Retribution
7. Stigmatization
8. Normative insulation
9. Habituation

The outline should not be construed as a theory about crime or punishment and certainly not as a theory about deterrence. As suggested in Chapter 1, it is not possible to list *specific and demonstrably relevant* extralegal conditions, and the list of preventive consequences of punishment does not mean that all of them are truly important. There is virtually no truly systematic evidence to show that each postulated phenomenon actually prevents crimes, let alone how much. They are only *possible* preventive consequences of punishments. However, those consequences take on special significance because each of them could be related to the properties of punishment that are emphasized by the deterrence doctrine. For example, both incapacitation and normative insulation probably vary directly with the severity (length) of imprisonment. Accordingly, given a relation between crime rates and severity of imprisonment, that relation could reflect at least two consequences of punishment other than deterrence.

If it were possible to measure each of the possible preventive consequences, research evidence would probably indicate that the list should be reduced. Some of the variables (e.g., reformation) may have only a very negligible impact on the conventional crime rate. However, until such time that the phenomena can be measured, the list is useful in analyzing research findings on the deterrence question. If nothing else, it serves as a reminder that virtually any finding in past deterrence research is subject to all manner of interpretations.

Four

Properties of Legal Punishments

Any statement of the deterrence doctrine as a theory will incorporate three notions—punishment, deterrence, and crime rates. However, even if two theorists have the same conception of deterrence, focus on the same type of deterrence (e.g., absolute), limit their theories to the same type of crime, and generalize about the same kind of crime rate (e.g., categorical), their conceptualization of "legal punishment" could be quite divergent.

The point is not just that theorists' definitions of punishment may differ.[1] Additionally, assertions about deterrence are virtually meaningless unless they refer to specific *properties* of punishment, and for that reason alone the assertion that punishment deters crime is neither informative nor testable. Even Beccaria and Bentham spoke in terms of the celerity, certainty, and severity of punishment; but it does not follow that a deterrence theory will make assertions about all of those properties or only those properties. As just one possibility, a theorist may conclude that celerity is irrelevant for some types of deterrence; and there are far more specific properties of punishment than those recognized by Beccaria or Benthem. To illustrate, the severity of prescribed punishments (e.g., statutory penalties) and the severity of actual punishments are distinct properties.

A theory that does not recognize such distinctions is vague, but a theorist must do even more. Any deterrence theory is untestable unless it encompasses stipulations as to (1) the procedure for numerical repre-

---

[1]Here, as elsewhere, the word "punishment" is to be construed as restricted to *legal* punishment.

sentation of properties of punishment, (2) the requisite kinds of data, and (3) the methods for gathering those data. Yet those considerations receive very little attention in versions of the deterrence doctrine, and even the identification of specific properties of punishment has been neglected. Although a statement of deterrence theory would be premature at this stage, possibly relevant properties of punishment can be identified, along with *suggested* procedures for their numerical representation. Work along that line at least provides theorists with a range of alternatives.

Appropriate Units of Comparison

No one would entertain the idea that prescribed punishments for criminal homicide in, say, Georgia determine the first-degree murder rate in another state. That is a tacit recognition that a punishment deters an individual only in some context (if at all). Up to this point, such a context has been designated in various ways (e.g., a jurisdiction, a population, a metropolitan area). However, in formulating a deterrence theory, the identification of the context should be taken as a critical step, for the identification determines the units that are to be compared in tests of the theory.

Two crime rates are not comparable unless they pertain to violations of the same criminal law. For example, if the laws of one jurisdiction are such that a sexual relation between first cousins is criminal, while in another jurisdiction the "legal definition" of incest excludes that relation, then the "criminal incest rates" for the two jurisdictions are not strictly comparable. What has been said of rates for a particular type of crime applies *a fortiori* for the total rate (all crimes combined), as the criminal laws of two jurisdictions may differ so much that one type of act (e.g., gambling) may be a crime in one but not in the other.

Since a deterrence theory necessarily makes assertions about crime rates, the question of comparability is crucial. Briefly, tests of a theory are not defensible without some assurance that the crime rates are at least approximately comparable; hence the choice of a "unit term" for a theory should be made in order to maximize comparability. The most feasible solution is to use the words "jurisdictional population" as the unit term in deterrence theories (or isolated deterrence propositions) and define it as two or more individuals who are subject to the same set of criminal laws (or the same criminal law when the concern is with a particular type of crime). Of course, the word "jurisdiction" in itself may have territorial connotations, but that is not inconsistent with the definition. Two or more residents of a particular territorial unit or all of the residents in the unit may be a jurisdictional population, and the same may be true of two or more individuals who were physically present in the territorial unit during some stipulated period. However, two or more residents do not constitute a jurisdictional population unless *all* of the territorial unit is subject to the same set of criminal laws. Similarly, two or more territorial units do not contain comparable jurisdictional populations unless the same set of criminal laws applies in all of those units. To illustrate, cities in the same state would qualify if municipal ordinances were ignored (i.e., if an act is a crime only by state criminal law). Similarly, states qualify but necessarily so only in regard to federal criminal laws. Finally, the present conceptualization permits a wide variety of comparisons in deterrence research (e.g., metropolitan areas in the same state, age groups in the same city).

Legal Punishment

As already indicated, there are numerous properties of punishment, but it is unlikely that all of them will be recognized in a sophisticated deterrence theory. In any case, a definition of "legal punishment" is needed preliminary to analyzing particular properties.

Legal Reactions to Crime

The deterrence doctrine assumes that some evaluations of conduct (norms) are laws. Another assumption is that violations of those evaluations are reacted to by persons in particular statuses in such a way that trained investigators would identify the violations as *crimes,* the persons as *legal officials,* the reactions as *legal,* and some of the legal reactions to crimes as *punitive.*

The immediate conceptual problem is that social scientists and even jurisprudents differ in their conceptions of law, legal officials, crime, and punishment. Definitions of those terms remain divergent after generations of debate; and it remains to be seen whether any definitions can be formulated so that they apply cross-culturally and historically, with applications to nonliterate peoples being especially debatable. No attempt is made here to define the three key terms—"law," "legal," and "official"—if only because no definition would resolve the debates. So it is assumed that the general meaning of those terms is sufficiently precise for present purposes.

With regard to identifying possible principal variables in a deterrence theory, it will suffice to define only "legal reactions to crime" and "legal punishments." Legal reactions to crimes are attempts by legal officials to (1) anticipate certain types of acts; (2) respond to allegations or other evidence of such acts; (3) label instances of such acts as criminal; (4) identify suspected perpetrators of such acts; (5) accuse suspected perpetrators; (6) seek confirmation of the accusations; and (7) rectify the consequences of the acts and/or punish the suspected perpetrators. In some societies one or more steps in the reaction process (e.g., seeking confirmation, staging a trial) may be absent or not clearly distinguishable; and legal systems differ sharply with regard to the organization of reactions to crime, especially in regard to the differentiation of reactors. (One reactor may perform all the reactions in the sequence, or each reaction may be performed by different reactors.) But all legal systems are alike in one respect: actual reactions to acts are supposedly governed by "prescribed reactions," meaning statements as to what legal officials *ought to do* in certain circumstances. Prescribed reactions may appear as statutes, or they may simply be statements made by legal officials.

The foregoing may appear as only a tortuous way of saying that crimes are subject to legal punishment, but a sophisticated theory of deterrence cannot be based on that oversimplification. Conceptualization of punishment haunts attempts to formulate a theory of deterrence, and there is no simple solution.

It is trite to say that imprisonment and fines are punishment. The statement is not a definition of punishment; at most it is only illustrative. Then consider the sequence of legal reactions to crimes in some Anglo-American jurisdictions: investigation, interrogation, arrest, indictment, trial, imprisonment (or fine or probation), parole, and loss of civil rights. Which of those "steps" are punishments? Any answer to that question must be consistent with the answer to a more general question: What is "punishment"? It will not do to answer "infliction of pain or discomfort," for that phrase ignores the distinction between intention and perception. That distinction is central in the typology of legal actions shown in Table 4-1. The typology makes the intention of legal officials a sufficient but not a necessary condition for a legal action to be a punishment. Intention is recognized for the simple reason that deterrence is commonly (if not universally) an aim of penal policy (Morris, 1966). Accordingly, any purported test of the deterrence doctrine is a tacit assessment of penal policy, and viewed that way there is reason to recognize the intention of those who prescribe legal reactions to crimes.

The typology also makes perception a sufficient but not a necessary condition for a legal action to be a punishment. That feature of the conceptualization is consistent with the idea of assessing penal policy, for any thorough assessment considers unintended consequences, and a type II action (unintended punishment) is one such instance. The recognition of perception also reflects a concern with the deterrence doctrine as a potential theory. Whatever the intention, an action may deter an individual if it is perceived by the individual as causing pain or discomfort. However, the perception of a legal action is not limited to the immediate object of the action (e.g., a convicted individual), and the point is not just recognition of vicarious punishment (e.g., executing the relatives of a convicted traitor). To the extent that legal reactions to instances of a particular type of crime are perceived by members of the jurisdictional population (including those who are not immediate objects of the action) as causing pain or discomfort, the type of crime may be deterred. But no attempt is made to distinguish between types of legal action by referring to the proportion of individuals who perceive them one way or another, since any distinction along that line would be arbitrary. Yet the typology does not preclude recognition that one kind of legal action may deter individuals more than others because a greater proportion of the members of the population perceive it as punitive.

The typology reflects a definition of punishment that is not limited to "intention," a conceptualization that stems from and is relative to a concern with deterrence. Anticipating the argument that a type II action by an official is not legal punishment, that argument ignores the perception of the object of the action and the public at large, which is especially important in contemplating deterrence. If members of a jurisdictional

Table 4-1. A Typology of Actions by Legal Officials

	Action Prescribed with the Intent of Inflicting Pain or Discomfort	Action Not Prescribed with the Intent of Inflicting Pain of Discomfort
Action Perceived by Some Members of the Jurisdictional Population as Causing Pain or Discomfort	Type I: Congruent Punishment	Type II: Unintended Punishment
Action Not Perceived by Any Member of the Jurisdictional Population as Causing Pain or Discomfort	Type III: Ineffective Punishment*	Type IV: Nonpunitive Action

*Appearances to the contrary, this class of actions is not a logical contradiction or null class, not even if officials who prescribe legal actions are considered members of the jurisdictional population. They may prescribe an action with the intention of causing pain or discomfort and yet come to recognize that the intended consequence is not realized. For that matter, the statutes of criminal law, having been enacted generations before, may be far removed from both the intention and the perceptions of those who could alter them.

population do not perceive a legal action as causing pain or discomfort, it is difficult to see how they could be deterred by that action, whatever the intention of those who prescribed the action. Indeed, *by definition* type III actions (ineffective punishments) cannot deter individuals from committing a crime.

To summarize, a legal punishment or penalty is a legal action in response to the conduct of someone, administered so that the action (1) is perceived by some members of the jurisdictional population as causing someone pain or discomfort or (2) was prescribed with the intention of causing someone pain or discomfort.[2] Of course, there are various considerations and issues that the definition does not speak to directly, one having to do with the persons who undertake the actions in question. Those persons need not be (though they commonly are) legal officials, meaning that they could be members of the public at large. However, a punishment is legal if and only if it is prescribed by an authority (see Benn, 1973:19), and that prescription extends to the identification of appropriate actors (officials or otherwise).

A legal action is not punishment unless it is a response to the conduct of particular individuals (otherwise, a legislative tax increase could be construed as punishment); but the conceptualization admits the possibility of vicarious punishment (i.e., one person is punished for the conduct of another). Admission of that possibility will not please those who seek to defend the utilitarian justification of punishment. Faced with the claim that the utilitarian rationale extends to the punishment of the innocent (Armstrong, 1971), the defenders of that rationale have argued that causing an individual pain or discomfort is not punishment unless that individual has committed a crime or has been found guilty (see Baier,

---

[2]The definition excludes "anticipatory reactions" to crimes, that is, actions taken by legal officials to further the detection of crimes and the apprehension of offenders, as when radar equipment is used by the police to detect speeding. Insofar as members of the public are aware of such actions, they may perceive them as painful or discomforting in one sense or another; but such actions are not responses to the conduct of particular individuals or, stated another way, particular crimes. Viewed that way, the actions are no more a punishment than is the construction of a prison. True, anticipatory reactions may increase the perceived certainty of punishment, but there are all manner of practices that could have the same result, some of which are clearly alien to conventional conceptions of punishment (e.g., a program to increase police traffic patrols is hardly punishment in itself). Stating the argument more generally, if punishment is construed so broadly that it includes virtually all activities of legal officials, then it becomes impossible to bring evidence to bear on the deterrence doctrine. In particular, a more inclusive conception of punishment than that adopted here precludes numerical representation of the properties of punishment (e.g., certainty, severity). To be sure, various properties of punishment (objective and perceived certainty in particular) may reflect all manner of activities by legal officials, but the deterrence doctrine takes the magnitudes of properties as given.

1972; Quinton, 1972). Whatever merits the argument may have in regard to justifying punishment, the present definition admits vicarious punishment on the presumption that it may be a deterrent.

Analytical Types of Punishment

The present emphasis on "perception" in the definition of legal punishment cannot be justified by appealing to classical or contemporary versions of the deterrence doctrine. Beccaria and Bentham scarcely recognized the problem in defining legal punishment, and the same is true of some recent assessments of the deterrence research (e.g., Tittle and Logan, 1973). Both proponents and opponents of the doctrine focus on statutory penalties (e.g., imprisonment) and simply take procedural reactions (e.g., arrest) for granted. They are taken for granted, evidently, because all statutory penalties in Western countries presuppose procedural steps. (In Anglo-American jurisdictions individuals are imprisoned only after a trial.) Yet it is difficult to identify a procedural reaction (e.g., interrogation, arrest, or trial) that would not qualify as a punishment, and those procedural reactions do not loom large in research or in theorizing on deterrence only because of a preoccupation with statutory penalties.

Suppose that in jurisdictions A and B the statutory penalty for robbery is imprisonment; and in *both* jurisdictions during a given year the proportion of reported instances of robbery that resulted in imprisonment is 0.15. However, in jurisdiction A only 0.60 of the reported instances resulted in an interrogation of a suspect, only 0.35 resulted in arrest, and only 0.25 resulted in a trial. By contrast, in jurisdiction B the corresponding figures for procedural punishments are interrogation, 0.95; arrest, 0.80; and trial, 0.70. As such, the certainty of procedural punishments is far greater in B than in A; and presuming that those punishments are viewed by most members of both jurisdictional populations as punitive (a cause of pain or discomfort), legal reactions to robbery would deter much more in B than in A, even though the certainty of imprisonment is the same for the two jurisdictions.

Conceptualizations of punishment should extend to the identification of classes of punishment, and conventional terms are not adequate for that purpose. No special significance can be attached to statutory punishments as a class, for instances of them (e.g., fines, jail sentences, imprisonment) have no properties in common that are relevant in contemplating deterrence. Nor will it do to speak of "major" punishments because that class virtually defies a meaningful definition.

The proposed solution is to distinguish two major types of punishment. One type, the *procedural,* includes any legally prescribed action in the investigation or adjudication of an alleged crime, commencing with such actions as interrogation of suspects and ending with such actions as trials. The other major type of punishments is designated as *substantive,* and it includes any legally prescribed action after the investigation and adjudication of an alleged crime. Common instances of substantive punishments in Western countries are fines, incarceration, and executions; but the class also extends to probation, parole, and what is known as "loss of civil rights."

No claim is made that this simple typology of punishments is demonstrably superior to alternatives, and the same may be said of the definition of punishment (supra). In the final analysis, the adequacy of typologies or definitions cannot be assessed thoroughly until attempts are made to use them in theories, and the present ones are formulated only in regard to their eventual use in deterrence theories. The primary rationale for the types of punishment is that they are consistent with the definition of punishment, which is to say that procedural reactions to crime may be punitive even though unintended (type II in Table 4-1), while substantive reactions are likely to be both intended and perceived as punitive (type I in Table 4-1). So the two major types reflect the distinctions introduced in Table 4-1, with a tacit denial of the significance of type III punishments in that table (instances of which may be substantive or procedural). However, the two major types diverge from those recognized in Table 4-1 largely because they are defined in terms of the way criminal law is commonly administered. Hence, the two major types are thought to be significant in that they bear indirectly on central considerations in the very definition of punishment and reflect the organizational features of criminal justice.

Substantive punishments are particularly difficult to describe in less abstract terms, primarily because they are not limited to fines, incarceration, or executions. The only way to avoid ethnocentric distinctions is to speak in terms of additional analytical types.

It is generally the case that only legal officials can incarcerate an individual, confiscate an individual's money or property, or execute an individual with impunity. Stated more abstractly, individuals have certain rights that limit what others can do to them. When anyone legally violates those rights with impunity and the violation is perceived or intended to cause pain or discomfort, it is an "abrogative" punishment. The most common and distinctive abrogative punishments in Western countries are fines and executions.

Another type of substantive punishment could be designated as "loss of civil rights," but the meaning of that term is not the same in all legal systems (see Damaska, 1968a, 1968b; Neithercutt, 1969), and even in the United States that class of punishments can be defined only enumeratively (e.g., loss of right to vote, loss of right to hold office). For that matter, the term itself is misleading; it should be "loss of legal privileges." To illustrate, an adult who has not been convicted of a felony is not legally punished for either voting or refraining from voting. In that sense, each adult has a privilege, and a legal punishment may take the form of depriving a particular adult of certain privileges. Rather than use the cumbersome phrase "loss of legal privileges," such punishments are designated as "deprivative."

In all countries any citizen has certain legal duties, acts that an individual cannot omit with impunity. The nature of those duties are not the same for all individuals, but a legal punishment can take the form of increasing the duties of individuals (i.e., imposing additional duties). Such punishments are here designated as "impositional." They are much rarer than abrogative or deprivative punishments, and in many cases an impositional punishment is reported in newspapers as an oddity (e.g., a judge orders someone to pick up litter along the streets for two hours each day over a week). However, probation is in part an impositional punishment and for the rest largely deprivative. So probation must be characterized as deprivative-impositional and it should be recognized that imprisonment *may be* abrogative-impositional. The major purpose is to distinguish those punishments from procedural punishments, and all of them occur after the adjudication of an alleged crime.

The theoretical significance of the foregoing types of substantive punishments cannot be determined at this stage in deterrence research; hence very little additional attention is devoted to them. However, the purpose is to set the scene for eventual generalizations about deterrence that transcend such conventional and ethnocentric distinctions as fines, incarceration, executions, probation, and parole. Those generalizations will be oriented around one central question: Which types of punishment deter individuals more than others? Answers to that question must await much more research, and it is doubtful that the question can be answered without introducing contingencies or conditions. Nonetheless, eventually it will be advantageous to attempt answers in terms of analytical types of punishment rather than in terms of conventionally recognized types in Western countries.

Implications for Penal Policy

Both laymen and legislators evidently think of criminal sanctions largely in terms of substantive punishments, such as fines, incarceration, and executions. Those reactions to crime are undoubtedly perceived by the public as painful or discomforting; but insofar as deterrence is the goal of a penal policy, that policy is incomplete if it takes procedural punishments as given.

The subject of penal policy takes on special significance in the case of the United States, where critics of the criminal justice system never tire of criticizing it as "retributive" (see, e.g., Menninger, 1966). That line of criticism is misleading in that it presupposes a unified penal policy with explicit principles, which is a far cry from the mishmash criminal justice system in the United States or in any component jurisdiction. Nonetheless, the preoccupation of American legislators with the severity of substantive punishments suggests a predominantly retributive orientation. However, barbaric though it may be, a retributive orientation is more consistent with commonly accepted principles of justice than is a deterrence orientation. Specifically, an emphasis on increasing the certainty of procedural punishments as a means to deterrence is likely to result in the punishment of innocent people. The more general point is that striving for deterrence readily runs contrary to commonly accepted principles of justice. Moreover, if those principles are paramount, then there are far worse things than a retributive penal policy, a point that is seemingly lost on advocates of "therapeutic treatment" of criminals (Menninger, 1973) but not on some social critics (especially Lewis, 1971).

Prescribed Punishments

Threat of punishment is central in the deterrence doctrine, and there are two ways that individuals come to perceive a threat. One way is through an experience relating to actual punishments; that is, an individual may (1) be punished on accusation of having committed an act, (2) witness others being punished, or (3) be informed that someone has been punished. The other way is normative. In any social unit the members share beliefs to some extent in regard to *appropriate* reactions to acts, including punitive reactions. Some of those beliefs may be shared only by a minority, and a particular belief may or may not correspond to actual reactions, especially if those who subscribe to it are powerless. If a belief concerning appropriate reactions to acts is enforced by individuals in *special* statuses who use unlimited coercion, then one may properly speak of that belief as a law.

As emphasized by Kelsen (1945), criminal laws stipulate "negative sanctions," meaning prescribed reactions that some if not all members of the public view as punitive. Even though such sanctions are commonly stipulated in statutory law, they need not be written, codified, or even promulgated; and for that reason the term "prescribed punishments" is used here as a generic designation of a class of *reactions* to acts, one that is not limited to statutory penalties. The point is that an individual may perceive a threat of punishment on (1) reading a statute, (2) being informed that a particular type of act is against the law, or (3) being informed of the prescribed punishment for a type of act. In each case, the subsequent perception of a threat of punishment *does not* stem from experience pertaining to actual punishments.

Classical versions of the deterrence doctrine clearly assume that knowledge of prescribed punishments in itself may deter, but that assumption is debatable. It may well be that actual punishments deter some individuals independently of prescribed punishments, deter more individuals, and deter them more effectively. That possibility poses one of many questions that must be confronted in formulating a deterrence theory.

Officials and legislators in particular evidently presume that prescribed punishments deter, but it does not follow that one can make any predictions about differences in crime rates from prescribed punishments alone. Suppose the prescribed punishment for possession of marijuana is a $500 fine in one jurisdiction but two years imprisonment in another. It might appear that the deterrence doctrine anticipates a lower rate of marijuana possession in the second jurisdiction, but such a prediction reflects a presumption—that the prescribed punishment is perceived as more "severe" in the second jurisdiction. Moreover, the prediction ignores the correspondence between prescribed and actual punishments in the two jurisdictions, that is, the "certainty" of the prescribed punishment. Even though severity and certainty are properties of prescribed punishments, they are not somehow "objective" properties in the sense that the color black is a property of crows. Although criminal codes prescribe punishments, the celerity, certainty, and severity of those punishments are not actually given by the code. Accordingly, even if prescribed punishments deter, the way in which they do can be analyzed only in terms of their properties.

Properties of Legal Punishment: Certainty

The deterrence doctrine seemingly asserts an inverse relation between the certainty of punishment of a type of crime and the crime rate. The assertion is especially important because certainty of punishment is likely to be the principal variable in any deterrence theory. It receives extensive attention in classical versions of the deterrence doctrine, and to date few research findings question that emphasis (see, e.g., Logan, 1972b; Antunes and Hunt, 1973).

Requisite Data

According to the classical theory of justice, the punishment of a crime should depend on the offense, not the offender. In Western countries the classical theory has given way to individualization of justice, with a greater emphasis on differential treatment of offenders, ostensibly with a view to rehabilitation. Correlatively, juries and judges have been given greater discretion in passing sentence. Such discretion is precluded when a *specific* penalty is prescribed by statute for each type of crime. With the passing of classical justice, specificity has declined to the point that a felon may be sentenced to (1) imprisonment, (2) payment of a fine, (3) probation, (4) imprisonment and payment of a fine, or (5) payment of a fine and probation. Actually, the sentence is more problematical than the five alternatives suggest, for the length of imprisonment or probation and the amount of the fine may be left (within broad limits) to judicial discretion.

A *specific* prescribed punishment for a type of crime simplifies the numerical representation of certainty, but *alternative* punishments do not create an insoluble problem. For example, if the alternative punishments for shoplifting are six months in jail, a fine of $200, probation, six months in jail and a fine of $200, or probation and a fine of $200, then the certainty of punishment for shoplifting is simply the proportion of reported instances that result in *any one* of those alternative punishments.

Alternative substantive punishments complicate the analysis of certainty, and the analysis is incomplete unless it includes procedural punishments. Table 4-2 illustrates one method of inclusion. Observe that the numbers represent actual legal reactions to felony theft as processual steps.[3] Therefore, a suspected offender *may be* counted more than once, and those imprisoned, fined, or placed on probation are counted four times (each major step in the process). Steps I, II, III are sequential, while the subclasses of step IV (substantive punishments) are mutually exclusive. Thus, in some of the jurisdictions there are at least two alternative prescribed substantive punishments for felony theft, but in assessing certainty it makes no difference which alternative is imposed in particular instances. Moreover, the method for assessing certainty would be the same even if the substantive punishments were specific in each jurisdiction.

[3] The table is an oversimplification in that all conceivable steps in the legal reaction process are not considered (arraignment is one possible step excluded). However, the method of analysis applies regardless of the number of steps. Then observe the underlying assumption—that each procedural step (e.g., arrest) is perceived as punitive by some members of the jurisdictional population.

Table 4-2. *Actual Legal Punishments of Felony Theft in Three Hypothetical Jurisdictional Populations during a Year*

	Number of Instances*		
Types of Punishments	Population A	Population B	Population C
I. Interrogation of Suspects†	325	1,600	800
II. Arrest†	200	1,480	650
III. Trial†	125	1,275	520
IV. (1) Imprisonment, (2) Fines, (3) Probation, (4) Imprisonment and Fine, *or* (5) Probation and Fine‡	50	1,050	400
TOTAL (ΣX)	700	5,405	2,370

*Instances of felony theft (Nc) as identified by the police: population A, 350 cases; population B, 2,000 cases; and population C, 800 cases.
†Procedural punishments.
‡All subtypes are substantive punishments.

An Illustrative Measure

To assess the overall objective certainty of punishment,[4] numbers pertaining to steps in the reaction process must be combined and expressed relative to the total reported instances of the crime in question (typically, those reported by the police). That is accomplished by the following formula for expressing the overall objective certainty of punishment: $OOC = \Sigma X/[(Tp)(Nc)]$, where the X values are like those shown in Table 4-2, Tp is the number of types of procedural punishments and substantive punishments (ignoring alternative kinds), and Nc is the total reported instances of the crime. Thus OOC is 0.50 for jurisdiction A {that is, $700/[(4)(350)]$}, 0.68 for jurisdiction B, and 0.74 for jurisdiction C.

For practical reasons alone, in deterrence research Nc may be "crimes reported by the police," but perennial questions about the reliability of such incidence statistics cast doubts not only on official crime rates but also on all measures of objective certainty in which Nc is based on those statistics. To the extent that instances of a type of crime are not reported to or by the police, the objective certainty of punishment is overestimated. It is pointless to argue that unreported crimes are irrelevant in deterrence research, for individuals may commit crimes on the presumption that they will go undetected (as in the case of shoplifting) or unreported (as in the case of rape). However, the exclusion of unreported crimes in tests of deterrence propositions about the certainty of punishment does not necessarily result in either positive or negative test

[4]The word "objective" is used to indicate that two investigators working independently could conceivably agree in the numerical representation of the property for any jurisdiction. However, the significance of that label for the property cannot be fully appreciated until a related but distinct property, perceived certainty, is considered.

outcomes. Consider a jurisdiction in which only 30 of 200 annual instances of a type of crime, X, were detected and reported by the police. Then suppose that the *actual X* rate was greater than that for any other type of crime, while the official X rate (based on 30 cases) was less than the official rate for any other type of crime. Now suppose that 24 of the 30 official instances of X resulted in imprisonment and that the "official certainty ratio" (i.e., 24/30) was greater for X than for any other type of crime. The combination of a low official rate and a high certainty of imprisonment may appear to be only spurious support for the deterrence doctrine, the argument being that the *actual* rate for X was high relative to other types of crimes. However, if actual X cases were to be considered, then the certainty of imprisonment for X was low (24/200); hence X would not be inconsistent with the deterrence doctrine. Indeed, had only a few (say, 6) of the 30 official cases of X resulted in imprisonment, then the combination of a low official rate and a low certainty of imprisonment would have been spurious negative evidence.

Only one other point can be made about the problem—purported evidence of the *absolute unreliability* of official figures on the incidence of crime can be very misleading when contemplating the reliability of measures of the certainty of punishment. That evidence appears in the form of data on "unofficial reports of crime", either reports of alleged victims or self-reported criminality (see, e.g., Biderman, 1967; Doleschal, 1970; Ennis, 1967; and Reiss, 1973). Those data clearly indicate that official figures grossly underestimate the true incidence of crime. However, as shown in Chapter 2, the correlation among types of crimes between "official incidence" and "unofficial incidence" is substantial, which suggests that the *relative reliability* of official crime figures may be much greater than critics have recognized. The crucial point for present purposes is that among types of crimes there is likely to be a close relation between two measures of the objective certainty of punishment, one in which Nc is based on official figures and the other in which Nc is based on unofficial figures. In brief, either of the two measures could be used to test deterrence propositions without appreciably divergent test results.

Other Illustrative Measures

One possible objection to the measure of overall objective certainty *(OOC)* is that all types of punishment are treated as equally important, even though some are surely perceived as more severe than others. Quite true, but severity is not the property of punishment in question. However, the certainty of some types of punishment may deter individuals more than do other types (independent of differential severity), and that possbility can be examined by employing two special measures of objective certainty. *Specific objective certainty* refers to a particular type of punishment, and the formula is SOC = Xt/Nc, where Xt is the total number of actual punishments of the type in question. Thus, *SOC* for arrest in jurisdiction A is 0.57 (that is, 200/350), and *SOC* for *some* kind of substantive punishment (type IV) is 0.14 (that is, 50/350). Here, as elsewhere, even though the certainty figure is given for a type of punishment, it actually pertains to a type of crime (felony theft in the case of Table 4-2).

Given alternative substantive punishments, one may speak of the *relative objective certainty* of each alternative. The formula in such a case is ROC = Xa/Xn, where Xa is the total number of instances of the alternative substantive punishment in question, and Xn is the total number of actual substantive punishments (regardless of type). Thus, suppose that in jurisdiction A 30 individuals were sentenced to imprisonment; *ROC* for imprisonment would be 0.60 (i.e., 30/50). Then suppose that ten individuals were sentenced to imprisonment and a fine; *ROC* for that substantive multiple punishment would be 0.20 (i.e., 10/50).

Since legal reactions to crimes take place through steps, the certainty of any step is contingent on the certainty of all previous steps. In recognition of that contingency, for certain purposes it may be desirable to compute a measure of *sequential specific objective certainty* for each type of punishment. The formula is SSOC = Xt/Xp, where Xt, as before, is the total number of instances of the type of punishment in question (e.g., trial), and Xp is the total number of instances of the preceding type of punishment. Thus, again taking jurisdiction A as the illustrative case, *SSOC* for trial would be 0.63 (that is, 125/200), and it would be 0.40 for *some* substantive punishment (regardless of type). If 25 of the 50 instances of substantive punishments were imprisonment, then *SSOC* for that type of punishment would be 0.20 (i.e., 25/125).

Other Considerations

Although not a mathematical necessity, an inverse relation may hold among jurisdictions between the number of types of legal reactions and some of the measures of objective certainty. That relation is also likely when comparing types of crimes in the same jurisdiction if the reaction process comprises more steps for some crimes than for others. However, when objective certainty is greater for some jurisdictions or types of crimes than it is for others, the reason for the difference is not directly relevant in contemplating deterrence.

The sheer variety of measures may be bewildering and irritating. However, we simply do not know which kind of measure is appropriate for tests of deterrence theories, and a great deal of exploratory research with alternative measures is needed to reach a conclusion.[5] In any case, it is idle for a theorist to make assertions about the certainty of punishment and pretend that the assertions are testable without stipulating measures.

Different measures of objective certainty are particularly relevant in contemplating evidential problems and questions as to how deterrence operates. Suppose there is an inverse relation between the crime rate and *only one* measure of objective certainty, *SOC* for imprisonment. That finding would suggest that certainty deters only insofar as the punishment is severe, but the possibility of incapacitating effects would also be suggested. Now suppose that the crime rate is inversely related only to *SSOC* for imprisonment. That finding would suggest that the type of crime in question is committed largely by "professionals," who are concerned with the certainty of particular substantive punishments. Of course, in pursuing a theory of deterrence one may long for something firmer than mere suggestive findings in exploratory research, but the only alternative is to rely on sheer intuition.

Prosecutorial Relabeling

In actual research both the number and the nature of the steps in the reaction process may be different from those shown in Table 4-2, but the formulas for various measures can be applied regardless of the steps in the reaction process. However, when it comes to gathering requisite data, there are several practical problems and choices that could be crucial in testing a deterrence theory.

The first choice has to do with four numbers pertaining to a given type of crime and punishments in a particular jurisdiction: (1) *Cp*, the number of such crimes reported by the police in "official incidence statistics" for some period; (2) *Pp*, the number of such *Cp* cases that resulted in the application of at least one of the prescribed punishments for that type of crime; (3) *Op*, the number of such *Cp* cases that resulted in the application of some other prescribed punishment (i.e., a punishment other than one of those prescribed for the type of crime in question); and (4) *Sc*, the number of individuals punished as though they had committed the type of crime in question even though their acts were not so labeled by the police in the official incidence statistics. The *Op* and *Sc* numbers are in large part manifestations of what is known in Anglo-American jurisdictions as a "reduction in charge," commonly a case where the accused pleads guilty to a crime other than that originally charged (see Blumberg, 1967; Sudnow, 1965). The goal of the accused

---

[5]The hope is that all alternative measures are so highly correlated that a choice among them would be inconsequential.

in such "plea bargaining" is to avoid a severe substantive punishment, and to that end he or she pleads guilty to a "lesser crime" (e.g., when initially charged with first-degree murder, the accused may negotiate with the prosecution to reduce the charge to manslaughter). The goal of the prosecutors in such a case is, of course, to avoid a possibly long and costly trial, one in which there would be no assurance of a conviction.

Although relevant, the terms "reduction in charge" and "plea bargaining" are not adequate in assessing the certainty of punishment. For one thing, it is logically possible for the initial charge to be "increased" during the legal reaction process, and for that reason alone the phenomenon in question is here designated "prosecutorial relabeling." As for plea bargaining, it does not necessarily result in a change in the initial charge or in the type of crime recorded by the police in their official incidence statistics. Rather, if there are alternative prescribed substantive punishments (e.g., a fine *or* imprisonment), the accused may plead guilty to the offense (not a lesser one) in return for some assurance of avoiding the more severe sentence. Such bargaining does have a bearing on the severity of punishment, but it is not a problem in assessing the certainty of punishment.

The major problem is the treatment of the Op and Sc cases, and the problem arises because Cp cases are the basis for computing not only crime rates in deterrence research but also the denominator in formulas for expressing the certainty of punishment. At first glance, it may appear that all Sc cases should be excluded in assessing certainty, since those cases tend to inflate the certainty of punishment for the type of crime in question. To illustrate, suppose the police indentify 60 cases of robbery, but 30 of those cases are subsequently "reduced" to assault, and the 30 individuals are punished as though they had committed assault. The punishment statistics for assault would be misleading, for it could be that the number of individuals punished for assault exceeded the number of cases identified by the police as "assaults." Nonetheless, misleading or not, such Sc numbers are relevant in contemplating deterrence.

On reading or otherwise being informed that someone has been punished for assault, members of the public may come to perceive the certainty of punishment for that type of crime as greater than they would have otherwise. Similarly, if the 30 cases of robbery reduced to assault are ignored in computing the certainty of punishment for robbery, it is as though those 30 individuals were not punished at all (i.e., as though they were not arrested). Yet the associates of those 30 individuals are likely to know that the individuals were punished.

As the foregoing suggests, there is no truly defensible basis for ignoring Op and Sc cases in computing the certainty of punishment for a particular type of crime, that is, for basing the measure of certainty only on the ratio of Pp to Cp. Moreover, the inclusion of Op and Sp cases does not require any special formulas, and the data $(Pp, Op,$ and Sc cases) can be entered in a table like 4-2 with only one modification. The labels for the procedural and substantive punishments are changed so that all Op and Sc cases can be tabulated along with Pp cases.

The suggestion is not that measures of certainty should always be based on data that include Op and/or Sc cases. A measure that encompasses those cases is a different measure from one based on Pp cases alone, and the distinction is not incorporated in the identification of the various measures only because it would complicate explication. Moreover, only through exploratory research can the significance of the distinction be determined. It could be that the relation between the crime rate and a measure of the certainty of punishment depends on the inclusion or exclusion of the two types of cases (i.e., Op and Sc). No less important, experimentation with the alternatives could suggest insights as to how deterrence operates. If the inclusion of Op cases results in a much closer relation between measures of certainty and the crime rate, that alone suggests that the type of crime is committed largely by professionals, who reckon certainty in terms of reduction in charges and plea bargaining. Conversely, if the inclusion of Sc cases results in a much closer relation between the crime rate and the measure of certainty, then that outcome would indicate that individuals may be deterred despite considerable ignorance of how the judicial system actually operates.

Other Complications

The notion of the certainty of punishment is complicated for reasons other than prosecutorial relabeling. Suppose the prescribed punishment for robbery in a particular state is not less than 10 nor more than 15 years imprisonment. If a convicted offender *receives* a 10-, 11-, 12-, 13-, 14-, or 15-year sentence, has the prescribed punishment actually been applied? It is not the indeterminate range of the prescribed sentence that poses a problem, for if a convicted offender serves as much as the minimum stipulated sentence, then a prescribed punishment has been imposed. However, taking paroles, pardons, and other commutations of punishment into consideration, sentences actually served cannot be inferred correctly from sentences received (even ignoring deaths and escapes). Sentences actually served can be determined only by tracing cases (e.g., all robberies reported by the police in 1974) through the legal reaction process over several decades, which is not feasible. The only practical alternative is to gather data on reactions to crimes up to the time of the trials and the initiation of the sentences. However, initiation of a sentence is different from sentence received, just as both are different from sentence actually imposed (or "executed"). Thus, if the accused *receives* a sentence of 15 years imprisonment, the sentence is initiated on the first day of incarceration, but the sentence imposed depends on the amount of time actually served. Similarly, if a convicted felon pays only part of a fine, the sentence has been initiated. Excluding capital crimes and execution, the step from sentence received to initiation of a sentence is the most certain one in the reaction process. So, with those exceptions, "sentence received" and "sentence initiated" can be equated (for research purposes) without substantial error.

All deterrence research is concerned with crime rates for a particular period. Thus, suppose an investigator compares the 1974 robbery rates of states. If the investigator is concerned with the relation between those rates and the objective certainty of punishment for robbery, an attempt could be made to trace each reported case in each state through the reaction process, with the intention of ascertaining the *number of 1974 cases* that eventually result in interrogation, arrest, trial, conviction, and the initiation of a sentence. Such a "projected cohort" approach requires enormous resources, and it would be a very lengthy undertaking. (Some cases labeled by the police as robberies during 1974 will not reach a trial or be otherwise terminated for several years.) Moreover, it is difficult to see how reactions to cases after 1974 could have any impact on the 1974 crime rate.

The alternative is a "retrospective cohort" analysis, in which crimes reported by the police during a particular year in the past (e.g., 1970) are traced through the reaction process up to the present point in time (e.g., the end of 1974) just before or during the years for the crime rates (e.g., 1974 and/or 1975). One disadvantage of the strategy is that not all cases will have been terminated by the end of the period, and the selection of a range of years is bound to be arbitrary. However, experimentation may reveal that within narrow limits the choice of a range of years makes no major difference. If it does make a major difference, then the alternatives can lead to insights as to how deterrence operates. To illustrate, suppose that one version of OOC is based on Nc for 1965–1973, with all of the cases during those nine years traced through the reaction process up to the end of 1974. Then suppose that another version of OOC is based on Nc for 1973, with all of the cases traced through the reaction process up to the end of 1974. Finally, suppose that the second version of OOC is much more inversely related to the 1974 crime rate. If so, the suggestion would be that perception of certainty is based much more on recent cases. Should just the reverse be the case, the suggestion would be that public perception of certainty develops from somewhat diffuse experience over a long period.

If a retrospective cohort analysis is not feasible, then the only other alternative is the "estimational" approach. If the crime rates are for 1974, then legal reactions during *that year* to instances of the crime that occurred during or prior to 1974 are taken to be indicative of eventual legal reactions to 1974 cases. Suppose the *average annual* number of rapes over 1972–1974 in a particular jurisdiction is 80. Now suppose that in 1974 the police interrogated 72 different individuals on suspicion of rape, that 64 arrests for rape were made in 1974, and that 38 trials resulted in a conviction, with the convicted offender being sentenced to imprisonment. Those numbers would be entered in a table like 4-2, and Nc (number of cases) would be 80 (the average annual nunber over 1972 –1974) in computing the measure of certainty. All such numbers would be estimates, and the estimates would be adequate for deterrence research only to the extent that (1) the annual number of crimes and reactions to them have been uniform over 1972–1974, (2) the ratio Pp/(Op + Sc) is constant among the units of comparison (either types of crimes or jurisdictions), and (3) the proportion of punishments (e.g., imprisonments) in the form of concurrent or consecutive sentences is uniform among the units of comparison.

In most research the choice among alternative ways of gathering data is dictated by practical considerations; but even with unlimited time and resources, the choice among alternatives is not obvious. Yet it may be that for some jurisdictions the choice makes no appreciable difference. To illustrate, consider three versions of *OOC:* one based on a retrospective cohort analysis, one based on a projected cohort analysis, and one based on an estimational analysis. Suppose that among several jurisdictions (or types of crimes in the same jurisdiction) there is a close direct relation between any two versions of the measure. If so, the outcome in a test of some deterrence proposition would not depend on the choice of kinds of data. With that possibility in mind, a great deal of purely exploratory work is needed to determine the relation between versions of the same measure of certainty (projected cohort, retrospective cohort, and estimational). If the alternatives are not closely correlated, the situation would be complicated, and it would not be a technical problem divorced from theory. We know very little about the way individuals perceive the certainty of punishment. If they perceive it in reference to cases over a long period, then measures of certainty should not be restricted to cases during the year of the crime rate or even during the preceding year. In any case, when testing deterrence propositions several versions of each measure of certainty should be employed, and that strategy might yield insights as to how deterrence operates.

Perceived Certainty

Most of the recent research on the deterrence question has taken the certainty of punishment as "objectively given" (see, e.g., Logan, 1972b). But there is every reason to suppose that deterrence depends on the perception of certainty rather than on the objective certainty; indeed, it is difficult to imagine the deterrence doctrine being interpreted otherwise.[6] Accepting that argument, it is not surprising that most tests of deterrence propositions about certainty have not yielded truly impressive positive evidence, for to date *no* test pertaining to official crime rates has considered perceived certainty.

Data on perceived certainty can be gathered only through survey research. Each member in a sample of a jurisdictional population would be asked at least one question, something like the following: Of the last 100 cases of robbery here in (jurisdiction name), what is your *guess* as to the number that resulted in the arrest of a suspect? Of course, the exact wording of the question would depend on the type of crime and the type of legal reaction under consideration, with several members asked the same question about each type of reaction (e.g., interrogation, arrest, trial, and imprisonment) and each type of crime.

Given responses to such perceptual questions, the data would be arranged as shown in Table 4-2, and all of the measures of certainty would apply as though the data pertained to *actual* legal reactions. Each number in the table (e.g., number of arrests) would be an average of the guesses made by the population members about the certainty of a particular type of reaction, and *Nc* would be 100. To distinguish measures of perceived certainty from measures of objective certainty, the former are designated as *OPC, SPC, RPC,* or *SSPC.*

Given *OOC* values (overall objective certainty), *OPC* values (overall

[6]The point is that the objective certainty of punishment is related to the crime rate only to the extent that objective certainty is directly correlated with perceived certainty. However, an interpretation of the deterrence doctrine is especially difficult when it comes to assumptions about the objective certainty of punishment (see Zimring and Hawkins, 1973:158–172). For one thing, it could be argued that the doctrine does not assert any relation between the crime rate and objective certainty, which is to say that only perceived certainty is relevant. Yet at various points both Beccaria and Bentham clearly suggest that perception of certainty is a function of actual punishments, and the nature of that relation is a central consideration when it comes to the policy implications of the deterrence doctrine. Even so, it should be recognized that the perception of certainty of punishment may be a function of some facet of actual punishments other than what is here designated as "objective certainty."

perceived certainty), and crime rates for jurisdictions (or types of crime within the same jurisdiction), the empirical interrelations among those variables would have great theoretical import. Extensive commentary on that import is reserved for Chapter 6, and a few general observations must suffice at this point. If there is no close direct relation between the *OOC* values and *OPC* values, recent purported tests of the deterrence doctrine would become subject to even more criticism, and grave doubts would be cast on related penal policies. The latter point can be stated as a question: Why attempt to deter crime by increasing the objective certainty of punishment when there is no reason to anticipate a subsequent increase in perceived certainty? As for theoretical import, observe that a negligible relation between *OOC* and *OPC* values would not preclude a close *inverse* relation between *OOC* values and crime rates, but it could not be attributed to deterrence. The inverse relation might reflect some preventive consequence of punishment other than deterrence (e.g., incapacitation).

Radically Different Strategies

The foregoing methods are seemingly consistent with the meaning of "certainty of punishment" in all versions of the deterrence doctrine. However, since those versions do not speak to questions about the numerical representation of properties, all manner of methods could be used to analyze the certainty of punishment. That is particularly the case if a theorist assumes that actual punishments contribute to general deterrence by furthering the perception of certainty by the public at large.

Observe again that in most of the formulas pertaining to objective certainty the number of reported crimes enters into the denominator. Yet it may be that in some if not all jurisdictional populations a substantial number of members do not come to perceive the certainty of punishment as "high" or "low" in reference to the *ratio* of punishments to crimes. Rather, their perceptions could be a function of the sheer number of punishments or, more likely, the number reported in news media.[7] That possibility deserves consideration regardless of the relation between a measure of *objective* certainty and a measure of *perceived* certainty. Should there be no relation, the deterrence doctrine would not be refuted; but objective certainty of punishment would have to be reconceptualized, and the present measures would no longer be relevant. However, even if a close direct relation between a measure of objective certainty and a measure of perceived certainty does hold, the number of media-reported punishments would still be relevant in answering a

[7]Needless to say, the amount of space or time devoted to accounts of punishment may be much more relevant than is the sheer number of such accounts.

question: How does that relation obtain? The validity of the deterrence doctrine does hinge on that question, but any answer would have enormous policy implications.

Suppose it is found that both measures of objective certainty and measures of perceived certainty vary directly with the number of media-reported punishments. That finding would suggest that the two measures of certainty (objective and perceived) are related only through their mutual relation with the number of media-reported punishments. However, if only the measure of perceived certainty is closely related to the number of media-reported punishments, then it would be difficult to see how general deterrence could be furthered by increasing the objective certainty of punishment. Even the sheer number of punishments (not as a ratio to crimes) could be irrelevant, which is to say that among some jurisdictions or for some types of crimes in the same jurisdiction there may not be a close direct relation between the number of actual punishments and the number of media-reported punishments. That possibility may appear to be farfetched, but it is less so when one realizes that publicizing punishments is commonly left to the whim of news agencies.

Properties of Punishment: Severity

From Beccaria and Bentham to the present, all versions of the deterrence doctrine assert that the deterrent efficacy of punishments depends on their severity, but doubts about the significance of severity are raised by the claim that certainty is more important (see Zimring and Hawkins, 1973:161). In any case, the notion of severity of punishment is a very complicated one; hence the present analysis of that property focuses on terminological distinctions and measurement problems.

Normative Severity

Suppose that in a particular jurisdiction the prescribed prison term is 30 years for rape and 15 years for robbery. As such, no one would question that the prescribed punishment is more severe for rape, but the judgment pertains to *normative severity* (the severity of prescribed punishment) and not to *actual severity* (the severity of actual punishments). The import of the distinction is best explicated by considering *actual* legal reactions to crimes in the *same* two jurisdictions. Suppose that over two years the police reported 45 rapes, 15 of which resulted in someone receiving a prison sentence of 30 years, with none of the remaining cases resulting in a conviction. Now suppose that during the same period the police reported 200 cases of robbery, 120 of which resulted in someone receiving a sentence of 15 years imprisonment, with none of the remaining cases resulting in a conviction. Given those figures *and* the contrast in the prescribed punishment, for which of the two types of crimes was the severity of punishment the greatest? Even ignoring procedural punishments, the question is difficult because there are two defensible answers. It could be argued that the punishment for robbery was more severe because proportionally fewer rapists received a prison sentence; but that argument blurs the distinction between the certainty and the severity of particular punishments, and it could be that individuals are deterred (it at all) more by normative severity than by the severity of actual punishments. But that is only a supposition, and the problem is not avoided by arguing that actual punishments have to do with certainty, not with severity. Consider two jurisdictions, *A* and *B*, where the statutory punishment for murder is life imprisonment or death. The normative severity may well be the same for the two jurisdictions (depending on how those two punishments are perceived), but suppose that in *A* 60 percent of the reported murders resulted in a sentence of life imprisonment and 20 percent resulted in a death sentence. Now suppose that the figures were reversed for jurisdiction *B*, that is, 20 percent of the murder case resulted in a sentence of life imprisonment and 60 percent in a capital sentence. As such, the objective certainty of a substantive punishment would be 0.80 for both jurisdictions. Of course, the *relative* certainty of the two alternative substantive punishments was not the same for the two jurisdictions, but that difference in itself reveals nothing about the severity of actual punishments. Indeed, if the *perceived* severity of each substantive punishment is not the same in two jurisdictions, then the two jurisdictions may differ with regard to the relative certainty of each alternative punishment but not with regard to the overall severity of actual punishments.

In the light of the foregoing, a theorist would be ill-advised to ignore the distinction between normative severity and actual severity. Of course, it could be that there is a close direct relation between those two; but that cannot be known a priori; hence there is a pressing need for purely exploratory research on the question. However, several difficult problems pertaining to the numerical representation of severity must be dealt with before exploratory research is feasible.

Perceptions of Severity

No one is likely to question that five years imprisonment is more severe (i.e., more painful or discomforting) than a $300 fine, or that ten years imprisonment is more severe than five years. But it is naive to assume that investigators can agree in judging even the relative severity of all legal reactions to crime.

Problems in assessing severity are not peculiar to exotic cultures. Consider some questions about common substantive punishments in Anglo-American jurisdictions. What numerical value would represent the severity of ten years imprisonment? Surely it is not "10." Then which is the more severe, a 30-day jail sentence or a $3,000 fine? Finally, if a numerical value represents the severity of a particular type of legal reaction to crime in California, to what extent does that value also represent the severity for the same type in, say, Mississippi?

All such questions suggest that investigators are not likely to agree in assessing the severity of punishments if they employ their own standards of pain or discomfort. Of course, one can entertain the possibility of some objective procedure for assessing severity, but it is difficult to imagine any defensible procedure that ignores perceptions of individuals who are subject to the criminal law in question. That is all the more true when assessing severity as it pertains to deterrence. After all, no legal action can deter if it is not perceived as punitive by those who are subject to it, and whether or not actions deter supposedly depends in part on the degree to which they are perceived as severe.

The attention devoted to perceived severity may appear inordinate and labored. Yet conceptualizations of severity in all versions of the deterrence doctrine do not provide explicit directions for the numerical representation of perceived severity.

The perceived severity of a particular type of legal action (e.g., execution) depends, of course, on judgments made and stated by members of the jurisdictional population. But soliciting, assessing, and converting such statements into numerical values is a difficult procedure. One strategy reduces to asking individuals questions of the following form: How severe do you consider X to be: (1) mildly severe, (2) fairly severe, or (3) very severe? Answers to such a question cannot be the basis for an interval measure of severity unless one assumes that the difference between response categories (1) and (2) is equal to the difference between (2) and (3). There is no basis for such an assumption. Moreover, the vast majority of answers to such questions, at least in the United States, are likely to be similar. Not so surprisingly, Americans tend to regard most statutory penalties (e.g., ten years imprisonment) as very severe. An extension of the response categories from (1) to (5), with the first being "very mild" and the last being "very severe", would not preclude a concentration of responses in the extreme category ("very severe").

Proposed Procedure

Perceptions of the severity of legal reactions can be expressed *ordinally* (e.g., reaction *X* is more severe than reaction *Y*), and it could be that individuals actually perceive severity largely in an ordinal sense. So one appropriate strategy is to ask members to compare the various types of legal reactions to crime in the jurisdiction according to their *relative* severity. There may be 50 or more distinct types of legal reactions (including the procedural), and it is not feasible for individuals to rank all of them in order of perceived severity. However, a "severity question" can be worded as follows: Considering *X* and *Y*, which do you think is more severe? If there are 50 types of legal reactions, then there would be 1,225 different questions; that is, $(50^2 - 50)/2$. Each question should be asked of, say, at least 100 members; but each member may be asked 50 such questions (selected at random), and so the sample would comprise 2,450 individuals.

The perceived severity of a particular type of punishment could be computed by the following formula: $PS = [Ms + (Ae/2)]/[(Np - 1)(Nr)]$, where Ms is the number of instances in which a respondent has judged the type of punishment to be more severe than the other type, Ae is the number of instances in which the judgment is approximately equal, Np is the number of types of legal punishment, and Nr is that total number of respondents. To illustrate the use of the formula, suppose that it is applied to data on the perceived severity of execution as one of 40 types of legal reactions to crimes. So 39 questions would be asked about the severity of execution relative to other punishments, one being: Which do you think is the most severe legal punishment for a crime, execution or life imprisonment? Suppose that the question is posed to each of 100 individuals (a random sample of the jurisdictional population) and that 70 of them answered "execution," 20 answered "about the same," and 10 answered "life imprisonment." Suppose further that all individuals answered "execution" in response to the other 38 questions (where execution is one of the two punishments), with the number of responses totaling 3,800 (in addition to the 100 questions about execution and life imprisonment). As such, the perceived severity of execution would be $PS = [3,870 + (20/2)]/[(39)(100)] = .994$.

Questions about severity would include both procedural and substantive punishments. The inclusion of all types of punishment may appear unnecessary, the argument being that the relative severity of some types is obvious. Thus, since arrest is a necessary condition for a trial, it may appear that the latter is necessarily more severe than the former; but it is *logically* possible for a respondent to perceive arrest as more severe than a trial. Moreover, the ratio of the *magnitude* of the perceived severity of a trial to the magnitude of the perceived severity of an arrest cannot be known a priori, and eventually research on severity should be extended to a consideration of magnitudes. With that end in mind, respondents should be asked two questions about each pair of punishments, *X* and *Y:* Which of the two, *X* or *Y*, do you consider to be the more severe? If the number 1 represents the severity of *X* or *Y* (the one designated as less severe), what number would you assign to *X* or *Y* (the one designated as more severe)? Should a respondent say that *X* is the more severe, the *S* value of *Y* would be 1, and the *S* value of *X* would depend on the number given by the respondent in answering the second question.

Once a large number of respondents have assessed each pair of legal reactions, then the magnitude of the perceived severity of any particular type of reaction can be computed as follows: MPS = $[\Sigma_s- ([Np - 1][Nr])]/[(Np - 1)(Nr)]$. A *MPS* value of 0.000 would indicate that all respondents regarded the type of reaction as less severe than any other type, and there is no upper limit to *MPS*.

Any *MPS* value would be relative not only to a particular jurisdictional population but also to the types of punishment compared, but the procedure could be modified to realize "absolute" values. The appropriate severity question with that end in mind would be something like this: If zero is no pain or discomfort, what number would you say represents the pain or discomfort of *X*? Given responses to such a question, the *absolute magnitude* of the perceived severity for any type of punishment could be computed as follows: AMPS = $\Sigma S/Nr$. The *AMPS* value would probably depend appreciably on the wording of the question, and it may be that some respondents simply cannot assess severity in such an absolute way. In any case, it could be that only one of the three measures of severity is inversely related to the crime rate; hence still another line of exploratory research should be undertaken before formulating what purports to be a testable deterrence theory.

Additional Problems

Consider the following statement in a hypothetical criminal code: The punishment for rape in the first degree shall be 20 years imprisonment, with no probation or suspended sentence. That statement is clearly a prescribed reaction, that is, anyone convicted of first-degree rape *ought* to be sentenced to 20 years imprisonment. However, those who receive that sentence may not actually serve 20 years, with the actual time served depending on parole and/or other commutative practices.

Unless the distinction between sentence *received* and sentence *imposed* is recognized, questions pertaining to the perceived severity of punishments are ambiguous. Thus, if a question simply refers to 20 years imprisonment, some respondents may interpret it as actually serving 20 years, while others may think of it as receiving a sentence of 20 years. The first group are much more likely to perceive 20 years imprisonment as more severe than does the second group. Accordingly, to avoid ambiguity and ensure comparable responses, the severity questions should be worded in a manner suggested by one of the following phrases: receiving a prison sentence of 20 years, actually serving 20 years in prison, receiving a sentence of probation for 2 years, actually being on probation for 2 years.

The application of the preceding formulas is somewhat independent of the way questions about severity are worded; but there are two versions of each measure, one based on responses to questions about the severity of sentences received and the other on responses to questions about sentences actually imposed. So we have *PSI* and *PSR*, *MPSR* and *MPSI*, *AMPSR* and *AMPSI*, with *R* denoting sentence received and *I* denoting sentence imposed.

Of course, it could be argued that one is deterred (if at all) in anticipation of the sentence that may be imposed, not the sentence that may be received; but some individuals may be deterred by the very prospect of receiving a sentence (perhaps of any kind) without looking beyond that point in the reaction process. Even if individuals are concerned exclusively with the sentence actually imposed, their knowledge of sentences actually served may be so limited that they judge the severity of the threatened actual punishment for a particular type of crime largely by reference to the prescribed punishment. Finally, it is the prescribed sentence that limits the sentence actually imposed.

It would simplify matters considerably to think of sentences received as normative reactions (i.e., statements as to what *ought* to happen) and sentence imposed as actual reactions, but that distinction will not bear examination. When a judge passes sentence on a convicted felon, it is no less an actual reaction than is the incarceration of the felon. Furthermore, either of the two actual reactions may or may not be consistent with the prescribed punishment. Thus, if the prescribed punishment for arson is five years imprisonment, a convicted arsonist cannot be sentenced to more or less than five years of imprisonment without the sentence being contrary to the prescribed punishment. However, when a convicted felon is sentenced to the "correct" prison term, he or she may serve less than the stipulated time without the imposed (actual) punishment being contrary to the prescribed punishment. That is the case because, after a sentence is received, another set of prescribed punishments becomes operative, with those prescriptions having to do with parole, pardons, and other commutative practices.

At first glance it may appear that the foregoing problems and complexities would be circumvented by speaking of "threatened punishments" rather than "prescribed punishments," but the change in terminology only gives rise to a difficult question: What is the threatened punishment for any particular type of crime? Surely it is not entirely a matter of actual punishments. The question is all the more difficult because the severity of threatened punishments cannot be analyzed defensibly without reference to public perception, and it is ambiguous to ask questions about severity without distinguishing between sentence received and sentence imposed. Consider the problem as it would be manifested in the analysis of a particular crime. Suppose that the prescribed punishment for manslaughter is 15 years imprisonment, but parole practices are such that a convict *may be* released on serving one-third of the sentence received. Accordingly, questions about the severity of punishment for manslaughter could be worded various ways, even ignoring the possibility of probation. Thus, the question could refer to receiving a sentence of 15 years, actually serving a sentence of 15 years, actually serving 5 years, or actually serving between 5 and 15 years.

The most feasible reduction of complexity is to analyze the severity of prescribed punishments in terms of the sentences that one *could receive* on conviction and to word related questions about severity accordingly. One rationale is that the prescribed sentence sets limits on the sentence actually imposed. However, the proposed solution is more complicated than it may appear. Suppose that the statutory penalty for auto theft is not less than two years imprisonment or more than five years, a fine of not less than $500 or more than $2,000, or both such imprisonment and such a fine. Suppose further that the probation laws in the jurisdiction state that persons convicted of auto theft can be sentenced to probation for not less than two or more than five years. So there would be at least six prescribed punishments, and the severity of *the* prescribed punishment for auto theft could not be expressed numerically without asking members of the jurisdictional population questions about the severity of the six sentences that could be received: two years imprisonment, five years imprisonment, a fine of $500, a fine of $2,000, two years probation, and five years probation. Even considering only the maximum and minimum of each punishment (e.g., ignoring the possibility of a fine of $1,500), all manner of *PSR, MPSR,* or *AMPSR* values could be taken as representing the perceived severity of the prescribed punishment for auto theft, and that is especially true if probation does not preclude the possibility of a fine. So *PSR, MPSR,* or *AMPSR* for auto theft could be the lowest severity value (probably that for two years of probation), the greatest severity value (probably the *combined* values for a prison sentence of five years and a fine of $2,000), or an average of all possible sentences, including multiple punishments (e.g., a fine of $500 and imprisonment for five years).

The foregoing should make it clear that a focus on sentence received does not resolve all problems in assessing the severity of prescribed punishments; additionally, when alternative punishments are prescribed for a type of crime, there are several *PSR, MPSR,* or *AMPSR* values that can be *assigned* to that type of crime. The proposed solution in the case of substantive punishments is to consider only the prescribed punishment or the prescribed multiple punishment (e.g., $2,000 fine and five years imprisonment) that has the highest *PSR, MPSR,* or *AMPSR* value.

As the first consideration in an illustrative application of the procedure, observe that a *PSR, MPSR,* or *AMPSR* value *never* refers to a type of crime; rather, each value refers to a prescribed punishment (procedural or substantive). However, the computation of a *PSR, MPSR,* or *AMPSR* value for particular types of punishment (procedural and substantive) is a step toward computing a value that represents the normative severity of punishment for a particular type of crime.

Suppose that *PSR* values have been computed for all types of punishment as follows: interrogation, 0.00; arrest, 0.01; trial, 0.03; conviction, 0.07; probation for one year, 0.08; probation for five years, 0.10; fine of $1,000, 0.06; fine of $5,000, 0.12; imprisonment for one year, 0.18; and imprisonment for five years, 0.48. Now suppose that all of the procedural punishments apply to grand theft and that the substantive punishment for that type of crime is stipulated in the criminal code as follows: First, the punishment for grand theft shall be not less than one or more than five years imprisonment, a fine of not less than $1,000 or more than $5,000, or both such a fine and such a term of imprisonment; and, second, at the discretion of the magistrate, a person convicted of grand theft may be sentenced to probation for not less than one or more than five years but without the imposition of a fine.

Given the alternative prescribed punishments for grand theft, all manner of *PSR* values (including averages) could be taken as representing the normative severity of punishment, *NSP,* for that type of crime. However, the proposed procedure simplifies matters by considering all procedural punishments (since they are not mutually exclusive) but only that prescribed combination of substantive punishments with the greatest *PSR* value, which for grand theft is a fine of $5,000 *and* imprisonment for five years. So *NSP* for grand theft would be $0.00 + 0.01 + 0.03 + 0.07 + 0.12 + 0.48 = 0.71$.

Although the procedure simplifies matters, it does not solve all problems. For one thing, rather than base *NSP* on *PSR* values, *NSP* could be based on *MPSR* values or *AMPSR* values. A defensible choice is unlikely without exploratory research along the lines previously indicated, which would include the question of the feasibility of asking respondents to judge the severity of punishments in terms of absolute magnitude. A demonstration that respondents can express their judgments in terms of absolute magnitudes (which enter into *AMPSR* values) would greatly facilitate research on the deterrence question. If *NSP* is based on *PSR* or *MPSR* values, then *NSP* values should only be used to compare types of crime in the same jurisdiction.

Even if it does prove feasible to compute *AMPSR* values, the proposed procedure is subject to question. Recall that the procedure simplifies matters by focusing on the substantive punishment or the combination of substantive punishments that has the greatest perceived severity value; but we know very little about how individuals perceive the severity of the punishment of a particular type of crime, especially when there are alternative substantive punishments. What degree of severity is most important to them—the minimum, some kind of average, or the maximum? Stated another way, are individuals deterred primarily by their consideration of minimum severity, average severity, or maximum severity? The proposed procedure does not answer the question, nor is it one that can be answered readily (if at all). In any case, there is a need for exploratory research on the nine alternative versions of *NSP*, as shown in Table 4-3. To illustrate, by reconsidering *NSP* for grand theft, we have the following range of alternative values (each of which is limited to some combination of *PSR* values):

$$NSP_1 = 0.00 + 0.01 + 0.03 + 0.07 + 0.06 = 0.17$$

$$NSP_2 = 0.00 + 0.01 + 0.03 + 0.07 + [0.08 + 0.10 + 0.06 + 0.12 \\ + 0.18 + 0.48 + (0.06 + 0.18) + (0.06 + 0.48) + (0.12 \\ + 0.18) + (0.12 + 0.48)/10] = 0.28$$

$$NSP_3 = 0.00 + 0.01 + 0.03 + 0.07 + (0.12 + 0.48) = 0.71$$

If comparisons of types of crime in the same jurisdiction or comparisons of the same type of crime in different jurisdictions reveal a close direct relation among all of the nine alternative versions of *NSP*, then the proposed procedure (which prescribes use of NSP_3, NSP_6, or NSP_9) could be adopted with greater confidence.

Table 4-3.   Alternative Ways for the Numerical Representation of the Normative Severity of Punishment for a Particular Type of Crime

Alternative Substantive Punishments*	Perceptions of the Severity of Prescribed Punishments		
	Ordinal (PSR)	*Magnitude (MPSR)*	*Absolute Magnitude (AMPSR)*
Minimum Perceived Severity	NSP_1	NSP_4	NSP_7
Average Perceived Severity	NSP_2	NSP_5	NSP_8
Maximum Perceived Severity	NSP_3	NSP_6	NSP_9

*Including combinations of punishments (e.g., imprisonment for one year and a fine of $5,000) that are prescribed as alternatives.

Severity of Actual Punishments

The severity of actual punishments is no more objectively given than is the severity of prescribed punishments. Indeed, the severity of actual punishments cannot be assessed defensibly without a perceived severity value for each type of prescribed punishment, or at least for those that have been applied in some instances.

At first glance it may appear that the perceived severity values would have to be *PSI, MPSI,* or *AMPSI,* meaning that the perceptions would have to pertain to sentences actually imposed. Again, however, passing sentence on a convicted felon is no less an actual legal reaction than is the incarceration of the felon or the felon's payment of a fine. So a truly complete investigation of the severity of actual punishments would include an analysis of both sentences received and sentences imposed (as well as of procedural punishments). In the case of sentences received, those sentences are analyzed in terms of *PSR, MPSR,* or *AMPSR,* while sentences actually imposed are analyzed in terms of *PSI, MPSI,* or *AMPSI.*

Fortunately, one general method can be employed for the numerical representation of the severity of actual punishments, whether sentences received or sentences imposed are being considered. That method is illustrated by Table 4-4; and the formula for the severity of actual punishments for a particular type of crime is SALP $= \Sigma(P)(Sv)$, where P and Sv are values for each type of punishment as shown in Table 4-4. Applying the formula to the data in that table, we have SALP $=$ $[(1.000)(.001)] + [(0.500 + 0.002)] \ldots + [(0.225)(0.150)] = 0.060$.

Research on the severity of actual punishments is complicated be-

Table 4-4. Data on Actual Legal Punishments of
Embezzlement in a Hypothetical Jurisdiction

Types of Actual Punishment	Number of Cases	Proportion of Cases (P)*	Perceived Severity Value (Sv)†
	Col. 1	Col. 2	Col. 3
Interrogation of Suspect	200	1.000	.001
Arrest of a Suspect	100	.500	.002
Trial of a Suspect	85	.425	.006
Conviction of a Suspect	45	.225	.010
Probation, 3 Years‡	10	.050	.017
Probation, 5 Years‡	2	.010	.020
Fine of $10,000‡	20	.100	.017
Probation of 3 Years, Fine of $5,000‡	2	.010	.030
Imprisonment, 2 Years‡	5	.025	.160
Imprisonment, 5 Years‡	6	.030	.400
Loss of Civil Rights‡	45	.225	.150

*Number of cases divided by the maximum number for any type of punishment (200 in this instance).

†PSR values are shown, but they could be any of the other five versions of a perceived severity value (PSI, MPSR, MPSI, AMPSR, or AMPSI).

‡Sentence received if the Sv values are PSR, MPSR, or AMPSR, but sentence actually imposed (served) if the Sv values are PSI, MPSI, or AMPSI.

cause, as shown in Table 4-5, there are at least 18 versions of *SALP*.[8] The different versions are of theoretical significance, but they also entail practical considerations. Suppose that an investigator is concerned with the severity of actual punishments of robbery in Los Angeles. If the research is concerned with deterrence, then the investigator would compute the Los Angeles robbery rate for, say, 1973. Although the investigator could deal with the actual punishments of those robberies that occurred in Los Angeles during 1973, limited resources might preclude tracing each case through the legal reaction process over several years; and the actual punishments after 1973 could scarcely have a deterrent impact on the 1973 rate. True, the investigator could consider only those reactions to 1973

[8]One of the problems defies solution, that being the exclusion of cases of crime not reported to the police. The problem is similar to that confronted in assessing the certainty of punishment, and the same conclusion holds. Specifically, the exclusion of crimes not reported to the police from measures of the perceived severity of actual punishment does not necessarily result in spurious evidence (one way or another) in tests of deterrence propositions pertaining to the severity of actual punishments.

Table 4-5. Alternative Versions of SALP*

	Sentences Received or Imposed† Relative to Three Periods‡					
Type of Severity Value	Received in Y for a Crime in Y	Received in Y for a Crime in W, X, or Y	Received in X or Y for a Crime in W, X, or Y	Imposed in Y for a Crime in X or Y	Imposed in Y for a Crime in W, X, or Y	Imposed in X or Y for a Crime in W, X, or Y
PSR	$SALP_1$	$SALP_2$	$SALP_3$	−	−	−
MPSR	$SALP_4$	$SALP_5$	$SALP_6$	−	−−	−
AMPSR	$SALP_7$	$SALP_8$	$SALP_9$	−	−	−
PSI	−	−	−	$SALP_{10}$	$SALP_{11}$	$SALP_{12}$
MPSI	−	−	−	$SALP_{13}$	$SALP_{14}$	$SALP_{15}$
AMPSI	−	−	−	$SALP_{16}$	$SALP_{17}$	$SALP_{18}$

*Each *SALP* value always refers to a particular type of crime.
†Sentence completed or served.
‡Y is the period for which the crime rate is computed (e.g., 1973), X is some definite and finite period prior to Y (e.g., 1969–1972), and W is any time prior to X (e.g., prior to 1969).

cases that occurred by the end of 1973, but the reaction process would not be completed for many cases by the end of 1973. With that point in mind, the investigator is not likely to compute versions 1, 4, or 7 of *SALP* (see Table 4-5). Alternatively, the investigator could analyze all procedural punishments of robbery and all sentences received for robbery during 1973 regardless of when the robberies occurred. That analysis would end with the computation of version 2, 5, or 8 of *SALP*. However, it could be argued that in 1973 individuals were deterred (if at all) by punishments that took place prior to 1973 as well as during 1973. So the investigator could consider procedural punishments of robbery and sentences received for robbery during 1969–1973 regardless of when those robberies occurred, and the end product would be version 3, 6, or 9 of *SALP*.

The problems are magnified even more when contemplating sentences imposed. The length of time that individuals will serve on probation, in prison, and/or on parole for a robbery that took place in 1973 will not be known for years, which precludes versions 10, 13, or 16 of *SALP*. Alternatively, the investigator could analyze the sentences that individuals have served on completion of those sentences *in 1973* regardless of when the individuals allegedly committed robbery, and by that route compute $SALP_{11}$, $SALP_{14}$, or $SALP_{17}$. However, presuming that deterrence is furthered by knowledge of sentences actually served, that knowledge may well extend over several years prior to 1973, and with that posibility in mind the investigator may elect to compute $SALP_{12}$ $SALP_{15}$, or $SALP_{18}$. Whatever the choice, procedural punishments should be analyzed for the same years, that is, either 1973 or 1969–1973.

With reference to Table 4-5, note that Y could be for a period longer than one year (e.g., 1973) and X could be a period longer or shorter than four years (e.g., 1969–1972). The length of those periods could make a difference, but hopefully exploratory research will show that the character of punishment is so stable from year to year that the length of the period chosen is of no significance. Similarly, exploratory research may show that there is a close direct relation between any two of the 18 versions of $SALP$ shown in Table 4-5, a finding that would greatly simplify tests of a deterrence theory.

Presumptive Severity

All of the foregoing procedures are alien to recent research on the relation between severity of punishment and crime rates (e.g., Logan, 1972b) because that research did not extend to perceived severity. Rather, the investigators took the magnitude of imprisonment (e.g., median number of months served on release) as indicative of the severity of that type of actual punishment.

Since no one would question that, say, three years of imprisonment would be perceived by virtually anyone as more severe than one year, a concern with magnitudes of punishment is defensible. However, it should be recognized that investigators have dealt with *presumptive* severity, not perceived severity, and that the strategy has some definite limits. For one thing, granted that three years of imprisonment is perceived as more severe than one year, it does not follow that the former is perceived as three times more severe than the latter. Furthermore, two figures pertaining to the magnitude of punishment can be *compared* only if they pertain to the same type of punishment (e.g., length of imprisonment), and magnitudes cannot be *combined* if they pertain to different types of punishment. The latter limitation calls for an illustration. If some individuals are fined for a particular type of crime and others are incarcerated for the same crime, the average amount of fines and the average length of incarceration cannot be added to express the overall severity of actual punishments. The same is true of the magnitude of prescribed punishments. Thus, if the prescribed punishment for a type of crime is two years imprisonment and/or a $10,000 fine, those two magnitudes cannot be combined to represent the overall severity of prescribed punishments for that type of crime. Finally, for some types of actual punishments, there are alternative kinds of data for an assessment of presumptive severity, just as there are alternatives in the way of data on perceived severity. In the case of actual imprisonments for a particular type of crime, if the crime rate is for, say, 1974, then investigators could consider (1) average prison sentences received in 1974, (2) average prison sentences received during a period prior to 1974, (3) average prison sentences actually served on release in 1974, (4) average prison sentences actually served on release during a period prior to 1974, and/ or (5) average prison sentences served by those who remained incarcerated at some point in 1974 (e.g., the beginning of the year or the end of the year). Actually, those five possibilities are only suggestive, and hopefully exploratory research will show that any two versions of the presumptive severity of actual punishments are so highly correlated that a choice between them is inconsequential.

As previously suggested, the presumptive severity of prescribed punishments and the presumptive severity of actual punishments are distinct properties. However, when either property is a variable in a deterrence theory, the theorist is likely to assume that there is a close direct relation between presumptive severity and perceived severity. If that relation does not hold, then presumptive severity is not relevant in tests of a deterrence theory, not even if there is a close inverse relation between the presumptive severity of actual punishments and the crime rate. Given that situation, the most obvious interpretation would be that the relation between presumptive severity and the crime rate reflects some preventive mechanism other than deterrence, such as incapacitation.

Properties of Punishment: Celerity

Although Beccaria and Bentham emphasized the importance of celeritous punishment, celerity is the most debatable variable in the deterrence doctrine. The only rationale for an emphasis on celerity is found in experimental psychology, notably research on "operant" behavior, classical (Pavlovian) conditioning, or aversive conditioning. Whatever the form of conditioning attempted in experimental work (largely on animals), it is not effective if there is a long delay between the stimulus or reinforcer and the response that is to be established or repressed (Johnston, 1972; Singer, 1970; and Solomon, 1964). Thus, in the case of aversive conditioning, a response pattern may not be repressed effectively if there is a delay longer than six seconds between a response and the aversive or noxious stimuli (e.g., an electrical shock). Since legal punishments (even procedural) are commonly delayed for days if not months or years, it is difficult to see how experimental findings support the assumption that differences among jurisdictions or types of crime can be attributed even in part to contrasts in the celerity of punishment. In any case, one would surely be pressed to argue that the importance of the celerity extends beyond specific deterrence.

As for absolute and restrictive deterrence, the celerity of punishment may be totally irrelevant. If one witnesses the punishment of someone accused of a crime or is otherwise informed of such punishment, it is difficult to see how the deterrent impact of that experience would depend on the interval between the crime and the punishment. For that matter, since human beings relate experiences over long periods, the importance of celeritous punishment is debatable even in the case of specific deterrence. Even the supposition that immediate punishment is more dreaded than delayed punishment is questionable, for it could be that some individuals view the delay in legal punishment as no less discomforting than the punishment itself.

Research Procedure

Whatever the theoretical justification for considering the celerity of punishment as relevant, it is the simplest deterrence variable as far as research procedure goes. Since police and judicial records typically note the date at which particular kinds of official actions are taken, it is feasible to calculate the average amount of time between the alleged commission of an offense and arrest, trial, or sentencing. By that route one can calculate the average *objective* celerity of each step in the reaction process for each type of offense.

Research on the *perceived* celerity of punishment is complicated by the fact that we know virtually nothing about such perceptions, not even whether individuals are able and willing to make guesses. Assuming that they are, members of a jurisdictional population could be asked questions like: Considering the last 100 cases of burglary here in (jurisdiction name) that resulted in the arrest of a suspect, what is your guess as to the average number of days between the time of the burglary and the arrest? Only simple calculations would be required to compute "average perceived celerity" for each step in legal reactions to particular types of crime.

Cognitive Properties

Consider the following questions as posed to members of a jurisdictional population:

Question 1. Which do you consider to be the most severe punishment—a jail sentence of 30 days or a $3,000 fine?

Question 2.   Of the last 100 cases of robbery here in (jurisdiction name), what number do you think resulted in a suspect being sentenced to imprisonment?

Responses to the first question would indicate the relative perceived severity of the two punishments, but the responses would in no way indicate that the respondents know the types of crime for which those punishments are prescribed. Similarly, responses to the second question would pertain to the perceived certainty of receiving a prison sentence for robbery, but the responses would not be evidence that the respondents knew beforehand that imprisonment is the prescribed punishment for that crime. Finally, a response to either question would not reveal whether the respondent's conception of robbery is consistent with the legal definition of that crime.

All the foregoing reduces to one consideration—there are "cognitive properties" of punishment and crimes which cannot be analyzed in terms of the celerity, certainty, or severity of punishment. Such cognitive properties are crucial in contemplating the deterrence doctrine, but they have been ignored in all versions of the doctrine and in all deterrence research.

In recent purported tests of the deterrence doctrine, investigators have examined the relation between crime rates and (1) the presumptive severity of prescribed punishments, (2) the presumptive severity of the actual punishments, or (3) the objective certainty of punishments. Such tests may be justified one way or another, but they do not directly substantiate the argument that punishment deters an individual only to the extent that it is *perceived* as certain and severe. However, that argument can be construed as implying an assumption—that in contemplating a crime the individual "knows" the prescribed punishment. Restating the assumption as a question: Can a statutory penalty deter an individual from a crime if the individual does not know that penalty? A negative answer may appear obvious, but while the deterrence doctrine entails some sort of cognitive assumption, the "appropriate" assumption is most debatable. In any case, what are here designated as cognitive properties are analytically distinct from perceptions of the certainty and severity of punishment. The distinction may appear paradoxical; but observe again that the responses to questions 1 and 2 (supra) would not reveal knowledge of prescribed punishments.

Cognitive Properties: Conceptions of Criminal Acts

Cognitive properties of punishment are not limited to knowledge of the prescribed or actual punishments of crimes, at least not with regard to formulating and testing deterrence theories. Consider this question: If a man correctly believes that the prescribed punishment for incest is five years imprisonment, how can that belief deter him from seducing his stepdaughter unless he also believes that the act would be incest as legally defined in that jurisdiction? As the question suggests, knowledge of the law does not deter an individual unless that knowledge extends to *conceptions of criminal acts.*

The question is not just whether one perceives a contemplated act as "criminal"; additionally, when prescribed punishments differ by type of crime, individuals tend to misperceive the threatened punishment for a crime if they misperceive the relation between types of acts and types of crimes. That is, one may be deterred from committing an act not just by the belief that it would be a crime but also by the belief that it would be a *particular type of crime,* for the type of crime determines the punishment (or the range of alternative punishments).

Of course, if someone identifies a contemplated act as criminal and, therefore, subject to *some kind* of punishment, that identification alone could be sufficient to deter that individual. The argument is not far-fetched, especially if one assumes that the typical citizen perceives any kind of punishment as sufficiently severe and certain to refrain from any act. As such, the certainty and severity of punishment would be of minor importance in comparison to the amount of agreement between conceptions of criminal acts held by the police and those held by the public at large, with the crime rate being an inverse function of the amount of agreement. The ultimate extension of the argument is to deny the relevance of punishment altogether; that is, to assert that the typical citizen refrains from a contemplated act if he or she perceives it as a crime, with the omission dictated by respect for the law rather than by fear of punishment.

All versions of the last argument are most debatable, with the most obvious objection being that the argument exaggerates habitual or uncritical conformity to laws. Moreover, the argument probably does not apply equally to all jurisdictions, and it is particularly dubious when extended to societies characterized by marked racial, ethnic, or class conflict. No less important, even if in all jurisdictions a small minority of the citizenry govern their conduct with the certainty and severity of punishment in mind, those minorities could account for the differences in the crime rates of jurisdictions (i.e., some minority members are deterred more in some jurisdictions than in others), and those differences are crucial in assessing evidence on the deterrence question.

No cognitive property is more difficult to analyze than "conceptions of criminal acts." To illustrate, it may appear that any act may or may not be a crime and, if a crime, it must be one type or another. However, such judgments necessarily require a criterion, and it is difficult to imagine that there can be an absolute, objective standard. The only relevant standard *in the context of deterrence* is the evaluation of acts by legal officials, the police in particular. After all, it is the police who make the official decision to designate an act as a crime and typify it (e.g., robbery). Judgments or decisions by other legal officials (including jurors) are relevant only if they are the basis for reporting official statistics on the incidence of crimes.

So we reach a conclusion—whether an act contributes to the official crime rate depends on the identification of it by the police in the jurisdiction. Stating the matter another way and in the form of an illustration: If the police officer and the individual both identify a particular act as a crime and as statutory rape, then to that extent the individual "knows the law." Conversely, if the police officer identifies the act as statutory rape but the individual identifies it as "shacking up," then to that extent the individual is ignorant of the law.

All of the foregoing arguments are stated in very general terms, and none of them speaks directly to the central question: How is the relation between the properties of punishment and the crime rate contingent on the public's conceptions of criminal acts? That question can be answered by reference to Table 4-6.

To the extent that only type I acts are contemplated in each jurisdictional population being compared, there *may be* a close inverse relation between some property of punishment and the rate for type A crimes. If members of some populations refrain from a type I act because they perceive the punishment as likely but members of some of the other populations commit type I acts because they perceive punishment for it as unlikely, then the official rate for the corresponding type of crime (A) will vary from one population to the next, since the police will label the acts as a type A crime. Correlatively, if the perceived certainty of punishment does deter individuals, then that property of punishment will vary inversely with the A crime rate among the jurisdictions. Additionally, it may well be that the A crime rate also varies inversely with the objective certainty of punishment for type A crimes.

What has been said of type I acts and type A crimes applies also to type V acts and type B crimes. However, the situation is radically different when it comes to acts of types III, VI, VII, or VIII. To the extent that all acts in each of the jurisdictional populations are type III or VI, the A or B crime rate will not vary from one jurisdiction to the next (because the police do not label the acts as crimes), not even if the jurisdictions differ sharply with regard to properties of punishment for type A and type B crimes. Hence, the properties and the crime rates would not

Table 4-6. *Typology of Contemplated Acts*

	If the Act Were Committed and Observed by or Reported to the Police, They Would Label the Act as Some Type of Crime		If the Act Were Committed and Observed by or Reported to the Police, They Would Not Label the Act as Any Type of Crime
	Police Would Label the Act as a Type A Crime	Police Would Label the Act as a Type B Crime	
Prospective Actor Believes the Act Would Be Labeled by the Police as a Type A Crime if Observed by or Reported to Them	Type I	Type II	Type III
Prospective Actor Believes the Act Would Be Labeled by the Police as a Type B Crime if Observed by or Reported to Them	Type IV	Type V	Type VI
Prospective Actor Believes the Act Would Not Be Labeled by the Police as Any Type of Crime if Observed by or Reported to Them	Type VII	Type VIII	Type IX

vary inversely. Describing the condition another way, in the case of type III and type VI acts, individuals are deterred (if at all) from acts that the police do not label as crimes. The paradox goes the other way in the case of type VII or type VIII acts, for there can be no deterrence; the simple reason being that the members of the populations do not view the acts as crimes (even though the police do). The incidence of type A and type B crimes might well vary from one jurisdiction to the next, but the variation would reflect extralegal conditions, not deterrence.

The remaining types of acts are even more complicated. To the extent that type II acts are committed in each jurisdictional population, the type B crime rate may be inversely related to properties of punishment but only to the properties of punishment for type A crimes. Conversely, to the extent that type IV acts are committed in each jurisdictional population, the type A crime rate may be inversely related to the properties of punishment for type B crimes. Of course, Table 4-6 is an oversimplification, being restricted to only two types of crimes. However, it is sufficient to suggest an important possibility. To the extent that the police and the public differ in their conceptions of a particular type of crime, then deterrence from that particular type of crime could be a function of the properties of punishment for *all* types of crimes. Thus, if the punishment for all types of crimes is markedly certain, severe, etc., then the citizenry may be deterred from *any type of crime,* despite disagreement between the police and the public as to what constitutes an instance of each type of crime. However, if the disagreement reaches the point of acts like type VII and type VIII, then deterrence is precluded by purely cognitive considerations alone.

Numerical Representation

The central notion is "consensus in identification of acts," that is, agreement between police officers and members of the public in their identification of a particular act as to whether it is a crime, and if so, what type of crime. Previous commentary has clarified the meaning of the notion, but when it comes to numerical representation of the property, there are some horrendous problems.

It will not do to ask individuals to define types of crime (e.g., second-degree burglary) and then compare their definitions with those in a criminal code. For one thing, it could be argued that legal definitions of a type of crime are incomplete without reference to court rulings; and, in any case, a complete, explicit, and clear-cut definition of a type of crime may not be found either in the code or in court rulings. For example, in the Arizona criminal code, simple assault is evidently any assault other than aggravated assault, and "aggravated assault" is defined by a description of nine conditions (running some 250 words) that constitute such an assault (Bolin, 1972:16–17). So if Arizona residents were asked to define "aggravated assault," it would be most difficult to assess the "correctness" of their definitions. For that matter, even if the police and all other members of the jurisdictional population used the exact language of the criminal code (or a court ruling) in defining a type of crime, the police and other members might disagree in classifying *particular* acts as instances of that type.

The only feasible solution is to prepare accounts of acts that police have identified as instances of a particular type of crime (e.g., manslaughter), with accounts of, say, ten such acts selected at random and edited in order to terminate each account at the point where there was legal intervention. Given a random sample of members of a jurisdictional population, the sample would be divided (randomly) into ten subsamples, and the members of each subsample would be asked to read an account of a case (the same case for each subsample) and then answer two questions. First, do you consider the incident to have been a crime? Second, if you consider it to have been a crime, what type of crime do you think it was? In responding to the second question, each individual would be supplied with a list of, say, nine types of crime, including the type of crime in question, and ending with the response category "none of these types". Of course, the procedure would inflate agreement between the police and the public, for it would commence with acts that the police have identified as a particular type of crime, and on the basis of chance alone one out of every ten respondents would be expected to agree with the police identification.[9] However, it would be the only "manageable" procedure, since asking respondents to identify the type of crime without a "legal" list creates all manner of problems (e.g., deciding whether or not a response of "rape" is the equivalent of "forcible rape," when the latter is the police label).

Given responses to the two questions, "general consensus" (henceforth *GC*) is simply the proportion of all residents who answered the first question affirmatively. "Specific consensus," or consensus as to type of crime (henceforth *SC*), is the proportion of those residents who answered the first question affirmatively and agreed further with the police in identifying the type of crime.

A Theoretical-Conceptual Issue

Appearances to the contrary, the foregoing is not a categorical acceptance of the radical version of the labeling perspective in the study of deviance, according to which a particular act is a crime if and only if it is so labeled by a legal official (for critiques see Gibbs, 1972c; Schur, 1969, 1971). The underlying issue is not peculiar to crime, as the same "labeling argument" could be made about the typification of any act, or any object for that matter. Thus, an object is a planet if and only if it is so labeled by astronomers, and an act is a forward pass in football if and only if it is so labeled by a referee. If one recoils at the epistemological implications of such statements (sensing rightly that they are indicative of an uncritical nominalism that borders on solipsism), then the objection applies also to the radical labeling perspective in the study of

[9]Since the amount of agreement by chance presumably would be constant from one type of crime to the next, the problem is not a serious one. A more serious problem is that the procedure ignores disagreements *among police officers* when it comes to the identification of criminal acts (see Ferracuti et al., 1962).

deviance. What that perspective ignores, or tacitly rejects, is the notion of *types of acts.*

The rejoinder is, of course, that no act is an instance of a particular type unless so labeled by someone; but the rejoinder conveniently ignores a crucial question: Why is there any agreement in the labeling of acts by independent observers? It would be foolish to deny that such agreement is commonly realized, and it is difficult to imagine everyday social activities without agreement in perceptions or labeling. Granted alternative criteria of reality, it is hardly radical to argue that agreement in labeling acts is evidence that types of acts are real. Without each agreement, there could be no order or uniformity in social interaction, for *ego* (one party to the interaction) would have no basis for anticipating how *alter* (the other party) would respond to ego's acts. Yet no claim is made that absolute agreement in identification of acts with regard to type is realized (i.e., in all instances and by all individuals). It could be that the amount of agreement between police officers and the public varies substantially from one jurisdiction to the next, and such variation would be crucial in formulating a deterrence theory.

Policy Issues and Additional Theoretical Considerations

It might appear that crime would be rampant in a jurisdiction with a very low *GC* value, since the residents might commit acts without knowledge that the police were likely to regard those acts as crimes. That possibility is one of many that should be considered in exploratory research on deterrence, but it is questionable to assume that a low *GC* value is necessarily associated with a high crime rate. To illustrate, suppose that a large proportion of a jurisdictional population does not identify the seduction of a niece as criminal incest, whereas the police identify it as such. Even so, it would not follow that the act is common in that population, since the members may refrain either out of conscience or in recognition of social condemnation (both having to do with extralegal inhibitory factors). Yet a population with a low *GC* value and a low crime rate would be significant because it would indicate that deterrence is at most only sufficient for a low crime rate.

Whatever the theoretical significance of a low *GC* value for a type of crime in a particular jurisdiction, it would have a direct bearing on penal policy. If the rate for that crime is especially high in the jurisdiction, it would be most questionable to increase the statutory penalty. When members of a population are unaware of what the police regard as crimes, they cannot be deterred by penalties, however certain and severe.

Theoretical considerations and policy issues are especially compli-cated when there is a high *GC* value but a low *SC* value for types of crime, meaning that the citizens agree with the police in identifying acts as crimes but not in identifying the type of crime. Suppose that is the case for several types of crimes (i.e., a high *GC* value but a low *SC* value for each type). The policy issue comes down to a question: How could the rate for some type of crime be reduced by an increase in the objective certainty and/or presumptive severity of punishment when the populace and the police disagree in identifying instances of that crime? Common sense would suggest that an increase in certainty or severity would not lower the rate *through deterrence,* and that may well be the case. However, certain and severe punishments for *crimes in general* could result in low rates for all types of crimes *through deterrence* even though *SC* is low for each type of crime; that is, if *GC* is high and the punishment for all types of crimes is perceived as severe and certain, then the inability of the citi-zenry to distinguish types of crimes correctly might not be relevant. That possibility alone justifies exploratory research on the following question: Given a particular type of crime, is the relation between the rate and the certainty-severity of punishment for that crime more inverse than the relation between the rate and the certainty-severity of punishment for crimes in general?

Evidence that *general* certainty-severity of punishment (the average for all crimes) is more important than *specific* certainty-severity of punish-ment (that for particular types of crime) would pose a policy issue. It would suggest that the concern of legislators with increasing the severity of punishment for particular types of crimes is misplaced.

The possibility in question has implications for a deterrence theory as well as for policy. Should it be found that general certainty-severity of punishment varies inversely with the rate for particular types of crime, then still another variable would have to be recognized in formu-lating a deterrence theory. If nothing else, general certainty-severity would have to be controlled in some way in tests of a deterrence theory.

An emphasis on cognitive properties could lead to findings that cast doubts on the idea of deterrence in toto and related penal policies. Sup-pose investigators find a fairly close inverse relation between *GC* and the rate for any particular type of crime; that is, whether the rate is high or low in a particular population depends on the proportion of the popu-lation that agrees with the police in identifying acts as crimes. Suppose further that the inverse relation holds even when all other properties of punishment are somehow controlled or taken into account. The finding would suggest that conformity to the law is largely a function of "knowl-edge of the law," not of fear of punishment. As for policy implications, the finding would suggest that attempts to reduce crime by increasing the severity of punishment are pointless. Even if punishments have the enculturating consequences alluded to in Chapter 3, they are likely to correct only the misconceptions of those punished, not the populace in general. One's misconception of fraud is hardly corrected in reading that someone has been punished for that offense.

Cognitive Properties: Knowledge of Prescribed Punishments

Even if all members of a population agree with the police in their identification of criminal acts, it would not follow that they know the prescribed punishment for each type of crime. That cognitive property is crucial if only because it is central in what appears to be a devastating criticism of the deterrence doctrine. The criticism commences with the argument that one cannot be deterred from committing a crime unless one *knows the* prescribed punishment or alternatives. If that argument is accepted, then the deterrence doctrine appears to be patently absurd, for casual observations and a few isolated studies (e.g., California Assembly Committee on Criminal Procedure, 1968) clearly indicate that individuals are commonly ignorant of the prescribed punishments for each type of crime. However, the immediate issue is not the extent of such ignorance; rather it is the assertion that an individual cannot be deterred from committing a crime unless he or she knows the prescribed punishments. If that assertion means that an individual must have accurate and precise knowledge, then the deterrence doctrine is indeed dubious. There is very little systematic data on the subject, but contemplate the likely responses of Americans in a particular jurisdiction to the following question: What do you think the legal punishment is for rape? The majority of the responses are likely to be something like these: "ten years in the pen," "five years imprisonment," "at least three years in jail," "death," "life imprisonment." None of those responses may be accurate (i.e., they differ from the statutory penalty), but who would question that most Americans regard all of the punishments mentioned as severe. Then consider a comparison of felony theft, burglary, and armed robbery in a particular jurisdiction. Suppose that the maximum statutory penalty is 5 years for felony theft, 10 years for burglary, and 15 years for armed robbery. Then suppose that individuals are asked to estimate the maximum statutory prison sentence for the three crimes, with the responses expressed in the average number of years of imprisonment: felony theft, 2.3; burglary, 6.4; and armed robbery 21.7. Those figures would indicate that public knowledge of statutory penalties is scarcely accurate; nonetheless, the *rank order* of the statutory maximums and the *rank order* of the estimates are identical for the three types of crime.

All of the foregoing reduces to two arguments. First, the deterrence doctrine need not be interpreted as asserting that any individual's knowledge of prescribed punishment for crimes is accurate. Second, research should consider only the relative accuracy of the public's knowledge of prescribed punishments for crimes.

Numerical Representation

The initial step in conducting research would be the preparation of a list of, say, 20 diverse types of crimes and statutory sentence or combinations of sentences with the highest perceived severity value for each type of crime. Given such a list and presuming that robbery is on the list, members of the population would be asked the following question: Which of these sentences is the maximum provided by law when someone is convicted of robbery? The respondent would make a choice from the list of punishments, only one of which is the statutory penalty or combination of penalties for robbery that represents maximum severity.

Whatever the type of punishment designated by a respondent, it is assigned a *perceived severity value, Sv,* which has been computed before hand by one of the procedures previously described. To illustrate briefly, suppose that one respondent designates "five years of imprisonment and a $5,000 fine" as the punishment for robbery, with the *Sv* value for those punishments combined being 0.670; that another respondent designates "life imprisonment," with the *Sv* value for the punishment being 0.926; and that still another respondent designates "two years imprisonment," with the *Sv* value for that punishment being 0.270. The average of the values would be 0.622; and if the sample of respondents were limited to three individuals, the value (0.622) would represent the *knowledge of prescribed punishment* (henceforth, *KPP*) for robbery in that jurisdiction.

The same procedure would be followed in computing a *KPP* value for any type of crime, and the *KPP* values would be comparable in that the respondents would have designated the maximum statutory penalty for each type of crime from the same list of punishments. However, it would be questionable to compare the *KPP* value of the same type of crime in different jurisdictions, especially if the related *Sv* values were not computed by the *AMPS* formula (absolute magnitude of perceived severity). If the *MPS* or *PS* formula is used, then the *KPP* value for a type of crime would be relative to a particular jurisdiction. When that is the case, the most defensible comparison of *KPP* values would be among types of crimes in the same jurisdiction. Those comparisons would take the form of a test of deterrence proposition: Among types of crimes in the same jurisdiction, there is an inverse relation between *KPP* values and the crime rate.

Three additional limitations of the proposed procedure should be recognized. Since respondents always make a choice from a list of maximum statutory sentences and one is correct for the crime in question, by chance alone some of the choices are likely to be correct. Thus, if asked to designate the maximum statutory sentence for robbery from a list of, say, 20 punishments, then 1 out of every 20 respondents would be expected to designate the correct punishment. However, "chance expectation" is the same for all types of crimes, and in that sense the *KPP* values of the different crimes considered are comparable.

Another limitation is more serious. Observe that the procedure is oversimplified in that respondents are asked to designate the maximum statutory sentence; hence their knowledge of the minimum remains unexamined. That point is significant because virtually nothing is known about the relative importance of maximum and minimum punishments in relation to deterrence. Of course, the same procedure can be used to compute *KPP* values that are based on the respondents' designations of minimum statutory sentences for the types of crimes in question. Indeed, exploratory research should consider the relation between two sets of *KPP* values for a list of crimes, one based on designations of maximum sentences and one based on designations of minimum sentences. If the two sets of values are directly related, the finding would constitute evidence that tests of a deterrence theory can employ either version of the procedure for computing *KPP* values. Of course, it could be that the two sets of values are not closely correlated. If so, the strategic question would be: What is the relation between each set of *KPP* values and the crime rate? It could be that one set of *KPP* values is much more inversely related to crime rates than is the other set. Still another possibility is that the *sum* of the two kinds of *KPP* values is much more inversely related to the crime rate than is either kind alone. That finding would not simplify tests of a deterrence theory, but it would further knowledge of deterrence, with the suggestion being that individuals are somehow sensitive to both the maximum and the minimum statutory penalties. All of the foregoing possibilities are illustrative of the need for exploratory research when a defensible choice cannot be made between alternative procedures for the numerical representation of a particular property.

The final limitation of the procedure for computing *KPP* values is simple and perhaps not particularly serious. Note that respondents are not asked to identify procedural punishments. That consideration is excluded because the vast majority of respondents are likely to know that interrogation, arrest, trial, and conviction are prescribed for all crimes, felonies in particular.

A Complicated Distinction

If one argues that individuals cannot be deterred from a type of crime unless they know (in an absolute sense) the prescribed punishment or punishments for that crime, then the argument poses an irresolvable issue. The counterargument is, of course, that accurate knowledge of prescribed punishments is not even a necessary condition for deterrence. More specifically, the proposed procedure for computing *KPP* values rests on the assumption that the only necessary condition is a fairly close relation between the normative severity of prescribed punishment *(NSP* values) and knowledge of prescribed punishment *(KPP* values). Evidence can be brought to bear on that assumption through exploratory research, that is, by examining the relation between *NSP* values and *KPP* values among types of crimes in the same jurisdiction. The findings could be crucial in attempts to state the deterrence doctrine as a systematic theory.

To clarify the distinction between *NSP* and *KPP* values, consider a hypothetical jurisdiction in which the statutory penalty for robbery is ten years imprisonment. By asking respondents about the severity of that prescribed punishment, an investigator can compute a *NSP* value for robbery in that jurisdiction. Whatever that value may be, it in no way indicates that members of the jurisdictional population know that ten years imprisonment is the statutory sentence for robbery. Indeed, *NSP* values are computed for a type of crime without asking individuals to identify the statutory penalties (maximum or minimum). That particular type of identification is solicited only when computing *KPP* values for a type of crime. Accordingly, the two properties are logically independent, and it is possible that there is no relation whatever between *NSP* values and *KPP* values among types of crime. However, if there is no relation, then it would be pointless to entertain the idea that prescribed punishments deter crimes in direct ratio to their severity. Conversely, to the extent that *NSP* values and *KPP* values vary directly, there is a basis for the idea that the severity of prescribed punishments somehow plays a role in deterrence. Of course, even if there is no relation between *NSP* values and *KPP* values, it could be that *NSP* values are much more inversely related to crime rates than are *KPP* values. Such a finding would indicate that the relation between the severity of prescribed punishments and the crime rates reflects some consequences of punishment other than deterrence.

Demonstration of a negligible relation between *NSP* values and *KPP* values would have implications for penal policy no less than for deterrence theory. The finding would question attempts to further deterrence by increasing the magnitude of prescribed punishments (i.e., presumptive severity) for particular types of crimes.

Implications of Complexity

This chapter has identified nine properties of punishments of crimes as possibly relevant in contemplating a deterrence theory, those nine being (1) objective certainty, (2) perceived certainty, (3) perceived severity of prescribed punishments, (4) perceived severity of actual punishments, (5) presumptive severity of actual punishments, (6) objective celerity, (7) perceived celerity, (8) presumptive severity of prescribed punishments, and (9) knowledge of prescribed punishments. Needless to say, the prospect of treating all nine properties in a deterrence theory is foreboding; hence it would be desirable to dismiss some of the properties as irrelevant. But such selectivity cannot be justified at this stage, and even the doubts previously expressed about the relevance of celerity are largely impressionistic. A final complication is introduced by the recognition that some of the properties of punishment may be relevant (if at all) only in contemplating a particular type of deterrence, that is, absolute, restrictive, or specific. There are only two excuses for not being more selective in the recognition of possibly relevant properties of punishment: first, the subject has not been treated systematically in previous conceptualizations of the deterrence doctrine; and, second, deterrence research has been largely limited to two properties of punishment, objective certainty and presumptive severity.

All of the foregoing should make it clear that the methodology of deterrence research cannot be simple unless one is willing to tolerate oversimplified, incomplete, and crude investigations. However, one may well ask: Given so many properties of legal punishment, how can the citizenry possibly assess the threat of punishment realistically?

The question deserves attention if only because it touches on a policy issue. Whatever the merits of the individualization of justice, it has complicated criminal law and its enforcement to the point that the typical citizen is unlikely to have even approximately accurate knowledge of legal penalties. Alternative sentences, indefinite sentences, indeterminate sentences, probation, and parole are in themselves sufficient to make the criminal justice system virtually incomprehensible to laymen. The point is that the complexity of criminal law may preclude deterrence.

Five

Some Research Findings

Jurisprudents commonly bemoan the paucity of deterrence research; but the investigations number in the hundreds, and many of them are "systematic" according to any reasonable standard. The scope of the investigations is another matter. Most of them have been limited to one or two properties of punishment, and none of them have controlled for both extralegal conditions and preventive mechanisms other than deterrence. Given those shortcomings, a survey of research findings cannot be particularly profitable; but it is necessary if only to describe the limitations of deterrence studies in detail.

Limits of the Survey

This survey is limited to systematic research; hence it excludes anecdotal reports, accounts of isolated crimes, and arguments about the nature of human nature. Systematic research is difficult to define, but two alternative criteria are especially relevant in classifying deterrence investigations: (1) comparisons must extend to the crime rates of at least two jurisdictional populations that differ in regard to some property of punishment; *or* (2) comparisons must extend to rates for at least two *types of crimes* in the same jurisdiction, with those types differing in regard to some property of punishment. Those criteria exclude (1) statements about punishment purportedly made by "criminals," (2) observations on human or animal behavior in laboratory situations, (3) allegations about the rationality or irrationality of human behavior, and (4) assertions about the consequences of extralegal punishments outside of laboratory situations. Those phenomena are ignored primarily because the deterrence doctrine is interpreted as asserting nothing whatever about any of them. As a case in point, the assertion that people have starved rather than eaten cattle during a famine may or may not be construed as compelling evidence about the irrationality of human behavior; but, in any case, it has no direct bearing on the deterrence doctrine. Similarly, what human beings or rats do in a laboratory situation is one thing; what a convict does on release from prison is another.

The emphasis on systematic research is dictated by more than space limitations; additionally, it reflects two arguments, the first being that only the empirical relation between properties of punishment and crime rates is *directly* relevant in assessing the deterrence doctrine. To illustrate, consider a *general* proposition: Individuals who perceive a threat of punishment for committing some type of act are more prone to refrain from it than are individuals who do not perceive any such threat. The proposition is more inclusive than the deterrence doctrine, which is *limited to* criminal acts and legal punishments; therefore, exceptions to the general proposition do not necessarily refute the deterrence doctrine. The second argument reduces to a condemnation of a common practice, that of reading all manner of assumptions "into" the deterrence doctrine. Thus, it is commonly alleged that the deterrence doctrine assumes that human behavior is governed by free will. The allegation is certainly disputable; and just the reverse can be argued, that the deterrence doctrine is deterministic.

A Typology of Studies of General Deterrence

Since the sheer volume of deterrence research precludes a universal inventory, this survey is restricted to illustrative instances of types of studies. Table 5-1 identifies 21 types of studies of general deterrence, and the typology serves to identify major shortcomings of those studies.

Kinds of Relations

Evidence can be brought to bear on virtually any assertion about general deterrence by examining the empirical relation between a property of punishment and the crime rate through (1) a comparison of different jurisdictions without regard to change in punishments, in which case the study is type A; or (2) an analysis of change, in which case the study is type B or type C. The central consideration in a longitudinal study (type B or type C) is that certain changes in some property of punishment should be followed (according to the deterrence doctrine) by a change in the crime rate. The first change may take the form of *an episode,* such as when (1) the *kind* of prescribed punishment is altered (e.g., imprisonment replaces the death penalty); (2) the magnitude of the prescribed punishment is modified; or (3) the procedure of law enforce-

Table 5-1. *A Typology of Studies of General Deterrence**

Properties of Legal Punishments Considered		Space-time Relation with Crime Rate		
		Cross-sectional or Synchronic‡	Longitudinal or Diachronic§	
			Episodic	Trend
Objective Certainty of Punishment Not Considered	Presumptive Severity of Prescribed Punishments†	Type IA	Type IB	Type IC
	Presumptive Severity of Actual Punishments	Type IIA	Type IIB	Type IIC
	Presumptive Severity of Prescribed Punishments† and Actual Punishments	Type IIIA	Type IIIB	Type IIIC
Objective Certainty of Punishment Considered	Presumptive Severity Not Considered	Type IVA	Type IVB	Type IVC
	Presumptive Severity of Prescribed Punishments†	Type VA	Type VB	Type VC
	Presumptive Severity of Actual Punishments	Type VIA	Type VIB	Type VIC
	Presumptive Severity of Prescribed Punishments† and Actual Punishments	Type VIIA	Type VIIB	Type VIIC

*Limited to systematic research on the relation between legal punishment and crime rates.

†Except in the case of capital punishment studies, "severity" refers to the magnitude of the kinds of punishments being considered (e.g., length of prison sentence). A statutory penalty is an instance of a prescribed punishment.

‡An examination of the relation between a property of punishment and the crime rate (among jurisdictional populations or types of crime in the same jurisdiction).

§An examination of the relation between *change* in some property of punishment and *change* in the crime rate.

ment is altered.[1] Research on trends in the crime rate after such an episode is a type *B* study. By contrast, if there are *two or more quantitative* changes in punishment (e.g., a series of increases in the statutory maximum fine, fluctuations in the average prison sentences served), then investigators can examine in a type *C* study the relation between *two trends:* changes in the crime rate and changes in the property of punishment.

The variety of possible empirical relations between the properties of punishment and the crime rate transcend the distinctions just described. Thus, in one study a time lag between change in the properties of punishment and change in the crime rate may be created, while in another study no allowance may be made for such a lag. Then observe that the relation between change in a property of punishment and change in the crime rate can be examined in two quite different ways. In the one case, the relation is examined for the *same* jurisdiction *over time;* that is, for *each* of two or more periods there is a value that represents change in a property of punishment and a value that represents change in the crime rate. In the other case, at least two jurisdictions are compared, and there are two values for each jurisdiction, one value representing change in some property of punishment during a period and the other representing change in the crime rate during a period. The two periods are the same for all jurisdictions; however, in either type of comparison (more than one jurisdiction *or* one jurisdiction over time), both values may represent the same period, or one of the values may represent change in punishment over a period (e.g., 1965–70) and the other value may represent change in the crime rate over a later period (e.g., 1970–1975).

Exlcusion of Perceptual Properties

Table 5-1 does not treat the inclusion or exclusion of perceptual properties of punishment (e.g., perceived certainty) as a distinguishing feature of particular studies. Briefly, to date *no* systematic research on the deterrence question has examined the relation between perceptual properties of legal punishment and official crime rates.[2] The exclusion of perceptual properties is the major shortcoming of deterrence re-

---

[1]Law-enforcement practices other than those designated as procedural punishments are not emphasized in this survey, primarily because some of them (e.g., the use of radar equipment to detect speeding motorists) cannot be analyzed in terms of properties of punishment. To be sure, some properties of punishment, especially objective certainty and perceived certainty, may largely reflect law-enforcement practices, but the deterrence doctrine takes properties of punishment *as given.*

[2]The point is emphasized because critics may question the allegation that perceptual properties of punishment have been ignored in deterrence research. They can do so by pointing to studies that have considered perceptual properties, but those studies are lim-

search taken as a whole, and the importance of that shortcoming cannot be exaggerated. Consider a finding of "no relation" between an objective property of punishment (e.g., objective certainty) and the crime rate. That finding would contradict a common deterrence assertion; but even if there is no relation between the objective certainty of imprisonment and the crime rate, it could be that the rate and the perceived certainty vary inversely. The point is that findings on the relation between the crime rate and the objective properties of punishment cannot be generalized to include perceptual properties without debatable assumptions.

Even studies of the severity of punishment have not been extended to perceptual properties. That is the case because virtually all studies have examined differences among jurisdictions with regard to the magnitude of the same kind of punishment (e.g., length of prison sentences), and the term "presumptive severity" is used in that sense in Table 5-1. The exceptions are instances where investigators have compared jurisdictions in which there is a statutory death penalty and jurisdictions in which there is no such prescribed punishment. In such cases, the assumption appears to be that the death penalty is perceived as more severe than any other kind of prescribed punishment. That assumption is plausible, and the same is true of the assumption that the perceived severity of imprisonment varies directly with the length of incarceration (presumptive severity). Nonetheless, such assumptions are not beyond question; hence the exclusion of the perceived severity of punishments (actual or prescribed) is one shortcoming of all deterrence studies.

Exclusion of Extralegal Conditions and Other Preventive Mechanisms

Unless indicated otherwise, no deterrence study has controlled for or otherwise taken into account (1) extralegal conditions that supposedly either inhibit or generate criminal acts *or* (2) possible preventive mechanisms other than deterrence.[3] Several investigators have speculated at length about the possible influence of those two factors in tests of deter-

---

ited to self-reported crimes (see, e.g., Waldo and Chiricos, 1972). The point is not that data on self-reported crimes are indefensible, but their use to test deterrence propositions (or any proposition about criminality) is a debatable strategy. In any case, regardless of the data on crimes, the perceptual properties of punishment have received very little attention in deterrence research.

[3]There are a few possible exceptions, such as Bean and Cushing's consideration (1971) of the proportion of black residents in their analysis of the relation among states between properties of punishment and the criminal homicide rate. The problem in that particular instance is that the nature of the relation between "proportion black" and the criminal homicide rate is most debatable. Surely the direct relation reported by Bean and Cushing does not hold universally (i.e., over time, cross-culturally, and internationally).

rence assertions, but speculation is a far cry from numerical representation and control.

When extralegal conditions and preventive mechanisms other than deterrence are ignored, the research findings are inherently disputable. Hence the present survey may appear pointless, especially if one demands conclusive evidence or a demonstration of causation. But those who make such demands should not even entertain the question of deterrence or, for that matter, any question about social phenomena.

Other Deficiencies

All systematic deterrence research has considered some kind of crime rate, usually the conventional rate. As explained in Chapter 2, the conventional rate is scarcely defensible; but it has been used so much in deterrence research that other types of rates are not identified in Table 5-1.

In using official crime statistics, deterrence investigators tacitly assume that those statistics are at least relatively reliable. Since that assumption is most debatable (see Beattie, 1960; Wilkins, 1963; and Wolfgang, 1963), the use of official crime statistics is a problem that haunts deterrence research in general. A less conspicuous limitation pertains to methods for estimating the objective certainty of punishment and expressing the presumptive severity of punishment (e.g., length of prison sentences). Briefly, as indicated in Chapter 4, there are various contending methods that can be used, and a host of problems (e.g., prosecutorial relabeling) are not peculiar to particular methods. Yet each deterrence study has relied on one method rather than a comparison of alternatives, and at best the investigators have done little more than recognize the problems.

If a deterrence study examines only the relation between the crime rate and the objective certainty of imprisonment, it is restricted not only to one property of punishment but also to one type of punishment (imprisonment). Typically, in addition to procedural punishments there are two or more prescribed alternative substantive punishments (e.g., fine, probation, imprisonment) for virtually any type of crime; hence a deterrence study is not complete if limited to only one type of punishment.

Stating the matter another way, the proportion black is not a variable in an accepted *theory* about criminal homicide. Unfortunately, the same observations apply to the other few instances in which investigators have introduced control variables in their attempts to test deterrence propositions (see, e.g., Kobrin et al., 1972; Tittle, 1969; and Tittle and Rowe, 1974).

That is another shortcoming of virtually all studies examined in this survey.

However, that shortcoming is likely to be misunderstood. It is not just that deterrence studies have been restricted largely to capital punishment and imprisonment; additionally, other punishments (e.g., probation, fines) have been ignored even though they were alternative substantive punishments for the type of crime in question. The exclusion of procedural punishments is no less glaring.[4] Since deterrence studies differ very little with regard to the types of punishment considered, that distinction is not recognized in Table 5-1. The paucity of systematic research on the deterrent efficacy of fines (see Samuels, 1970; Zimring and Hawkins, 1973:175–178) is especially unfortunate if only because fines are used so commonly as criminal sanctions.

Finally, note particularly that one investigation of deterrence may be treated as two or more distinct studies, depending on the properties of punishment considered *simultaneously*. Suppose an investigator considers the objective certainty of punishment, the presumptive severity of prescribed punishments, and the presumptive severity of actual punishments but does not consider their relation to the crime rate simultaneously (e.g., two of the properties are not controlled when the relation between the crime rate and the third property is examined). If so, the investigator has conducted three investigations, all of which are inferior to a type VII study (which treats three properties of punishment simultaneously).

Use of the Typology

Table 5-1 serves to avoid a monotonous litany of the limitations of deterrence studies. The identification of a study as, say, type IC reveals its major limitation—changes in *all* properties of punishment other than presumptive severity have been ignored. Further, regardless of the type, unless noted otherwise, the investigation did not take into account extralegal conditions or possible preventive mechanisms other than deterrence.

The very typification of deterrence studies is so damning that a word should be said in the way of mitigation. If a study excludes several properties of punishment, it may not be an oversight or a tacit denial

[4]For one notable exception, see Kobrin et al., 1972, esp. p. 258. The findings of that study do not provide truly impressive support for the deterrence doctrine, but they are sufficient to confirm the importance of what is here designated as procedural punishments (e.g., trial). Another notable exception (Tittle and Rowe, 1974) provides much more support for the deterrence doctrine, but the findings are limited to the certainty of arrest.

of the relevance of those properties. Rather, the exclusion may reflect practical considerations, limited research resources in particular.

Criteria for Considering Particular Studies

Given the vast amount of research on deterrence, studies could be selected in a survey so that the findings would appear to be conclusive evidence either for or against the deterrence doctrine; but such a biased selection would accomplish little, for past studies of deterrence are so defective that a thoughtful critic would not regard the findings as conclusive evidence one way or the other. Nor would anything be gained by selecting studies in such a way that a "representative" proportion of them would appear to support or refute the deterrence doctrine. Indeed, given that the deterrence doctrine can be construed in various ways and given the defects of past research, it would be misleading to create the impression that, say, two-thirds of the findings support the deterrence doctrine.

Rather than select studies with a view to assessing the "weight" of evidence, emphasis was placed on the strategic methodological features of studies. Even in that context, no attempt has been made to make the survey representative, since an atypical study may be important because it employs a novel methodology or because it illustrates some unusual methodological defect.

Type I Studies

Until the 1960's most deterrence research was concerned only with the presumptive severity of prescribed punishments. That focus reflected a preoccupation with the death penalty, and the preoccupation is understandable given the primacy of capital punishment in the long history of debates over penal policy. In any case, all studies of the deterrent efficacy of the death penalty have not been of the same type.

A Type IA Study on the Death Penalty

American states are strategic for deterrence research if only because legal definitions of some crimes are approximately comparable among states, while prescribed punishments and actual punishments vary from state to state. Thus, since the death penalty has been abolished in some states but retained in others, it is not surprising that much research on the deterrent efficacy of the death penalty has taken the form of interstate comparisons.

In a well-known investigation, Vold (1952) compared the annual criminal homicide rates of three groups of states, selected so that there were three contiguous states in each group, with at least one of the states being "abolitionist" and at least one being "capital." The rates were based on police reports of criminal homicides over 1933–1951, and some of those rates are shown for each state in Table 5-2. The table is only illustrative, restricted as it is to 1935, 1940, 1945, and 1950; but data for other years would not alter any conclusions.

There is no truly uniform and clear-cut difference that holds for all states and all years; but, overall, the capital states had higher criminal homicide rates than did the abolition states. Specifically, only in 6 of the 24 comparisons is the rate for an abolition state greater than the rate for a contiguous capital state, and those 6 differences are not substantial by any reasonable standard.

Vold's data are consistent with those of other similar investigations (e.g., Sellin, 1967c; Schuessler, 1952), though that is hardly surprising, since the investigators used the same kind of statistics and undertook essentially the same comparisons. Nonetheless, one would be hard pressed to find any evidence that death-penalty jurisdictions have lower crime rates (on the average) than other jurisdictions.

Paradoxically, however, there are several reasons for not regarding

Table 5-2. *Criminal Homicide Rates for Each of Nine States Grouped by Contiguity* *

States	Criminal Homicide Rates Per 100,000 Population for Each of Four Years			
	1935	1940	1945	1950
Group I States				
Michigan (Abolitionist)	3.3	3.2	4.1	4.1
Ohio (Death Penalty† Optional)	7.0	4.8	5.4	4.1
Indiana (Death Penalty† Optional)	4.7	4.0	5.1	4.6
Group II States				
Wisconsin (Abolitionist)	0.9	1.3	1.3	0.8
Minnesota (Abolitionist)	1.6	1.1	1.2	1.6
Iowa (Death Penalty† Optional)	2.8	1.0	1.6	1.3
Group III States				
Rhode Island (Abolitionist)	1.7	1.3	0.8	1.1
Massachusetts (Death Penalty† Mandatory)	1.2	1.0	1.2	1.0
Connecticut (Death Penalty† Mandatory)	1.7	2.1	1.4	1.3

*From Vold (1952:4), who used rates based on homicides reported as criminal by the police.
†All references to the death penalty are for first-degree murder only.

the evidence presented by Vold and others as refuting the deterrence doctrine. For one thing, Vold did not consider the objective or the perceived certainty of execution, and that omission takes on special significance because it is a defect of virtually all research on the death penalty. Moreover, the certainty of punishment is ignored in two ways. Vold's research is a type I study because he *implicitly* compared the death penalty with an alternative prescribed punishment for ostensibly the same type of crime. The alternative in all abolitionist states is imprisonment; and that recognition gives rise to a question: What bearing do such comparisons have on the deterrence doctrine? They have no bearing unless it is presumed that the death penalty is perceived by the public as more severe than life imprisonment, and that is the basis for characterizing Vold's study as type I. Even so, the two prescribed punishments may well have differed also in regard to certainty. If it could be shown that the certainty of imprisonment was substantially greater than the certainty of the death penalty prior to its abolition, then the findings of Vold and other investigators would become all the more debatable. Defenders of the deterrence doctrine could then construe the findings as demonstrating what they have often argued—that the certainty of a punishment is more important than its severity.

Another point is that Vold's investigation and others like it do not compare *capital crime rates.* Rather, they compare criminal homicide rates (as in the case of Vold) or general homicide rates (which are based on cases of justifiable homicides, manslaughter, and negligent homicides as well as first-degree murder). The assumption is that such rates vary directly and closely with the capital murder rate, and it is understandable, for published data cannot be used to compute capital rates for American states. Nonetheless, the assumption is debatable, since it reduces to the assertion that the proportion of homicides or criminal homicides that are first-degree murder does not vary significantly among jurisdictions. As one instance of contrary evidence, over 1925–1941 in Middlesex county, Massachusetts, 119 individuals were convicted on a homicide charge, 26 percent of whom were convicted for first-degree murder. By contrast, the respective figures for Suffolk county were 43 individuals and 7 percent (Ehrmann, 1952). The divergence in proportions probably might have been even greater if the denominator represented the number of criminal homicides reported by the police (rather than the number of individuals convicted on some homicide charge) and the units of comparison were states or countries (rather than counties).

Granted the shortcomings of his research, Vold's technique was sophisticated in that he attempted to control for extralegal conditions. The underlying assumption is that the overall sociocultural features of contiguous states are similar. However, anyone familiar with Oregon, California, and Nevada will question the assumption, and our ignorance of the extralegal conditions that generate or inhibit first-degree murder precludes a thorough assessment of the "contiguity" strategy in making comparisons.

A Type IB Study on the Death Penalty

Prior to the 1960's the bulk of deterrence research focused on the death penalty. The findings of one such study, conducted by Sellin (1967b) on the abolition of capital punishment in eight American states, are summarized in Table 5-3.

The table permits comparison of homicide figures in several states before, during, and after the abolition of the death penalty. For five of seven states the homicide figure increased with abolition, but in only three of six states was there a decrease in the figure after reinstatement of the death penalty. Moreover, several changes in the homicide figures were inconsequential by any reasonable standard.

*Table 5-3. Figures on Homicide for Eight States: Before, during, and after Abolition of Capital Punishment**

States	Nature of the Figures on Homicide†	Before Abolition		During Abolition		After Reinstatement	
		Years	Figures	Years	Figures	Years	Figures
Arizona	Convictions for Murder‡	1915–1916	41.0	1917–1918	46.0	1919–1920	45.0
Colorado	Convictions for Murder	1891–1896	15.4	1897–1901	18.0	1902–1907	19.0
Delaware	Murders and Non-negligent Manslaughters	1956–1958	22.3	1959–1961	14.3	No Reinstatement Reported	
Iowa	Convictions for Murder	1864–1871	2.6	1872–1878	8.8	1879–1966	13.1
Kansas	Homicide Rate	No figures for Years Prior to 1907		1930–1934	6.5	1936–1940	3.8
Missouri	Homicide Rate	1911–1916	9.2	1917–1919	10.7	1920–1924	11.0
Oregon	Murderers Committed to Prison‡	1909–1914	59.0	1915–1920	36.0	Not Reported	
Washington	Homicide Rate	1908–1912	6.5	1913–1918	6.8	1920–1924	5.4

*This table was constructed from data in Sellin, 1967b. Data for Maine, South Dakota, and Tennessee were not reported in such a way as to permit tabular presentation.

†Unless indicated otherwise, the figures are for an average annual number, and the rates are per 100,000 population.

‡Total number (not average annual number).

Sellin's findings illustrate the negligible predictive power of the deterrence doctrine when extended to include a proposition about the relation between change in the presumptive severity of the statutory penalty for murder and change in the figures that have to do with criminal homicide. That proposition anticipates an increase in the crime rate when there is a decrease in the presumptive severity of the statutory penalty (e.g., substitution of some penalty for capital punishment), and it anticipates a decrease in the crime rate when there is an increase in the severity of statutory penalty (e.g., reinstatement of the death penalty). The predictive power of the proposition in these instances (Table 5-3) is clearly unimpressive. In only 8 of the 13 instances is the prediction correct, whereas 6 or 7 correct predictions would be expected on the basis of chance alone.

Of course, the "negative" evidence can be explained away on several grounds, such as ignoring the certainty of punishment or failing to control for change in extralegal conditions. Still another argument is that the homicide figures should have been restricted to the *incidence* of capital murders, which means that the general homicide rate and the figures relating to convictions are inappropriate. However, if the figures pertain to convictions for first-degree murder, it could be argued that jurors are reluctant to convict in a capital case; hence the figures would increase with abolition and fall with reinstatement.

Whatever the merits of the foregoing arguments, they cannot be extended to include a declaration that Sellin's findings are peculiar to the death penalty and to homicide. Schwartz (1968) has shown that the incidence of rape in Philadelphia did not decline after a marked increase in the presumptive severity of the prescribed punishment for that type of crime.

Observe that the data in Table 5-3 are limited to short run-changes in the incidence of homicide (of one kind of rate or another). Defenders of the deterrence doctrine could object to the findings for that reason, and their argument would include the assertion that the abolition or reinstatement of the death penalty is related only to long-run trends in the crime rate. However, the rationale for the argument is disputable. If the death penalty contributes to the social condemnation of capital crimes (or homicide in general), then the impact of abolition would not be manifested for at least a generation. Even so, that line of reasoning tacitly invokes normative validation, not deterrence, and there is no empirical evidence to support that reasoning. Several American states have been abolitionist for generations, and yet the comparisons made by Vold (1952) and Sellin (1967c) do not reveal any evidence that the crime rate is higher in "old abolitionist" states than in death-penalty states.

The foregoing observations are only suggestive of the arguments that can be made to refute evidence such as that reported in Table 5-3. Those arguments are counterproductive, for they preclude consensus in the assessment of any deterrence proposition. Consensus can be realized only if assessments focus on one question: What do the findings suggest about the predictive power of the deterrence proposition under examination? Again, in this case little can be said for the predictive power of the proposition. Accordingly, since Sellin's findings are hardly atypical, it is not difficult to understand why so many social scientists came to doubt the deterrence doctrine. Their only mistake was in assuming that evidence contrary to *one* deterrence proposition is sufficient for rejecting the deterrence doctrine in toto.

Of course, the emphasis on predictive power will not be to the liking of those who argue that no research finding has policy implications unless it purports to be a causal demonstration. But it is a mistake to assume that fundamental policy questions are even voiced in terms of causation. The central question is and always will be: If this policy is adopted, what will happen? An answer to that question *is* a prediction, and Sellin's findings simply do not provide a justifiable basis for predicting that homicide figures will increase with the abolition of the death penalty or decrease with its reinstatement.

A Special Problem with Type B Studies

Even when an increase in presumptive severity is followed by a sharp decrease in the crime rate, that relation is questionable evidence of an increase in deterrence, and the problem is not just that the finding pertains to only one episode. There is another problem, one that haunts *all* type B studies. Even though the problem is introduced here in connection with the presumptive severity of prescribed punishments, it is not limited to that property.

Defenders of the deterrence doctrine interpret a change in the crime rate that follows a change in the properties of punishment as an effect of the those properties. However, a change in the properties of punishment may be a response to changes in the crime rate, and that possibility takes on added significance when considered in connection with the notion of a "regression effect."

Changes in the crime rate are commonly cyclical. When that is the case, the "probability" of a further increase in the crime rate is less after several years of a consistent increase, while the probability of a further decrease in the rate is less after several years of a consistent decline. Now suppose that legislators or other officials are most likely to increase the magnitude of prescribed punishments (or to reinstate the death penalty) after several years of an increase in the crime rate. If so, a *decline* in the crime rate shortly after the change in the prescribed punishment would be expected on the basis of a regression effect alone, that is, apart from deterrence. Now suppose that a reduction in the magnitude of punishments (or the abolition of the death penalty) is most likely after the crime rate has been falling for a number of years. If so, an *increase* in the rate after the change in punishment would be expected on the basis of a regression effect alone, once again apart from deterrence.

Observe that the foregoing depicts the regression effect as operating so that findings appear to be consistent with the deterrence argument. Since such findings have not been realized in most type *B* studies, the evidence against the deterrence doctrine is all the more significant. However, in previous illustrative observations on the regression effect, the treatment of probability is grossly oversimplified, and the complexities defy exaggeration. Yet there are three incontestable points. First, the vast majority of type *B* studies of deterrence have either ignored the regression effect or treated it superficially. Second, the notable exceptions are limited primarily to a few studies of changes in punishments or enforcement practices pertaining to traffic offenses (e.g., Campbell and Ross, 1968; Glass, 1968; and Ross, 1973); and those studies clearly indicate that regression effects are not just a remote possibility. Third, it is surely plausible to assume that penal policies may be altered in response to trends (real or imagined) in the crime rate, and there are numerous instances where fears concerning crime trends or public indignation over particular crimes have apparently prompted officials to alter punishments (see, e.g., Schwartz, 1968; Samuelson, 1969).

The third point is crucial in contemplating further deterrence research. Specifically, arguments about regression effects should not appeal to plausibility alone, which is to say that more research should focus on the relation between changes in crime rates and *subsequent* changes in penal policies. The central question is whether there is a consistent relation between the two, and that question cannot be answered by research on only one jurisdiction (e.g., Samuelson, 1969). Of course, it may well be that the relation in question depends on the type of punishment (e.g., the death penalty) and/or the type of crime. The matter would be complicated even more should it be discovered that regardless of type of punishment or type of crime there is nothing approximating a uniform relation between trends in crime rates and subsequent changes in penal policy, with one alternative possibility being that policy changes could be responses to economic or political conditions rather than to trends in crime (see Rusche and Kirchheimer, 1939).

The question of a uniform relation is important because an answer could alter assessments of type *B* studies and determine future research strategies. However, a regression effect could operate in particular instances even if there is no uniform relation between crime-rate trends and subsequent changes in penal policy (i.e., a relation that holds generally for all jurisdictions, types of crimes, and/or types of punishment). If so, a regression effect would have to be treated as problematical in each investigation, and instances in which properties of punishment are altered after several years of a more or less constant crime rate would take on special significance. (The regression effect is minimal in such a case.) That is all the more significant since there does not appear to be a simple, standard way for dealing with the possibility of regression effects (see Campbell and Ross, 1968; Glass, 1968; and Ross, 1973).

Other Special Problems with Type B Studies

Doubts regarding the interpretation of type *B* findings are by no means limited to the possibility of regression effects. There are so many additional problems that only a few of the more obvious ones can be introduced. As before, the problems are illustrated by reference to the presumptive severity of prescribed punishments, but they are not limited to that property.

Consider a change in the prescribed punishment for "driving while intoxicated" from a fine to a prison sentence. Some police officers may view the new penalty as unduly harsh; consequently, they may arrest motorists on that charge only in the most flagrant or dangerous cases. Such enforcement practices would reduce the official crime rate below the previous level (when the punishment was milder), and the reduction would appear to be due to the increase in deterrence.

Just the opposite of the "underreporting effect" may occur. Proposals to increase the prescribed punishment for a type of crime are occasionally publicized; and the publicity is likely to draw the attention of police officers to that type of crime, with the consequence being that they will be more prone to report instances of it and arrest suspects. To illustrate, Andenaes (1952) attributed an increase in official reports of sexual offenses in Norway to a publicized change in the prescribed punishment of that type of crime.

Unfortunately, there is no reason to suppose that *underreporting* effects and *heightening* effects counterbalance when prescribed punishments are changed, and ordinarily an estimate of either effect is only a guess. The only partial solution is to focus research on types of crimes for which there are independent bases for estimating incidence (before and after change in the prescribed punishment). Research on traffic offenses is especially strategic, for investigators can (1) make observations on the behavior of motorists (e.g., Feest, 1968), (2) use official reports of violations, and (3) consider the incidence of traffic fatalities when analyzing offenses pertaining to speeding or driving while intoxicated (see Ross, 1973).

Since only one type *B* study has been considered in detail and the findings are contrary to the deterrence doctrine, it may appear that illustrations were selected to discredit the doctrine. Therefore, it should be pointed out that in the most elaborate and sophisticated deterrence study ever conducted, Ross (1973) reports compelling evidence that implementation of the British Road Safety Act did result in a sharp reduction in the number of incidents of individuals driving while intoxicated. The Act encompassed several measures, the most important being the prescribed use by the police of a device to estimate the alcohol consumption of motorists. Far from being content to document a decrease in the number of official violations after the Act, Ross considered so many alternative interpretations (i.e., other than an increase in deterrence) that nothing short of a full reading of his paper (1973) would do justice to the research. Among other things, he shows that the drop in offenses was due to more than a regression effect, and his consideration of trends in traffic fatalities (including reports on blood analysis to determine alcohol consumption before death) was one check on underreporting and heightening effects.

Unfortunately, the methodology of Ross's study is virtually unique, and there are few type *B* studies that can be considered as systematic research. The typical "finding" is nothing more than an observation by a journalist or an official that a change in some prescribed punishment or police practice (e.g., intensification of surveillance) was followed by a drop in the official crime rate. The objection is not just that contrary results are unlikely to be publicized (especially by the police) or even that the "experiment" did not utilize controls or recognize contending interpretations (i.e., other than the deterrence argument). No less important, a full report is typically never published in a scholarly journal; hence the evidence is not scrutinized by an impartial, critical, and informed audience. The point is illustrated by the widely publicized "Connecticut crackdown on speedsters" in December of 1955. After the Governor ordered stringent enforcement of harsher sanctions for speeding, official statistics showed a marked decline in the number of traffic fatalities and arrests for speeding, which the Governor attributed to the change in sanctions. However, after a detailed analysis of the evidence in two independent studies (Glass, 1968; Campbell and Ross, 1968), the investigators concluded that the decline in traffic fatalities (especially in 1956) may have been only a regression effect. Unfortunately, the investigators did not focus on the decline in arrests for speeding.

The quality of type *B* studies could be enhanced by an arrangement wherein individuals trained in criminology and research methods would work closely with law-enforcement agencies that are willing to experiment with prescribed punishments or enforcement practices. One obstacle to such an arrangement is that official agencies are reluctant to sponsor research that could discredit the deterrence doctrine; but the reluctance may reflect recognition that experimentation with legal sanctions (prescribed punishments or enforcement practices) is inherently controversial, for it is bound to be unfair to some individuals and perhaps represent a flagrant violation of due process. Only the strategic importance of type *B* deterrence studies justifies experimentation with punishment (if it can be justified at all). If the classical conception of "cause and effect" is to be paramount in deterrence research, then type *B* studies are crucial, especially if they incorporate the distinction between experimental and control conditions.

The Neglect of Type IC Studies

One inconspicuous limitation of deterrence research on capital punishment is that it cannot take the form of a type IC study. That type requires data on at least two changes (ideally several) in the *prescribed* punishment for a type of crime in a particular jurisdiction, with those changes being quantitative, so that investigators can speak of *amounts* of increase or decrease in presumptive severity (magnitude). The prediction suggested by the deterrence doctrine is an inverse relation (over time) between two trends—the presumptive severity of the prescribed punishment and the crime rate. However, for all practical purposes that prediction is testable only when the magnitude of the prescribed punishment is altered at least twice; an example would be when the maximum statutory term of imprisonment is increased (or decreased) during some period and decreased (or increased) during a later period. Abolition of the death penalty and its replacement with imprisonment does not qualify (for it is only one change), and even instances where the death penalty is replaced and subsequently reinstated would not be relevant unless the investigators have data on the *perceived* severity of the death penalty and imprisonment. Only such data can be used to express the amount of change in severity when imprisonment replaces the death penalty or vice versa.

There are numerous opportunities for conducting a type IC deterrence study since the statutory term of imprisonment and/or fine for each of several types of crime has been increased or decreased at least twice over recent decades in numerous jurisdictions. However, those opportunities have not been exploited. Rusche and Kirchheimer (1939) examined trends in punishment and crime rates in several European countries between World War I and II, but a close reading discloses a preoccupation on their part with changes in sentences actually received or served rather than in prescribed punishments. Given provisions for indefinite or indeterminate sentences, probation, and parole, changes in prescribed (statutory) punishments cannot be justifiably inferred from changes in actual punishments.

The very idea of a type IC study of deterrence is debatable, for such a study ignores *(inter alia)* the certainty of punishment and the severity of actual punishments. However, with regard to penal policy, there is a special justification for type IC studies. When increasing the magnitude of prescribed punishments, legislators are not altering the number of actual punishments. Hence their action suggests that they feel that an increase in the magnitude of a prescribed punishment (i.e., presumptive severity) will be sufficient in itself to bring about a decrease in the crime rate.

Type II Studies

Both type I and type II studies are defective in that they ignore *(inter alia)* the objective certainty of punishment. However, even though objective certainty has to do with actual punishments, it is logically distinct from the presumptive severity of actual punishments. There have been few studies of the relation between crime rates and the presumptive severity of actual punishments alone (i.e., a type II study), evidently because of the preoccupation of early investigators with the statutory death penalty. If capital punishment is the prescribed penalty for a particular type of crime in two or more jurisdictions, then one can assume that the presumptive severity of actual punishments of the crime is approximately the same in all of those jurisdictions. However, if the prescribed punishment is the same kind but noncapital (e.g., imprisonment) in all jurisdictions, then the presumptive severity of actual punishments may vary sharply among those jurisdictions, especially if the prescribed punishment is indefinite (e.g., two to ten years imprisonment) or indeterminate (e.g., not less than one year of imprisonment) in any jurisdiction. Stating the matter another way, only when the prescribed punishment is both the same kind and definite (e.g., five years imprisonment) can investigators justifiably argue that the presumptive severity of actual punishments is more or less constant among all jurisdictions. If there are qualitatively different alternative punishments (e.g., two years imprisonment and/or a $5,000 fine) in any jurisdiction, then the presumptive severity of actual punishments in those jurisdictions cannot be compared (i.e., they could be compared only with regard to the perceived severity of actual punishments). Here we can see a defect of the capital punishment studies. Since the death penalty ceased to be mandatory in most American states long ago, it is untenable to assume that the presumptive severity of actual punishments for *possibly* capital crimes is even approximately the same from state to state. Nonetheless, the assumption was accepted (perhaps uncritically) by early investigators of deterrence, with the consequences resulting in a large number of type I studies but few type II studies.

A Type IIA Study

Observe again that most early investigations of deterrence were restricted to one prescribed punishment, the death penalty. In recent years, the research has expanded not only to include other types of punishment but also to include the presumptive severity and the objective certainty of *actual* punishments. The first two of the recent studies (Gibbs, 1968; Tittle, 1969) reported findings that can be construed as consistent with the deterrence doctrine, but other investigators promptly challenged that interpretation. To that end, Chiricos and Waldo (1970) conducted a series of distinct studies, distinct in that they analyzed the relation between the crime rate and particular properties of punishment that they considered separately (i.e., they did not consider two or more properties simultaneously). In their type IIA study, they considered the difference among states in regard to the presumptive severity of actual punishments in the form of the "median length of sentence served" by state prisoners on release in a particular year. Their findings for six types of crimes are presented in Table 5-4.

Only 4 of the 12 correlation coefficients in Table 5-4 are negative, hence consistent with a deterrence prediction. Further, only the negative correlation for homicide is of an appreciable magnitude, and even that is not the case for homicide in the second period (1964–1966). Indeed, the findings indicate that the relation for some types of crimes is markedly unstable, which is yet another problem when interpreting the findings of deterrence research.

Chiricos and Waldo's findings on presumptive severity of imprisonment cannot be dismissed as unsubstantiated or as a product of a particular way of expressing statistical associations, for a subsequent investigation (Bailey et al., 1974) found essentially the same relations even though different measures of association were used, along with the same kind

Table 5-4.   Relations among States between Length of Imprisonment and Rates for Six Types of Crimes during Two Periods: 1960–1962 and 1964–1966*

| Types of Crimes | Phi Coefficients of Correlation | |
	Between Median Length of Imprisonment† and Average Annual Crime Rate, 1960–1962	Between Median Length of Imprisonment‡ and Average Annual Crime Rate, 1964–1966
	Col. 1	*Col. 2*
Homicide	−.33	−.03
Robbery	.12	.00
Assault	.32	−.08
Burglary	.25	.08
Larceny	.14	−.09
Auto Theft	.13	.12

*From Chiricos and Waldo (1970), who used figures on crime from *Uniform Crime Reports* and *National Prisoner Statistics*.

†Of prisoners released from state prisons in 1960 after serving a sentence for the type of crime in question.

‡Of prisoners released from state prisons in 1964 after serving a sentence for the type of crime in question.

of data for three periods (1950, 1960, and 1964). Of course, defenders of the deterrence doctrine can allege that both investigations employed the wrong kind of data, but that line of criticism is not constructive unless it stipulates the "right" kind of data. Alternatively, defenders of the doctrine can point to Chiricos and Waldo's failure to consider other properties of punishment in conjunction with the presumptive severity of prison sentences; but there is surely some justification for considering that property alone, especially given the possibility that long prison sentences are incapacitating. Given that possibility, the negligible correlations in Table 5-4 cast doubts on the idea that long prison sentences have *any* impact on the crime rate by means of deterrence or any other mechanism (see also Zimring and Hawkins, 1973:194–203). In conclusion, the only obvious way that defenders of the deterrence doctrine can dismiss Chiricos and Waldo's findings is to retreat to a conventional argument— that the severity of actual punishment in itself is not important (at least within very broad limits).

Type IIB Studies

Since all *B* studies deal with changes in the crime rate after some episode, a type IIB study is necessarily restricted either to a particular actual punishment or to more than one at about the same time. If the prescribed punishment is indefinite (e.g., not less than two or more than ten years imprisonment), then a particular sentence may be much greater than previous sentences for the same type of crime. Similarly, if there are alternative kinds of prescribed punishments, one of which is presumably much more severe than the other (e.g., a $200 fine or two years imprisonment), the "harsher" punishment may rarely be imposed. In either case, when someone receives what is ostensibly an exceptionally severe sentence, it is "exemplary" if the magistrate or the jury emphasizes the unusual character of the sentence. Given an exemplary sentence, the deterrence doctrine can be construed as predicting a decline in the crime rate. Consider Hood and Sparks's observations (1970:173): "It is also possible to point to a few instances in which changes in the law or its enforcement, or in the penalties provided, have been followed by sudden (though usually short-term) reductions in the offenses concerned. Two recent examples in England are the heavy prison sentences imposed on a group of young men convicted in 1958 of assaulting coloured people in the Notting Hill area of London, and the 'exemplary' sentences imposed by another judge on persons convicted of stealing from public telephones kiosks in Birmingham, where this offense had become especially prevalent. In each case, the imposition of heavier sentences was well-publicized, and was followed by a decline in the type of crime in question."

Observations on a few isolated cases (no matter how carefully documented) are hardly compelling evidence of deterrence, and that is the most obvious problem in assessing type IIB studies. Another problem is that a regression effect in the crime trend after the imposition of an exemplary sentence is especially likely, since judges or juries commonly resort to extreme measures when confronted with evidence of a rising crime rate (Zimring and Hawkins, 1973:44). Still another complication is that officials may take preventive steps that have nothing to do with deterrence. Consider Hood and Sparks's subsequent commentary (1970:173) on the British instances previously noted: "There are almost invariably a number of other factors present in situations of this kind, which could explain the observed fall in crime rates. In the case of the Birmingham telephone kiosk thefts, for example, the reduction in crime appears to have been due at least in part to the installation of coin boxes of a kind which were less easy to break open, as well as to better policing; and there is some evidence that the racial violence in Notting Hill was declining even before the severe sentences were imposed."

Still another problem with IIB studies is that exemplary sentences further general deterrence (if at all) only to the extent that they are publicized. Hence a type IIIB study is incomplete if the extent of publicity is not considered. When an exemplary sentence is not publicized, a decrease in the crime rate would be an anomaly; and in the same condition no change in the rate (not even an increase) would be crucial evidence for or against the deterrence doctrine. Tornudd (1968:122) has emphasized the importance of publicity in observations on the possible reasons why a change in actual legal reactions to drunkenness in three towns in Finland was not followed by any appreciable change in the number of arrests for that offense.

Type IIC Studies

The major advantage of a type *C* study over a type *B* study is that the evidence of a relation between a change in the crime rate and a change in punishment is not restricted to one case. Still another advantage of a type *C* study is that the "proportional quality" of change can be examined more systematically. Thus, if the average presumptive severity of actual punishments increases 50 percent during some period (e.g., 1965–1970) but only 10 percent during some subsequent period (e.g., 1970–1975), then the deterrence doctrine can be construed as predicting that the crime rate decreased during both periods but proportionately less in the last period.

Despite the advantages of a type *C* study, only approximations of it are reported in the literature, one being Rusche and Kirchheimer's analysis (1939) of the relation between trends in actual punishments and crime rates in England, France, Germany, and Italy (circa 1900–1932). Their statistics for Germany are fragmentary, and the English statistics are limited to 1911 and 1928, with the nature of the crime rates described poorly. Consequently, this analysis will consider only France and Italy, but it should be noted that Rusche and Kirchheimer reached the same conclusion for all four countries.

Table 5-5 shows rates for seven types of crimes and figures pertaining to actual punishments in France in 1900, 1910, 1922, and 1932. Since there were alternative kinds of punishments for each crime, no summary figure can be used to express change in the overall magnitude of punishment (i.e., overall presumptive severity). A summary figure would be feasible only if each type of punishment could be assigned a perceived severity value, S; and the summary figure for each year would be equal to ΣSP, where P is the proportion of cases in which an individual is sentenced to a particular type of punishment. In lieu of such a measure, an increase in the percentage of prison sentences of over one year is taken as indicative of an increase in presumptive severity, while the converse is true for prison sentences of less than a year. But it would be much better to have figures on average or median prison sentences;

Table 5-5.   Crime Rates and Punishments of Crime in France in 1900, 1910, 1922, and 1932 *

Years	Type of Crime	Crime Rate Per 10,000 Population	Percentage of Convictions by Type of Punishment†			
			Imprison- ment over One Year	Imprison- ment Not over One Year	Fine	Suspended Sentence
1900		10.24	4.54	80.01	8.92	23.2
1910		9.62	4.79	77.76	7.40	24.0
1922	Larceny	13.74	5.36	72.50	14.64	25.4
1932		11.94	3.63	74.83	13.97	28.0
1900		0.71	10.50	82.23	6.04	13.9
1910	Fraud	0.76	13.34	66.22	18.51	15.9
1922		0.82	9.11	81.58	7.00	13.7
1932		1.01	13.09	78.17	7.36	21.2
1900		1.03	3.75	85.94	8.96	21.2
1910	Embezzlement	1.47	4.93	80.83	10.75	21.7
1922		1.47	6.69	84.49	6.28	19.8
1932		1.81	7.39	76.62	13.59	24.5
1900	Outrages	3.30	0.50	66.38	33.05	19.5
1910	against	3.52	0.27	61.95	37.42	21.2
1922	Public	2.26	0.22	57.26	41.88	25.7
1932	Officials	1.59	0.03	51.74	47.69	28.7
1900		2.86	0.10	98.07	0.26	4.8
1910	Vagrancy	2.76	0.08	93.14	0.88	4.8
1922		2.28	0.23	88.91	0.90	4.7
1932		2.91	0.03	90.44	0.51	5.6
1900		8.76	0.50	48.95	49.73	26.6
1910	Intentional	8.61	1.34	47.14	50.29	30.3
1922	Assault	8.50	0.88	41.34	56.79	28.8
1932		8.70	0.71	31.32	66.86	31.8
1900		0.70	3.39	78.72	15.64	22.9
1910	Indecency	0.55	2.06	78.50	13.20	25.9
1922		0.57	2.87	82.35	10.59	19.0
1932		0.79	2.12	74.59	15.62	32.0

*From Rusche and Kirchheimer (1939:198).

†For reasons not made clear by Rusche and Kirchheimer, the percentages for a year exceed 100.

moreover, no inferences can be reached about change in the presumptive severity (amount) of the fines. Finally, change in the percentage of sentences that were suspended is at best only indicative of change in the presumptive severity of punishments in general. Despite such shortcomings, the figures warrant some general observations.

Whatever way one chooses to interpret the figures, for no type of crime is there evidence of any association between changes in actual punishments and changes in the crime rate. Far from being a relation between *proportionate* change, an increase in the presumptive severity of prison sentences does not even tend to be accompanied by or followed by a decrease in the crime rate.

Rusche and Kirchheimer present data like those in Table 5-5 for Italy (1906, 1910, 1922, and 1928) as well, and those data suggest the same conclusion. Again, there is no discernible association between change in the presumptive severity of actual punishments and change in the crime rate.

Rusche and Kirchheimer's findings cannot be construed as crucial evidence against the deterrence doctrine. That is the case because they considered only one property of punishment (presumptive severity of actual punishments), and they ignored extralegal conditions altogether. Nonetheless, the findings for all four countries suggest that type IIC studies are so inconclusive that they cannot be justified.

The Neglect of Type III Studies

In the recent revival of interest in the deterrence question, investigators (both sociologists and economists) have thrown part of the baby out with the bath. As a reaction against the preoccupation of early investigators with the statutory death penalty, recent investigators have completely ignored the presumptive severity of prescribed punishments. Hence, there have been few type I studies on prescribed punishments other than the death penalty (see Schwartz, 1968) and no type III studies at all.

The absence of type III studies is unfortunate. An assessment of the role of prescribed punishments in deterrence should not be based on research limited to the death penalty, especially since that research has been defective in several respects. The neglect of type III studies is unfortunate for a somewhat more complicated reason. Given indefinite sentences, indeterminate sentences, probation, and parole, there can be a great divergence between the presumptive severity of prescribed punishments and the presumptive severity of actual punishments. Of course, there may be an inverse relation between the presumptive severity of prescribed punishments and the crime rate, and that possibility can be examined by extending type I studies to include punishments other than the death penalty, with an emphasis on IA comparisons.

Even if the presumptive severity of prescribed or actual punishments is not related to the crime rate, the two considered together are another matter. But research along that line (type III studies) is difficult since indefinite sentences, indeterminate sentences, alternative punishments (e.g., fine or imprisonment, and probation) complicate an assessment of the presumptive severity of the prescribed punishment (or punishments) for a type of crime. The difficulty is not limited to prescribed punishments, since the actual punishments of a type of a crime may take various forms (e.g., fines, probation, imprisonment). So it may be that type III studies will have to be incomplete, meaning that they will have to focus on the presumptive severity of only one type of actual and prescribed punishment (e.g., imprisonment). A truly complete type III study would require data pertaining to the perceived severity of all kinds of prescribed and actual punishments, since the presumptive severity values of different kinds of punishment cannot be treated as additive.

Type IV Studies

Despite discontinuance of research on prescribed punishments, recent work has reflected an awareness that purported tests of the deterrence doctrine should consider several properties of punishment simultaneously. Hence, there have been only a few type IV studies, that is, investigations of the relation between the objective certainty of punishment and the crime rate, without regard to the severity of actual or prescribed punishments.

A Type IVA Study

Table 5-6 summarizes the findings of Chiricos and Waldo's study (1970) of the relation among states between the objective certainty of imprisonment and the crime rate. Observe that the statistical relation is shown for each of six types of crimes during three periods.

Of 18 correlation coefficients, *all but one* are in the direction predicted by the deterrence doctrine.[5] However, for two of the types of crimes (larceny and auto theft) the coefficients are negligible according to any reasonable standard, and for two other types (homicide and burglary) the coefficients are not uniformly and substantially negative in all periods. Finally, the differences among the types of crimes are not explained by any version of the deterrence doctrine, and they are puzzling.

[5]Just as it is questionable to identify generalizations as deterrence propostions or deterrence assertions, so it is questionable to speak of predictions derived from the deterrence doctrine. The deterrence doctrine is so vague that all manner of interpretations are defensible. All that can be said of the present interpretation (i.e., references to deterrence propositions, assertions, or predictions) is that it is based on a reading of several versions of the deterrence doctrine, including those set forth by Beccaria and Bentham.

Table 5-6.   Relations among States between Estimated Certainty of Imprisonment and Rates for Each of Six Types of Crimes in Three Periods*

| | Phi Coefficients of Correlation | | |
Types of Crimes	Between Estimated Certainty of Imprisonment, 1950, and Average Annual Crime Rates, 1950–1952†	Between Estimated Certainty of Imprisonment, 1960, and Average Annual Crime Rates, 1960-1962†	Between Estimated Certainty of Imprisonment, 1963, and Average Annual Crime Rates, 1963–1965†
	Col. 1	Col. 2	Col. 3
Homicide	.02	−.46	−.17
Robbery	−.26	−.33	−.25
Assault	−.35	−.38	−.42
Burglary	−.09	−.33	−.50
Larceny	−.04	−.17	−.15
Auto Theft	−.16	−.25	−.16

*From Chiricos and Waldo (1970), who used figures from Uniform Crime Reports and National Prisoner Statistics.

†The estimated certainty of imprisonment (Ci) for any year was computed as follows: $Ci = Ay/[(Cy + Cx)/2]$, where Ay is the number of individuals admitted during the year to a state prison who were sentenced for the type of crime in question, Cy is the number of crimes of that type reported by the police as having occurred in the state during the year, and Cx is the number of crimes reported for the preceding year.

For example, why should the correlation coefficients be negative and substantial in all three periods for assault only?

The foregoing qualifications notwithstanding, it is difficult to think of the statistics in Table 5-6 as being other than impressive support for the deterrence doctrine, especially since all other properties of punishment are ignored. However, Chiricos and Waldo (1970) question the correlation coefficients, arguing that they are statistical artifacts. The argument stems from recognition that the correlations are between two ratios, A/C and C/P, where A is the number of admissions to a state prison for a type of crime, C is the number of crimes of that type reported, and P is the population size of the state. Since C is the denominator of one ratio (certainty of imprisonment) and the numerator of the other (crime rate), Chiricos and Waldo argue that a negative correlation between the two ratios is a statistical artifact. It is difficult to follow their line of reasoning. For one thing, there are no rules of logic, mathematics, or statistics that would enable one to *deduce* the C/P ratio for a state given the A/C ratio (which could vary from 0.00 to 1.00 regardless of the C/P ratio). Chiricos and Waldo are content to invoke the notion of probability, but the meaning of that notion can be interpreted in all manner of ways. In any case, Chiricos and Waldo's attempt to demonstrate that the high probability of negative correlations is at variance with the conclusions reached by Tittle (1969) and Logan (1971, 1972b). Logan has treated the problem in detail (1972b), and he makes a forcible argument against the claim that the relations in question are spurious artifacts. The issue cannot be considered as resolved conclusively, but the critics have yet to question Logan's argument.

The Methodology of Type IVB Studies

Whereas only one case of an exceptionally severe exemplary sentence could conceivably further general deterrence, an isolated punishment has no appreciable impact on *objective* certainty, nor is there any basis for expecting an isolated case to further general deterrence through an increase in the *perceived* certainty of punishment. Accordingly, it may appear that a type IVB study of deterrence would be pointless, since the objective certainty of punishment is not a matter of an episode. Stated another way, no one is likely to assume that one episode will increase objective certainty to the point of reducing the crime rate through any mechanism.

Nonetheless, a type IVB study of deterrence is feasible if one thinks of an episode not as one isolated case of actual punishment but rather as a change in law-enforcement practices, such as an increase in police patrols, the publicized change to radar equipment in traffic surveillance, or the use of more lights in public places. Resorting to any of those surveillance measures is a tacit test of the deterrence doctrine if (1) it is assumed that the measure furthers the objective or perceived certainty of punishment for crimes and (2) the crime rate before the introduction of the measure is compared with the crime rate after the measure. In that sense, the police and other law-enforcement agents have tested the deterrence doctrine time and again, but none of those tests are considered here because they scarcely can be identified as deterrence studies. The problem is akin to that previously considered in discussing type *B* findings. Briefly, the tests in question are typically reported only in newspapers or in popular magazines, which is to say they are not reported fully or in a way that can be appraised by a critical and informed audience. Moreover, type IVB "tests" rarely employ controls (e.g., an increase in police patrols only in areas selected at random), and controls are all the more desirable in view of possible "displacement effects." To illustrate, a marked intensification of police patrols in some areas of a city may be followed by a decrease in crime in those areas but an increase in other areas, which would suggest that individuals simply shift their criminal activity.

Evidence of a displacement effect may be indicative of restrictive deterrence, but arguments along that line are very complicated, and the simple observation that the crime rate declined after some measure was taken is not adequate (regardless of the amount of decline in the rate). Further, evidence of a displacement effect complicates an attempt to assess the "cost-benefit" of any measure designed to increase the objective or perceived certainty of punishment, and that assessment has a crucial bearing on policy issues. So, whatever the advantages of a type IVB study in deterrence research, past work along that line has ignored all manner of interpretive problems.

A Type IVC Study

Assume that for each of several jurisdictions it is possible to compute a value that represents proportionate change in the *annual objective certainty* of imprisonment over some period (e.g., 1965–1970) and another value that represents proportionate change in the *annual crime rate* over the same period or some later period (e.g., 1965–1970, 1968–1974, or 1970–1975). Given such values, it could be argued that the deterrence doctrine asserts a prediction: Among those jurisdictions there will be an inverse relation between the two variables (i.e., change in the objective certainty of punishment and change in the crime rate). Chiricos and Waldo (1970) utilized published data on imprisonment and crime rates for American states to test such a prediction, and their findings are summarized in Table 5-7.

By any reasonable standard the prediction of an inverse relation is inconsistent with the findings. Observe that only 18 (33 percent) of the 54 correlations are in the predicted negative direction, far fewer than would be expected if they had occurred by chance alone. Moreover, none of the negative correlations are of a substantial magnitude, and for *no* type of crime are all coefficients negative.

The obvious questions pertaining to the findings in Table 5-7 have to do with the limitations of any type IVC study. However, there is a special question in this case, one pertaining to Chiricos and Waldo's choice of periods for examining change in the crime rate relative to change in the objective certainty of imprisonment. Since the deterrence doctrine does not stipulate what the two periods should be in such a test, investigators are free to consider whatever periods strike them as "logical," which is what Chiricos and Waldo did (1970:208). However, one must wonder why they did not consider the possibility of a shorter time lag between the two periods, including the case in which change in both variables occurs over the *same* period. Doubts grow on inspecting Table 5-7 carefully, for there does appear to be a pattern—the more the two periods overlap, the greater is the number of negative correlations. For example, in the fourth row the ratio of the number of "common" years to the number of "different" years is 8 to 7 or 1.14 to 1, and the number of negative correlations is 4. By contrast, in the bottom row there are no common years in the two periods, and there is only one negative correlation. Then examine the third row, where there is again only one

Table 5-7. Correlations between Change in the Objective Certainty of Imprisonment and Change in the Crime Rates among States*

Variables Correlated		Phi Coefficients of Correlation by Type of Offense					
Percentages Change in Objective Certainty of Imprisonment	Percentage Change in Crime Rate	Homicide	Robbery	Assault	Burglary	Larceny	Auto Theft
Over 1950–1960	Over 1955–1965	.10	.07	−.25	.07	−.02	.10
Over 1950–1960	Over 1959–1968	.43	.11	.11	.11	.16	.18
Over 1950–1960	Over 1960–1965	.19	.20	−.02	.25	.11	.24
Over 1950–1963	Over 1955–1965	.10	.25	−.33	−.02	−.11	−.26
Over 1950–1963	Over 1959–1968	.43	.29	−.16	−.5	.16	−.04
Over 1950–1963	Over 1960–1965	.38	.33	−.11	.1	.11	−.03
Over 1960–1963	Over 1962–1965	−.17	.13	.21	−.33	−.11	.00
Over 1960–1963	Over 1963–1966	.04	.00	.04	−.04	−.06	.05
Over 1960–1963	Over 1964–1967	.08	.08	.13	.04	−.02	.05

*From Chiricos and Waldo (1970). The certainty of imprisonment for a given type of crime, state, and year, y, is $Ay/[(Cy + Cx)/2]$, where Ay is the number of individuals admitted during the year to a state prison on a sentence for the type of crime in question, Cy is the number of crimes of that type reported by the police as having occurred in the state during the year, and Cx is the corresponding number of crimes for the preceding year. The crime rate for any year is *evidently* Cy/P, where P is the population size of the state. Unfortunately, Chiricos and Waldo do not indicate whether the P figure is a population estimate for the year or for the most proximate census year, nor do they report the number of states for each correlation. (Requisite data are not published for all states.) Finally, percentage change for a variable (certainty of imprisonment or crime rate) is $(V_2 − V_1)/V_1$, where V_1 is the value for one year (e.g., 1950) and V_2 the value for a later year (e.g., 1960).

negative correlation, and the ratio of common years to different years is 1 to 15 or 0.07 to 1.

The pattern in question is not a sufficient reason for rejecting Chiricos and Waldo's findings as being invalid or irrelevant. However, the pattern does suggest that a great deal of exploratory work on possible temporal relations between change in punishment and change in the crime rates needs to be conducted before a proper assessment of any type C study can be made. That need is reinforced by the fact that no version of the deterrence doctrine stipulates any particular "optimum" temporal relation. Still another consideration is the reliability of both the crime rates and the estimates of the certainty of imprisonment. There is every reason to question their reliability; and short-run changes, because they are not of an appreciable magnitude, could even run opposite in direction to the true amount of change. To illustrate, given an increase in the objective certainty of punishment for, say, robbery, of only 6 percent in one jurisdication over 1960–1963 and a decrease in another jurisdiction of only 4 percent for those years, then doubts about the reliability of the data alone raise questions about the difference in the direction of change in the two jurisdictions. Only in the case of substantial changes would the questions be allayed, but substantial changes in properties of punishment are likely only in the case of long-run trends.

The Neglect of Type V Studies

In shifting the focus of research from the death penalty to imprisonment, deterrence investigators have ceased to be concerned with the presumptive severity of prescribed punishments. Hence, for all practical purposes, there have been no type V deterrence studies. That is unfortunate for two reasons. First, there is a widespread belief that a severe prescribed punishment deters individuals only to the extent that it is certain, but that belief can be assessed only in a type V study. (Type VI studies are not directly relevant, for they deal with the presumptive severity of *actual* punishments.) Second, there is the widespread belief that the certainty of a prescribed punishment tends to vary inversely with the presumptive severity of that punishment; but that belief is based on very little systematic evidence,[6] and that will continue to be the case until type V studies are undertaken.

[6]Recent demonstrations (Bailey and Smith, 1972) of an inverse relation among states between the length of prison sentences served and the certainty of imprisonmeent are not directly relevant because they do not pertain to the presumptive severity of prescribed punishments. Most of the evidence concerning the relation between the severity of prescribed punishments and the certainty of punishment is restricted to historical observations on the death penalty in Britain, *circa* 1800 (see, e.g., Radzinowicz, 1948:83–163).

The findings of type V studies could be crucial in attempting to formulate a deterrence theory. At present there is scarcely any basis for even emphasizing prescribed punishments in formulating a deterrence theory, let alone for qualifying assertions about the relation between their severity and the crime rate (e.g., stipulating how the relation is contingent on the certainty of punishment). The policy implications of type V studies are even more obvious. Such studies might well show that the preoccupation of legislators with the severity of prescribed punishments is self-defeating, which is to say that beyond some point severity lessens deterrence by reducing certainty.

Subsequent commentary on type VI studies will indicate the form that type V studies could take. However, a type VB study would require very special circumstances, specifically, a situation in which (1) law-enforcement practices are modified so as to increase the objective certainty of punishment and (2) the presumptive severity of the prescribed punishments is increased. The closest approximation to such a study is Ross's analysis (1973) of the implementation of the British Road Safety Act, and that research (though very sophisticated) illustrates one of the problems with a type VB study. Ideally, the study should be conducted so that the findings reveal the relative importance of the two changes (increase in objective certainty and increase in the presumptive severity of prescribed punishments) in the promotion of deterrence. Ross could not take that step because his study was ex post facto; hence he could not incorporate experimental controls (i.e., the prescribed punishments were changed for all areas of the county, and the objective certainty of punishment was increased, ostensibly, in all areas).

Type VI Studies

With the advent of type VI studies, deterrence research became more sophisticated but only in that two properties of punishment were considered simultaneously, those two being the objective certainty of punishment and the presumptive severity of actual punishments. None of the other shortcomings of deterrence research (e.g., exclusion of perceptual properties) were eliminated, and type VI studies prematurely terminated a concern with prescribed punishments.

A Type VIA Study

Following a deterrence study (Gibbs, 1968) that was limited to criminal homicide, Tittle (1969) and Logan (1972b) extended the strategy (i.e., the same kind of measures) to include seven types of offenses. The data and findings of those two investigations are similar, hence it will suffice to consider only Logan's research.

All of the statistics in column 2 of Table 5-8 are consistent with a major deterrence proposition: There is an inverse relation between the objective certainty of punishment (in this case, imprisonment) and the crime rate among jurisdictions (in this case, states). All seven correlation coefficients are negative; but the relation is no more than moderately close for any type of offense, and there is considerable variation in the relation from one offense to the next. The variation is even greater when the logs of certainty and the crime rate are correlated (see column 3), and the relation is much closer for some offenses when the two variables are logged. Only moderately close inverse relations are not surprising, since only one property of punishment was considered and extralegal conditions were ignored. However, no version of the deterrence doctrine accounts for differences among types of offenses or anticipates the results of the log transformations.

No simple deterrence proposition about presumptive severity is consistent with the statistics in column 4, for only in the case of homicide is there an appreciable negative correlation between the length of prison sentence served and the crime rate. Since five of the coefficients are positive, the findings lend support to a widespread belief that the severity

Table 5-8. *Correlations between Properties of Legal Punishment and Crime Rates in the United States, Circa 1960* *

Offense Category	Number of States Compared†	Zero-order Product-Moment Coefficients of Correlation				Partial Correlations	
		r_{cy}	$r_{c'y'}$	r_{sy}	$r_{c's}$	$r_{c'y'.s}$	$r_{sy'.c}$
	Col. 1	Col. 2	Col. 3	Col. 4	Col. 5	Col. 6	Col. 7
Homicide	45	−.21	−.16	−.37	−.17	−.26	−.41
Robbery	47	−.51	−.56	−.06	−.17	−.56	−.20
Sex Offenses	48	−.53	−.73	.26	−.36	−.69	−.01
Assault	48	−.23	−.65	.14	−.54	−.66	−.34
Burglary	48	−.46	−.46	.07	−.38	−.46	−.13
Larceny	47	−.28	−.44	.12	−.57	−.44	−.18
Auto Theft	41	−.29	−.26	.19	−.17	−.23	.15

*From Logan, 1972b: Tables 1 and 4. Explication of variables: certainty of punishment, c = number of admissions to the state prison for the offense in 1960 and 1963 divided by number of instances of that type of offense reported by the police for 1959 and 1962; presumptive severity of imprisonment, s = mean length of time (in months) served by felony offenders for the offense upon their release from prison in 1960; crime rate, y = mean annual number of offenses in 1959 and 1962, divided by the population of the state as of 1960; c' = log of c; and y' = log of y. Logan's values were computed from data tabulated in the *Uniform Crime Reports* for the years indicated and in published reports of the U.S. Bureau of Prisons.

†Number of states for columns 2 and 3 (each offense) is 48.

of punishment is relatively unimportant in promoting deterrence. Of course, severe punishments may fail to deter because their imposition is uncertain, and the coefficients in column 5 are relevant in that connection. For each offense, the relation between presumptive severity and objective certainty is inverse, and for that reason alone one of the properties should be controlled when examining the relation between the crime rate and the other property. The relevant statistics in that connection are the partial correlations in columns 6 and 7. When the figures for presumptive severity are partialled (see column 6), the relation between the certainty of imprisonment and the crime rate is not changed appreciably for any offense; but when objective certainty is partialled (column 7), the relation between severity and the crime rate is more consistent with the deterrence doctrine. Six of the seven partial coefficients are negative; however, they are not substantial, hence doubts about the importance of the severity of punishment are not dispelled entirely.

Findings like those in Table 5-8 are the major reason why some sociologists and economists have concluded that the deterrence doctrine was dismissed prematurely. The difference between the more recent findings (since 1965) and the earlier findings (prior to 1955) is not merely a matter of interpretation. Rather, investigators shifted the focus of research from the presumptive severity of a particular *prescribed* punishment (the death penalty) to properties of another type of *actual* punishment (imprisonment). One suggested conclusion is that research findings are consistent with the deterrence doctrine only when they pertain to properties of actual punishment, and it is unfortunate that Logan's study and similar ones did not extend to an examination of the relation between crime rates and the presumptive severity of prescribed prison sentences. Should it be found that the relation is negligible, then there would be considerable justification for ignoring prescribed punishments in formulating a deterrence theory. However, the suggestion is not that type VI studies (such as Logan's) are adequate. Even if the exclusion of the presumptive severity of prescribed punishment can be justified, type VI studies cannot answer questions about perceptual properties of punishment (including prescribed punishments), extralegal conditions, or preventive mechanisms other than deterrence. For that matter, no type VI study has treated actual punishments thoroughly; and that will not be the case until the research takes into account celerity, procedural punishments, and alternative substantive punishments, probation and fines in particular.[7] So, while type VI studies have regenerated interest in the deterrence doctrine, they have left all manner of questions unanswered.

[7]The methodology and scope of type VI studies are not the only problems. It would be misleading to suggest that the findings can be generalized to all types of crimes and

The Neglect of Type VIB and VIC Studies

As previously indicated, in a type IVB study the investigator examines the crime rate before and after a change in law-enforcement practices (e.g., intensification of surveillance) that ostensibly increases the objective certainty of punishment. Such a study is incomplete unless it is extended to include a consideration of actual punishments, which is to say evidence of an actual increase in objective certainty. But even when objective certainty increases, there could be a decline in the presumptive severity of actual punishments; if so, the expected decline in the crime rate might not occur. All such possibilities would be considered in a type VIB study, but there are no instances of that type.

The findings of certain studies previously considered (Chiricos and Waldo, 1970; Rusche and Kirchheimer, 1939) indicate that change in the crime rate is not inversely related either to (1) change in the objective certainty of punishment or (2) change in the presumptive severity of actual punishments. However, those studies considered only one property of punishment; hence there is no way to know what the results would have been had the investigators controlled (statistically) for change in other properties. That control could be achieved in a type VIC study, and it is unfortunate that none have been conducted.

The Neglect of Type VII Studies

It is a telling commentary on the quality of deterrence research that no type VII study has ever been conducted, and that lacuna is difficult to understand. The simultaneous treatment of three properties of pun-

jurisdictions. Consider Beutel's research (1957) on "check violations" in Nebraska and Colorado, where it was found that the violation rate is not related to the objective certainty or the presumptive severity of punishment. That negative finding may be attributed to a very low objective certainty of punishment in all of the jurisdictions compared; that is, when all jurisdictions are characterized by a very low degree of objective certainty of punishment, then deterrence propositions are not supported (see Tittle and Rowe, 1974). Similarly, Zimring and Hawkins (1973:261) have cast doubts on the findings of type VIA studies by showing that the relations do not hold for criminal homicide when states are compared *within regions* (e.g., within the South). Yet it should be recognized that the variation in state criminal homicide rates is negligible within regions, and tests of deterrence propositions in such a situation are questionable unless all properties of punishment are considered and the data (including crime rates) represent something more than crude estimates. Nonetheless, the exceptions cast doubts on the findings of type VIA studies. Even the findings of no inverse relation between the crime rates and the presumptive severity of actual punishment cannot be taken as conclusive evidence that presumptive severity is irrelevant. The relation between presumptive severity and the crime rate may be contingent on the objective certainty of punishment in a way that cannot be fully revealed by conventional statistical techniques, such as partial correlation (see Erickson and Gibbs, 1973).

ishment (objective certainty, presumptive severity of prescribed punishments, and presumptive severity of actual punishments) would be a complicated undertaking, but any one of several conventional statistical techniques could be used (partial correlation being the simplest). No less important, the research is feasible, for relevant published data (including criminal statutes) are available for states.

Investigators cannot justifiably refrain from a type VII study by arguing that it would exclude perceptual properties of punishment. However, the inclusion of perceptual properties would require vast resources, and a type VII study could be a strategic preliminary step. Should a type VII study reveal that only the objective certainty of punishment is inversely related to the crime rate, then subsequent research on perceptual properties could be restricted justifiably to certainty. Nontheless, research on other perceptual properties would be desirable, but resources are so limited that the research might have to be restricted to what appears to be the one most strategic property of punishment. Only a type VII study would provide a defensible basis for identifying that property.

Specific Deterrence

The typology in Table 5-1 was designed to classify studies pertaining to general deterrence, and it cannot be applied readily to studies of specific deterrence. However, the distinction is not that specific deterrence studies are concerned with individuals rather than populations. All studies of specific deterrence deal with some form of a rate, such as the proportion of a group of individuals who have been imprisoned and then are convicted of another crime after release. The major difference is that in research on general deterrence the crime rate pertains to populations (e.g., the residents of states) in which some of the members may never have been punished for committing a crime, whereas in research on specific deterrence the crime rates pertain to populations in which all members have been punished. Still another difference is that research on general deterrence may consider change in prescribed punishments, which is not relevant in research on specific deterrence.

So in this section Table 5-1 is not utilized as it has been previously. However, the table still serves to identify various properties of punishment, and in that connection the most conspicuous shortcomings of specific deterrence studies are the properties of punishment that have been ignored in those studies.

A Study of Corporal Punishment

In 1944, Robert Caldwell reported a study of the criminal records of individuals sentenced in the courts of New Castle county, Delaware, over 1920–1940. The study was not methodologically sophisticated, but it has been cited time and again as evidence that severe punishment does not deter crime. One possible reason for the attention received by the study is that whipping (up to 60 lashes on the bare back) could be imposed by Delaware criminal courts on conviction for any of 24 crimes during the period.

Caldwell focused primarily on the postpunishment conviction record (in Delaware and elsewhere) of 320 individuals who were imprisoned and whipped at least once during 1920–1939. Much to Caldwell's credit, he recognized that the deterrent efficacy of corporal punishment could not be assessed without comparing those 320 individuals with others who were either sentenced to imprisonment or probation without being whipped. The nature of the comparisons and principal findings are shown in Table 5-9.

Observe that a definite pattern is present—in each category the proportion of individuals convicted for a crime *subsequent* to punishment tends to be *directly related* to the frequency and/or severity of the punishment. Of course, that generalization rests on the assumption that probation is perceived as less severe than whipping or imprisonment.

Several technical objections to Caldwell's methodology can be raised. It is not at all clear why Caldwell considered the 93 individuals who were sentenced to imprisonment or probation in 1928 (columns 3 and 4) in Table 5-9 rather than all individuals sentenced in the same way during 1920–1939. That year (1928) is the approximate midpoint of the period, but it would have been much better to have considered the same period for all six categories of offenders. Then observe that no allowance was made for possible differences in the length of imprisonment.

The importance of some of the foregoing criticisms are largely conjectural, but that is not the case for three other limitations of Caldwell's study. First, although not emphasized by Caldwell or those who have cited his findings, the study has bearing only on specific deterrence (i.e., the findings are not relevant in contemplating general deterrence). Second, since Caldwell presented no data on the frequency of offenses among individuals who have never been punished, his findings have bearing on the *marginal* deterrent efficacy of whipping, not its absolute efficacy. Third, differences in the postpunishment conviction rates as shown in Table 5-9 may well reflect contrasts among the categories of offenders prior to punishment.

The third consideration calls for elaboration. Some of Caldwell's statistics (1944:174–175) not shown in the table clearly reveal major prepunishment contrasts. Of those individuals who were not whipped in 1928, only 34 percent had been convicted of a crime before 1928. By contrast,

Table 5-9. Sentences Imposed by the Courts of New Castle County, Delaware, Circa 1920–1940*

Selected Characteristics of the Populations	Individuals Convicted for a Type of Crime that Could Have Resulted in a Sentence of Imprisonment and Whipping					
	64 Imprisoned and Whipped at Least Twice During 1920–1939	256 Imprisoned and Whipped Once During 1920–1939	67 Imprisoned but Not Whipped During 1928	26 Placed on Probation During 1928	62 Imprisoned but Not Whipped During 1940	58 Placed on Probation During 1940
	Col. 1	Col. 2	Col. 3	Col. 4	Col. 5	Col. 6
Percentage Subsequently Convicted for Any Type of Crime in Delaware or Elsewhere	65†	62‡	54§	42§	45¶	22¶
Percentage Subsequently Convicted for Some Major Type of Crime** in Delaware or Elsewhere	57†	49‡	43§	31§	Not Reported	Not Reported

*From untabulated data in the text of Caldwell (1944).
†Crimes committed after second whipping but prior to 1943.
‡Crimes committed after being whipped but prior to 1943.
§Crimes committed after 1928 but prior to 1943.
¶Crimes committed after completion of sentence but prior to 1943.
**Murder, manslaughter, robbery, aggravated assault, burglary, larceny, embezzlement, receiving stolen property, forgery, counterfeiting, rape, commercialized vice, violation of drug laws, bigamy, blackmail, kidnapping, and perjury.

of those whipped during 1928–1939, 69 percent had a record of a previous conviction (i.e., one that was prior to the conviction for which they were sentenced to a whipping). Further, Caldwell did not compare categories of individuals who were convicted for the same type of offense but received different sentences, and there is every reason to suppose that those who were whipped and imprisoned had been convicted of what is generally regarded as a more "serious" offense than those who were imprisoned but not whipped or those who were placed on probation. The crucial point is that regardless of the punishment the reconviction rate after punishment tends to be higher for individuals with more than one conviction and/or a conviction for a serious offense (homicide being a possible exception). Since Caldwell did not control for such prepunishment contrasts in his comparisons, an interpretation of his findings as evidence against the specific deterrence argument is debatable.

Another Study of Corporal Punishment

Over 1960–1964, a total of 604 boys absconded from Kingswood Classifying School (Royal Commission), and some of the boys were caned (one to eight strokes). The records of those instances were used by Clarke (1966) to conduct a study of corporal punishment and specific deterrence. Clarke's report includes an array of relevant findings, but space limitations make it necessary to consider only the figures in Table 5-10.

Of the 101 junior boys in Kingswood who were caned for their first offense, 11 or 10.9 percent, absconded again. By contrast, of the 65 junior boys who were not caned for their first offense, 26.2 percent absconded again. In the case of senior boys, the two corresponding percentage figures are 18.0 and 30.4. Thus, in each group the "absconding recidival rate" is more than 50 percent greater for boys who were not caned on the first offense.

Table 5-10. Reactions of Authorities in a British Approved School to Boys Who Absconded and Figures on Recidivism, 1960–1964*

Population	History of Absconding	Outcome of First Absconding†	
		Caned	Not Caned
Junior Boys	Absconded once	90	48
	Absconded twice	11	17
Senior Boys	Absconded once	164	71
	Absconded twice	36	31

*From Clarke (1966:371). Such schools are somewhat akin to reformatories or detention centers for juvenile delinquents in the United States.
†Boys who abscond may be caned and/or "detained."

As Clarke notes (1966:372), the findings in this case are not conclusive evidence of specific deterrence (not even if the differences are accepted as substantial), for it could be that caning is "selective" in the case of those boys who are not predisposed to repeat the offense. Canings were not administered randomly, and some kind of selectivity rather than deterrence could account for the differences in the recidival rates. However, Clarke was not able to show that any selective factor actually accounts for the differences. He says (1966:372): "In certain cases a boy may not be caned for his first absconding because in the judgment of the school he is going to abscond again whether he is caned or not." But the frequency of such judgments are not documented; hence the consequence of that postulated selectivity is conjectural.

A Study of Traffic Offenders

The figures in Table 5-11 pertain to 1,637 individuals in Israel who committed at least one traffic offense between January, 1960, and November, 1971. Those individuals are a subset of a random sample (3,864) of all the individuals who received a driving license in Israel over 1960–1969.

Observe that the punishments for the first offense are arranged (intuitively) in order of severity, with "warning" being considered the mildest reaction by authorities. Contrary to what advocates of the deterrence doctrine might expect, there appears to be a *direct* relation between the severity of the first punishment and the number of subsequent offenses. Thus, of those drivers who were warned on their first offense, 52.7 percent had no official record of subsequent offenses, whereas the corresponding percentage for those who lost their license was only 21.4 per-

Table 5-11. Punishment for First Traffic Offense and Total Number of Traffic Offenses for a Sample of Israeli Drivers, 1960–1971*

Type of Punishment for First Offense	Percentage Distribution by Number of Offenses						Number of Drivers
	1	2–5	6–10	11–15	16 or More	Total	
Warning	52.7	19.1	17.4	2.3	8.4	99.9	302
Choice of Fine or Court Hearing	37.7	20.2	23.4	4.6	13.9	99.8	915
Fine	39.7	17.6	18.9	6.5	17.1	99.8	375
Conditional License Cancellation	24.0	40.0	12.0	12.0	12.0	100.0	25
License Cancellation	21.4	35.7	21.4	0.0	21.4	99.9	14
Imprisonment, Conditional or Unconditional	33.3	16.7	16.7	16.7	16.7	100.1	6

*From Shoham (1974:65).

cent. The findings are debatable if only because of the small number of cases in the two most severe punishment categories, but that consideration is hardly a basis for rejecting the findings.

Shoham (1974) extended the analysis beyond Table 5-11, but the additional findings are scarcely less puzzling. Four variables were considered in relation to the number of offenses: (1) severity of punishment for first offense, (2) time between first and second offense, (3) time between commission of first offense and punishment, and (4) gravity of first offense. A multiple regression analysis indicated that the severity of punishment (first offense) accounts for a much greater proportion of the variance in the number of subsequent offenses than does any of the other three factors. But note that the finding is inconsistent with the deterrence doctrine, for as suggested by Table 5-11 the relation between the severity of punishment (first offense) and the number of subsequent offenses is *direct,* not inverse. The only question in that regard is that Shoham speaks of "severity of punishment" and "type of punishment" as if they were the same, and that is also the case for "type of offense" and "gravity of offense." Yet it is not clear how Shoham assigned severity values to punishments or gravity values to the types of offenses. Nonetheless, granted those reservations, it is difficult to see how the method (even if intuitive) could have produced such results.

The most obvious explanation of the findings has to do with selectivity. If it is assumed that punishments are severe for grave first offenses and that those who commit grave first offenses tend to be reckless drivers, then a direct relation between the severity of punishment (first offense) and the number of subsequent offenses would not be surprising. However, Shoham's findings (1974:66) indicate virtually no association between the gravity of the first offense and the number of subsequent offenses, even though there is some association (direct) between the severity of punishment and the gravity of the first offense.

Still another "deterrence prediction" is inconsistent with the findings. For all practical purposes, there is no association whatever between the celerity of punishment (time between first offense and sentencing) and the number of subsequent offenses. However, that finding does not come as a great surprise even to advocates of the deterrence doctrine, since the only evidence that the celerity of punishment contributes to deterrence is limited to experimental work on punishment (see Johnston, 1972; Singer, 1970; and Solomon, 1964).

Only one of Shoham findings is clearly consistent with a deterrence prediction: There is a direct relation between the severity of punishment for the first offense and the amount of time before the second offense. One can construe that relation as indicative of restrictive deterrence, but there is another puzzle. Even if those drivers who were severely punished (relatively speaking) for the first offense tend to "delay" their second offense, they eventually commit more offenses than those who were less severely punished for their first offense.

Shoham recognizes the puzzling character of the findings and concludes (1974:69) that one's driving record simply reflects "driving capability." However, that explanation hardly accounts for the direct relation between the severity of punishment and the number of subsequent offenses. In confronting that question, Shoham postulates that severe punishments increase the anxieties of drivers and lower their self-confidence, with the consequence being that they are poorer drivers and inclined to involuntary traffic violations. That line of reasoning is plausible, but it is clearly conjectural.

Additional Commentary

The findings of only three studies are hardly conclusive evidence on the question of specific deterrence, but not even a consideration of all relevant studies would alter the conclusion.[8] Briefly, few findings support the contention that individuals who have been punished for a crime are deterred from subsequent offenses, or for that matter that specific deterrence is a function of the severity of punishment. Certainly the findings are quite different from those that bear on the general deterrence argument (e.g., Gibbs, 1968; Logan, 1972b; and Bailey et al., 1974). Indeed, the evidence contradicts the specific deterrence argument so much that it is difficult to understand why recent surveys (Zimring and Hawkins, 1973; Tittle and Logan, 1973; and Tittle, 1974) failed to emphasize the point. Nothing is gained by creating the impression that arguments against the specific deterrent efficacy of imprisonment can be ignored (Tittle, 1974). Consider the widespread belief that over 50 percent of those released from prison are subsequently reimprisoned, and suppose that the true figure is more nearly 35 percent (Glaser, 1964). That revised figure is hardly impressive evidence of specific deterrence, especially since former convicts may commit offenses again and again without being reimprisoned. Even assuming that the remaining 65 percent (those not reimprisoned) commit no subsequent offenses, it would not follow that they have been deterred. Some may have been reformed by punishment, others may have been rehabilitated by a nonpunitive program in prison, and still others may simply cease their criminal acts because they are older or because they have returned to a changed environ-

[8]See particularly Lovald and Stub, 1968; Mecham, 1968; and Zimring and Hawkins, 1973:224–248.

ment (see Reitzes, 1955). The third possibility is especially important because lack of evidence in favor of rehabilitation or reform in prison does not justify the conclusion that those who are not reimprisoned (or, for that matter, those who commit no further crimes) have been deterred. Finally, what has been said of imprisonment applies generally to all kinds of conventional punishments; but the evidence in the case of imprisonment casts the gravest doubts on the specific deterrence argument, if only because incarceration appears far more severe than do fines or probation.

Despite the foregoing, proponents of the specific-deterrence argument can dismiss all research findings as irrelevant. Their contention is that the findings pertain at most to the marginal specific deterrent efficacy of particular punishments (e.g., whipping and imprisonment versus imprisonment alone) rather than absolute efficacy. Absolute efficacy can be assessed only by comparing the frequency of criminal acts in two populations: (1) individuals who have committed a criminal act but have gone unpunished and (2) individuals who have been punished for committing a criminal act. The rationale for the comparison is defensible, but it precludes any assertion that is in keeping with conventional interpretations of the specific deterrence doctrine—that individuals who have been punished for a crime refrain (or even typically refrain) from subsequent offenses. Rather, the assertion must be: Individuals who have been punished for committing a crime commit less subsequent offenses than those who have gone unpunished. Far from being platitudinously true, the assertion runs contrary to the belief that some individuals commit crimes in a "neurotic" quest for punishment (Alexander and Staub, 1956), and if that is the case it hardly taxes credulity to suppose that those who are punished seek punishment again. The assertion is also incompatible with another belief—that the stigmatizing or psychological consequences of punishment generate more crimes than punishment prevents. In any case, little is gained by an assertion about absolute specific deterrent efficacy without stipulating the method and requisite data for tests. Official crime data cannot be used to that end, and it is difficult to see how such an assertion could be tested without computing recidival and repetitive crime rates, with both based on self-reported crimes.

For reasons just suggested, there has been no systematic research on the absolute efficacy of punishments, but that is not the case for marginal efficacy. Numerous studies have compared some kind of official postpunishment recidival rate for two or more of the following populations: (1) individuals who have been incarcerated, (2) individuals who have been placed on probation, and (3) individuals who have been fined (see Davis, 1964; Hood, 1971; Kraus, 1974; Levin, 1971; Logan, 1972a; Radzinowicz and Wolfgang, 1971III; and Walker, 1968, 1969). Summarizing the findings very briefly, insofar as there is any substantial contrast among them at all, official postpunishment recidival rates tend to be higher for individuals who have been incarcerated. Those findings appear patently contrary to the belief that specific deterrence is realized in direct proportion to the severity of punishment.

Confronted with such findings, proponents of the specific deterrence argument can resort to still another evidential rationalization by pointing to two relations: first, regardless of punishment, the official recidival rates tend to be greater for individuals with a long record of arrests or convictions; and, second, individuals who have a long record of arrests or convictions are more likely to receive severe sentences (see Bailey, 1971; Hood, 1971; Radzinowicz and Wolfgang, 1971II, 1971III; Walker, 1968; and Wilkins, 1969). So the argument is that individuals who are punished the most severely are the "poorest risks," that is, the ones most likely to be repeaters regardless of the punishment.

The evidential rationalization just described is based on seemingly indisputable empirical premises, but it implies that severity of punishment varies inversely with the recidival rate (official or otherwise) if and only if the different punishments are imposed randomly on individuals. Given randomized punishments, there would be no selectivity, that is, the poorest risk would not tend to receive the most severe punishments.

The proposed randomization of punishments is surely defensible, but conventional interpretations of the specific-deterrence argument would have to be altered. Rather than merely assert that specific deterrence is realized to the extent that the punishment is severe, the assertion would have to require randomization of punishments. However, that version of the assertion would be untestable without a method of randomization. The method would not be difficult to formulate, but the feasibility of its application is another matter. Given the legal and ethical issues entailed in randomization of punishments (especially severe ones), judges are not likely to permit such research.

In light of the foregoing, one can perhaps understand van den Haag's argument (1969:145) that "lack of evidence of deterrence" is not evidence of "lack of deterrence." Unfortunately, van den Haag does not indicate what would be negative evidence, nor does he recognize that predictions derived from conventional interpretations of the specific-deterrence argument have been incorrect time and again. Such negative evidence (or call it what you will) can be ignored only by formulating a new theory of specific deterrence, one in which the assertions are either limited to absolute efficacy or require randomization of punishments.

Until that theory is formulated, the specific deterrence argument will continue to be a poor one, meaning that it simply creates no order in the world of events.

Unconventional Lines of Research

Certain kinds of research clearly have some bearing on the deterrence question even though they cannot be described by reference to the typology in Table 5-1. However, it would be a mistake to accept that typology as a criterion of relevant evidence rather than merely as a way of classifying conventional lines of research.

A Different Conception of a Crime Rate

Clarke's data (1966) on corporal punishment at the Kingswood Classifying School were previously analyzed in connection with specific deterrence, but his research also has bearing on the general deterrence question. If caning a boy for absconding deterred others, then the frequency of absconding should have declined more after that punishment was imposed than after an instance in which an absconder was not caned. Clarke analyzed the frequency of absconding in terms of the average number of days between the return of an absconder and the next absconding. If the average number is construed as indicative of change in the absconding rate (i.e., the greater the number, the greater the decline in the rate), then Clarke's investigation is a type IIB study. That is the case because one episode of a boy being caned can be viewed as an exemplary punishment (i.e., more severe than the alternative—detention). However, an instance of a boy being caned is not an obvious and dramatic change in punishment, and the measure of frequency is an unconventional form of a rate. Consequently, Clarke's study is treated as an unconventional line of research.

Table 5-12 summarizes Clarke's findings that have bearing on the question of general deterrence (restrictive deterrence in particular). For both groups of boys (juniors and seniors), the average number of days between the return of an absconder and the next case of absconding is greater when the returning absconder was caned. That difference is consistent with a deterrence prediction, but note that the difference is statistically significant only for senior boys. Moreover, Clarke did not examine the possibility of a regression effect, meaning that caning was more likely to be imposed after a period of an increase in the number of abscondings. However, he did take into account the possibility that what appears to be general deterrence is actually specific deterrence;

Table 5-12. *Corporal Punishment for Absconding from a British Approved School for Boys and Average Time between Abscondings, 1960–1964* *

Populations and Punishment Events	Average Number of Days between Return of an Absconder and Next Absconding	Statistical Significance of Difference between the Two Averages
Junior Boys		
127 Cases Where a Boy Was Caned for Absconding	14.09	Not Significant at .05 Level
82 Cases Where a Boy Was Not Caned for Absconding	11.10	
Senior Boys		
237 Cases Where a Boy Was Caned for Absconding	10.42	Significant at .05 Level
131 Cases Where a Boy Was Not Caned for Absconding	7.86	

*From Clarke (1966:372–373).

that is, if a boy refrained from absconding after being caned, his refraining would reduce the average number of days between abscondings. Clarke offers statistics to show that the difference for senior boys is independent of the subsequent absconding behavior of boys who were caned, and he concludes (1966:373) that "caning a senior boy for absconding deters other seniors from absconding."

As for the contrast between juniors and seniors, Clarke argues (1966:374): "It is possible that junior absconders are a more emotionally maladjusted group and their absconding may represent desire to escape. If this were so the threat of punishment might be expected to have little deterrent effect." The argument is sheer conjecture, and it ignores two points: first, even though the two groups were approximately of the same size, more seniors absconded; and, second, the average number of days between abscondings is much greater for juniors, especially in cases where the last absconder was caned. It is far less conjectural and relevant to point out that the certainty of caning for absconding was greater for seniors than for juniors (66 percent as compared to 61 percent in the case of first absconders). The contrast is not statistically significant, but it should be recognized that for both groups of boys the difference in the average number of days between abscondings is consistent with the deterrence prediction, and the only contrast is slightly more consistency in the case of senior boys.

A Field Experiment

In the typical laboratory experiment involving the punishment of humans, the punishments are probably perceived as far less severe than is a criminal sanction, and the responses of humans that are punished can hardly be construed as norm violations, let alone akin to criminal acts. The foregoing constitutes major limitations of experimental work on the deterrence question, but experimenters can control (within limits) the magnitude, frequency, and regularity of punishments. By contrast, in a purely observational study of crime and punishment, nothing is subject to control in a literal sense. However, the field experiment is a third alternative.

In field experiments only certain features of an otherwise "natural" situation are controlled by the investigators. Thus, in analyzing the deterrence question in a strictly legal context, the investigators cannot create types of criminal acts or control the prescribed punishments, and for all practical purposes the actual punishments are not subject to manipulation. But an experimenter can attempt to manipulate some properties of legal punishments, namely, those having to do with perception or cognition. That strategy was adopted by Schwartz and Orleans (1967) in an ingenious field experiment pertaining to federal income tax reports.

Having secured the cooperation of the Internal Revenue Service, the investigators selected a sample of individuals who had filed a 1961 tax return, with the individuals selected at random from high-income census tracts in a large urban area. Those individuals were divided on a purely random basis into three groups, identified as (1) sanction threat, (2) conscience approval, and (3) placebo. During the month prior to filing income tax returns for 1962, each member of each group was interviewed. Interview questions in the case of the "sanction threat" group were designed to make the subjects aware of the legal penalties for false tax reports, one being: "A jail sentence of three years could be imposed for willful failure to pay tax on interest. Under what conditions do you think the Government should impose a jail sentence?" Questions for the "conscience appeal" group were designed to accentuate moral reasons for compliance with tax laws, one being: "Would you consider a citizen's willful failure to pay tax on interest an indication that he is unwilling to do something for the country as a whole?" Members of the "placebo" group were also interviewed, evidently on the presumption that being interviewed in itself (i.e., apart from what is said) could have an effect, but the questions did not touch on the threat of sanctions or appeal to conscience. Finally, a fourth group of taxpayers, "the untreated controls," were not interviewed but considered in subsequent comparisons.

The experimental design minimized the differences among the groups prior to the interviews, including differences in their 1961 income tax reports. The 1962 income tax reports of each group differed in several respects (e.g., total deductions claimed) from their 1961 reports, but the logic of the design was devised so that a greater difference between the two tax returns (1961 and 1962) for some groups as opposed to others could be attributed to the contrast in the treatment of the groups. The investigators could not gain access to the records for particular individuals in any group; so, alternatively, they focused on *average* tax figures for each group as compiled by the Internal Revenue Service. Those figures are shown in Table 5-13, and note that each figure is the *average* difference between a 1962 tax figure and the corresponding 1961 figure for all individuals in a group.

Overall, in comparison to the two control groups (rows 3 and 4 of Table 5-13) both treatment groups (rows 1 and 2) increased their reported adjusted gross income *more*, increased their total deductions *less*, and increased their income tax *more*. The one exception is in column 3, which shows that the placebo group increased their total deductions claimed less than any other group.

Although some of the contrasts among the groups are statistically insignificant, the overall pattern clearly suggests that the implied threat of sanctions and the appeal to conscience do have an impact on behavior; and the findings indicate that the latter has the most impact for the behavior in question. Thus, the findings are important in that they support the deterrence doctrine but at the same time question the *relative* efficacy of severe punishments. Evidence gathered in a few other investigations suggests the same kind of conclusion, one of those investigations being a study in Utah (Mecham, 1968) of juvenile traffic violators who were assigned to four "treatment" groups on a random basis, with the treatment being a fine, driving restrictions, required attendance at a driving school, or a paper to be written on traffic safety. It was found that

*Table 5-13.　Statistics on Federal Income Tax Reports**

Group	Row Number	Number of Taxpayers	Average Differences: 1962 Dollars Minus 1961 Dollars		
			Adjusted Gross Income	Total Deductions	Income Tax after Credits
		Col. 1	Col. 2	Col. 3	Col. 4
Sanction Threat	1	87	181	273	11
Conscience Appeal	2	88	804	177	243
Placebo	3	88	−87	132	−40
Untreated Control	4	111	−13	320	−57

*From Schwartz and Orleans (1967:296).

during the subsequent year the proportion of juveniles with no further reported violations was greater in the group who wrote papers on traffic safety.

None of the findings of Schwartz and Orleans refute the deterrence doctrine unless the doctrine involves a declaration that punishment is the most effective means for realizing compliance to norms. Of course, the extent to which the findings can be generalized has yet to be determined; and it may well be that the pattern will not hold for other crimes, especially for those subject to more severe punishment than income tax evasion. Yet such considerations are not a denial of the significance of the research strategy employed by Schwartz and Orleans, nor do they preclude extension of the strategy.

When extending the strategy, investigators should think more in terms of specific properties of punishment and design field experiments accordingly. Schwartz and Orleans refer to "sanction threat," but that term is ambiguous. The questions posed in the interviews to accentuate the threat of punishment may have furthered (1) the perceived certainty of punishment, (2) public knowledge of prescribed punishments, (3) the perceived severity of prescribed punishments, and/or (4) cognition of the features of the crime in question. Such distinctions are perhaps not relevant at this point in field experimentation, but eventually experimental designs could be designed to reveal the most salient property of punishment in deterrence.

Actual Executions

It goes without saying that most studies of the deterrent efficacy of the death penalty have not been particularly imaginative, limited as they have been to simple comparisons of capital jurisdictions and abolitionist jurisdictions. However, a few investigations have focused on actual executions (see Savitz, 1967), and some of the investigators have displayed considerable ingenuity. That is true of Graves's study (1967) of daily patterns in the frequency of homicides during 1946–1955 in three California counties—Los Angeles, San Francisco, and Alameda.

During 1946–1955, executions in California were carried out on a Friday, and Graves evidently expected to find some daily trends in the number of homicides relative to "execution day." To that end he used the records of coroners in the three counties and computed the average daily number of homicides for each day of the week, with separate averages for execution weeks and nonexecution weeks (those just before and/or just after an execution week). The separate averages are necessary because there is a definite daily pattern in the frequency of homicides over a week regardless of whether executions are being held, with a sharp rise in the number on Saturday and Sunday. So the appropriate comparison for any day during an execution week is with the same day in a nonexecution week.

Graves's principal findings are summarized in Table 5-14, where there is a very definite but puzzling pattern in columns 1 and 2. The average number of homicides on Thursday and Friday (execution day and the day before) is much greater for execution weeks than for non-execution weeks, but the average number for Saturday and Sunday is much less for execution weeks than for nonexecution weeks. To use a causal description, it appears that a pending execution generates homicides, while the actual execution depresses the number of homicides.

Graves's study can be faulted on a few counts, such as (1) the absence of data on the publicity of executions, (2) the failure to differentiate homicides that were subsequently prosecuted as first-degree murder, and (3) the exclusion of weeks more than 14 days removed from an execution. But those considerations are minor in comparison to the fundamental problem. One may declare the "excess" homicides on Thursday and Friday of execution week as contrary to the deterrence doctrine, but advocates of the doctrine can point to the "deficiency" of homicides on Saturday and Sunday of execution weeks as supporting their argument. Graves himself attributes the Thursday-Friday excess to a "brutalizing effect," but he is willing to entertain the idea that the Saturday-Sunday "drop" reflects deterrence. However, the vagueness of the deterrence doctrine permits virtually any interpretation of Graves's findings. Think of the questions that are left to conjecture. Does an ac-

Table 5-14. *Homicides by Day of the Week over 1946–1955 in Three California Counties: Los Angeles, Alameda, and San Francisco**

Days of the Week	Average Number for 74 Weeks in Which There Was an Execution	Average Number for 116 Weeks before and/or after an Execution Week
	Col. 1	Col. 2
Monday	.459	.474
Tuesday	.473	.508
Wednesday	.486	.483
Thursday	.635	.483
Friday†	.649	.552
Saturday	.729	.948
Sunday	.797	.854

*From Graves (1967:330).
†Execution day in California.

tual execution somehow further the perceived certainty of the death penalty? Or is it that an actual execution somehow communicates the awesome severity of the death penalty? Of course, it could be neither, but the more general point is that the deterrence doctrine must be stated as a systematic theory before findings such as those of Graves can be rightly declared as either consistent or inconsistent with the doctrine. All that can be said for the moment is that it is difficult to imagine any deterrence theory that would be consistent with the excess of homicides on the day of execution.

Research Pertaining to Extralegal Punishment

As previously indicated, the present survey of evidence excludes research on the relation between the frequency of some type of act and extralegal punishments of that act. Such research is extremely diverse, encompassing investigations of (1) the relation between the frequency of cheating in school work and the conditions of "supervision" and (2) changes in the frequency of some act in a laboratory situation in which commission of the act is followed by an electric shock. Those investigations are excluded because the findings could not possibly falsify the deterrence doctrine insofar as the doctrine is restricted to propositions about the relation between crime rates and properties of legal punishments. However, it is readily admitted that the relevance of studies of extralegal punishments is debatable; indeed, the subject poses a most difficult question in attempting to assess the deterrence doctrine. Hence there is a rationale for examining a few extralegal studies, if only to illustrate some of the problems and issues entailed in treating the findings as evidence for or against the deterrence doctrine. The two studies considered subsequently are representative only in that the findings of one might be construed as contrary to the deterrence doctrine, while the findings of the other might be construed as consistent with the doctrine.

Misconduct in College: First Study

During 1961–1962, a survey (Salem and Bowers, 1970) was made of American colleges and universities to solicit information from deans and student-body presidents about formal sanctions for various types of student misconduct. Information was received from 838 schools, 100 of which were subsequently (1962–1963) selected for more extensive research, wherein questionnaires were sent to a sample of between 70 and 100 students in each school. The questionnaire asked students about *(inter alia)* their engagement in particular types of misconduct, their attitude (approval or disapproval) toward such misconduct, and their perception of the corresponding attitude of their peers (close friends or other student associates). Complete information was obtained on 92 colleges.

The investigators' analysis focused on: (I) violating alcohol-use rules, (II) getting drunk, (III) stealing library books, (IV) marking up library books, and (V) cheating in course work. For all but the fourth type it was found that from one college to the next, the percentage of students admitting to the misconduct varied *inversely* with the presumptive severity of the prescribed sanction.[9] However, it was subsequently found that for types of misconduct I, II, and III, the percentage of students who expressed personal disapproval of the misconduct varied *directly* with the severity of the prescribed sanction. The finding is significant because it suggests that the inverse relation between a self-reported rate of some type of misconduct and the severity of the prescribed sanction may reflect a more pronounced social condemnation of that misconduct in colleges where the prescribed sanctions are the most severe. That suggestion was supported even more by a comparison of self-reported violation rates in colleges where the amount of personal disapproval of the misconduct was more or less the same from one college to the next. For example, in colleges where 41–60 percent of the students expressed disapproval of getting drunk, the self-reported violation rate did not vary appreciably by type of sanction. Specifically, in colleges where the prescribed formal sanction was dismissal, the mean percentage of students who admitted to getting drunk was 32, as compared to 30 percent in colleges where suspension was the sanction, and 33 percent in colleges with a lesser penalty.

Two types of misconduct, marking up library books and cheating, were exceptions, meaning that the percentage of students expressing personal disapproval did not vary appreciably or regularly with the severity of the prescribed sanction. So for those two types of misconduct, the inverse relation between the severity of prescribed sanctions and the self-reported violation rates cannot be explained by differences among schools in regard to the amount of social condemnation (percentage of students expressing personal disapproval).[10] For that reason (evidently), Salem and Bowers considered cheating further; however, they devoted no more attention to marking up library books.

[9]The difference between the sanctions (e.g., fail course, be suspended or expelled) can be judged only intuitively, which is to say that it is not a matter of magnitude as in the case of varying lengths of imprisonment.
[10]This point was not emphasized by Salem and Bowers.

Twenty-eight colleges employed an "honor system," wherein students are admonished to report cheaters to the appropriate authority. Accordingly, Salem and Bowers examined the relation between self-reported cheating and the severity of prescribed sanctions, with colleges classified by both "normative climate" (amount of personal disapproval of cheating or perceived disapproval by peers) and "type of normative system" (presence or absence of the honor system). The major findings are summarized in Table 5-15.

In each panel, the self-reported cheating violations *tend* to vary inversely with the disapproval of cheating (personal or perceived). That relation is not surprising, but it is noteworthy that the relation tends to hold *regardless* of the prescribed sanction. However, the relation tends to be more uniform and accentuated as the prescribed sanction becomes more severe (compare, e.g., columns 1 and 3 in the first panel, that is, rows 1–4).

Just as the relation between the normative climate and the self-reported violation rates appears to be contingent on the severity of prescribed sanctions, so does the relation between the severity of prescribed sanctions and the violation rates appear to be contingent on normative climate, especially when the presence or absence of the honor system is recognized. Generally, the more cheating is disapproved of, the more the inverse relation between the severity of sanction and the self-reported violation rate is accentuated. (Compare rows 2 and 3, 6 and 7, 14 and 16, or 17 and 19.)

Salem and Bowers's supposition that the honor system makes a difference is consistent with Bonjean and McGee's findings (1965) on scholastic dishonesty, and the supposition is also supported by the data in Table 5-15. Observe that the violation rates (mean percentage of students who admit to cheating) is on the whole lower in colleges with the honor system (compare rows 1–4 with rows 5–8 or rows 13–16 with rows 17–20). However, that difference does not mean that the severity of prescribed sanctions is irrelevant. For example, the violation rate in row 7, column 3 (no honor system but severe sanction) is substantially lower than the corresponding rate in row 3, column 1 (honor system but mild prescribed sanction), even though the normative climate is approximately the same.

In colleges with an honor system, the mean percentage of students who expressed personal disapproval of cheating was 43, as compared to 33 percent for other colleges; but the difference is even greater for the percent of perceived peer disapproval, the two corresponding figures being 15 and 28 percent. The contrast led Salem and Bowers (1970:31) to suspect that "this heightened sense of peer disapproval is what con-

Table 5-15. *Percentage of College Students Admitting to Cheating, with Colleges Classified by Type of Normative System, Type of Normative Climate, and Type of Prescribed Sanction for Cheating: 92 United States Colleges, 1962–1963**

| | | | Percentage of Students Admitting to Cheating, Average of Schools Classified by Type of Sanction for Cheating | | |
| Colleges Distinguished by Type of Normative System and Normative Climate | Percentage Class | Row Number | Fail Specific Piece of Work or Less | Fail Course | Suspend or Expel |
			Col. 1	Col. 2	Col. 3
Honor-System Colleges	1–20	Row 1	†	†	†
Classified by Percentage of	21–40	Row 2	47	28	34
Students Who *Personally*	41–60	Row 3	52	33	24
Disapprove of Cheating	61–80	Row 4	39	†	11
Colleges *without* Honor	1–20	Row 5	62	71	†
System Classified by Percentage	21–40	Row 6	65	60	53
of Students Who *Personally*	41–60	Row 7	49	49	27
Disapprove of Cheating	61–80	Row 8	†	49	†
All Colleges Classified	1–20	Row 9	62	71	†
by Percentage of	21–40	Row 10	59	56	46
Students Who Personally	41–60	Row 11	50	40	25
Disapprove of Cheating	61–80	Row 12	39	49	11
Honor-System Colleges	1–20	Row 13	†	†	48
Classified by Percentage of	21–40	Row 14	44	36	34
Students Who Perceive Their	41–60	Row 15	47	33	29
Peers as Disapproving of Cheating	61–80	Row 16	40	25	19
Colleges *without* Honor System	1–20	Row 17	71	66	63
Classified by Percentage of	21–40	Row 18	57	58	57
Students Who Perceive Their	41–60	Row 19	44	40	31
Peers as Disapproving of Cheating	61–80	Row 20	47	46	†

*Table devised from figures reported in Salem and Bowers (1970:29, 30, and 32). Of the two types of normative systems, under the honor system students are commonly required to report fellow students for cheating. Normative climate is represented by the percentage of students who expressed personal disapproval of cheating or who perceived their peers (close friends or other student associates) as disapproving of cheating.
†No colleges in the class.

veys the deterrent force of formal sanctions under the honor system." Yet, as seen in the third and fourth panels of Table 5-15 (rows 13–16 and 17–20), when colleges are distinguished by the level of perceived peer disapproval of cheating, the inverse relation between the severity of prescribed sanctions and self-reported cheating tends to hold at all levels. The relation is more uniform and accentuated in the case of honor-system colleges (compare rows 14 and 18 or rows 15 and 19), but other comparisons (e.g., rows 2 and 14, rows 6 and 18) do not indicate that perceived peer disapproval of cheating conditions the impact of sanctions more than does personal disapproval. In any case, one need not invoke factors that are alien to the deterrence doctrine in accounting for the apparently greater impact of prescribed sanctions in honor-system colleges. As Salem and Bowers themselves observe (1970:32): "The honor system is . . . designed to increase the likelihood that formal sanctions will be brought to bear. The student's peers are directly responsible for activating the formal sanctioning machinery. As a result, formal sanctions, which are often imposed by a student court, are far less remote from the would-be offender." Although Salem and Bowers did not use the term, they clearly alluded to the "perceived certainty of punishment"; indeed, they espoused a conventional deterrence idea—that the relation between the severity of punishment and the violation rates is contingent on the certainty of punishment.

An assessment of Salem and Bowers's theoretical stance is difficult. They obviously entertained the idea that prescribed sanctions have at most only an indirect effect on violation rates, that is, by "strengthening the force of informal normative constraints" (Salem and Bowers, 1970:24), an argument stemming from Durkheim. However, it does not follow that the severity of prescribed sanctions are unrelated to cheating rates. Table 5-15 clearly shows that at some levels of the normative climate there is a relation between the severity of prescribed sanctions and the self-reported cheating in each of the two types of normative systems. Yet, elsewhere, Bowers and Salem (1972:429) claim that there is no such relation when the normative climate is "controlled."

Of course, Salem and Bowers may be arguing that informal normative constraints result in more conformity than do prescribed formal sanctions; but contemporary social scientists who entertain the deterrence doctrine do not necessarily deny that argument. In any case, Salem and Bowers's findings hardly represent clear-cut evidence in regard to the relative importance of formal and informal constraints, one way or another.

Still another consideration is that the findings indicate that prescribed formal sanctions deter some kinds of student misconduct more than others. That suggestion is consistent with Chambliss's argument (1967); but it does not contradict the deterrence doctrine, not even Beccaria's or Bentham's version, because the doctrine does not assert that all types of acts are equally deterrable.

One of the most commendable features of the research is the allowance made for "selectivity," that is, the possibility that youths select a college where their deviant proclivities are less subject to severe sanction. Much to their credit, Salem and Bowers had the foresight to ask the students if they had cheated in high school; and they found (1970:35) that "admitted cheaters" in high school are not prone to avoid colleges where the sanction for cheating is relatively severe.

In taking the social condemnation of acts into account, Salem and Bowers went beyond conventional deterrence research. Despite that sophistication, however, it should be recognized that a host of possibly relevant variables were excluded, some of the more obvious ones being (1) the rate of officially reported violations, (2) the objective certainty of punishment, (3) the perceived severity of actual punishments, (4) the knowledge of prescribed punishments, and (5) the perceived severity of prescribed punishments. Salem and Bowers considered only one variable, the presumptive severity of prescribed punishments, which may well be the least important property of punishment in regard to deterrence.

Another Study of Cheating in School

In an experiment on the threat of sanctions for cheating in three sociology classes (Tittle and Rowe, 1973), students took eight short examinations over the academic quarter (one examination a week). Instructors then graded the examination papers, recorded a grade for each student, returned the papers unmarked (i.e., as though ungraded) at the following class meeting, and the students were permitted to calculate their own grade (presumably after being informed of the correct answers). In the control class or group (26 students) no mention was made of cheating throughout the entire quarter; but on returning the papers for the fourth examination to the other two classes (the treatment groups, *A* and *B*), the instructor reminded the students that they were being trusted to grade their examinations honestly, thereby making a "moral appeal." Cheating was not mentioned again until the return of the seventh set of examination papers, at which time both classes (*A* and *B*) were informed that complaints about cheating made it necessary to "spot check" some papers to see if the grades were accurate. Finally, when the eighth set of examination papers was returned, both classes were informed (falsely) that a spot check had identified a cheater, who was to be penalized.

The amount of cheating was assessed in terms of the proportion of "opportunities utilized" by each student in each examination. To illustrate, since the maximum score on each examination was ten points, a student whose actual (correct) grade was six could cheat four points. If that student reported a grade of eight, then 50 percent of the cheating opportunities were "utilized." Given a percentage figure for each student on each examination, Tittle and Rowe then computed an average percentage figure for all classes, with a separate average for examinations 1–3, which involved no threat or moral appeal, examinations 4–6, which involved a moral appeal, examination 7, which involved the threat of a spot check, and examination 8, which involved a sanction threat. Those figures for the three classes are shown in Table 5-16.

In all three groups the moral appeal was followed by an increase in cheating, but the increase was small for two of the groups. However, after the threat of a spot check, cheating in treatment groups *A* and *B* declined sharply, and in the case of group *B* there was another substantial decline after the sanction threat. By contrast, in the control group (which was not exposed to a moral appeal or a threat of sanction), change in the amount of cheating from one set of examinations to the next was negligible. Both the decline in cheating and the difference between the treatment groups and the control group are statistically significant at 0.02 or less.

Much to their credit, Tittle and Rowe considered interpretations other than deterrence. To that end, they recalculated the cheating figures by another procedure, and the findings were not altered. Another line of analysis revealed no significant or relevant differences among the three classes in regard to age, sex, reason for enrolling, expected grade, motivation for earning a high grade, discrepancy between expected grade at the beginning of the quarter and actual grade, or major area of study.

The differences in the cheating records of the two treatment groups are puzzling, but Tittle and Rowe offer two plausible explanations. First, group *B* comprised 51 students, while group *A* only 30 students; hence the investigators attributed the greater decline in cheating among *A* students to a greater perceived certainty of detection resulting from a spot check of the examinations.[11] Second, they argue that the threats were less menacing for that group because of a tolerant instructor.

Just as the decline in cheating after a threat varied from group to group, so did it vary among individuals in each group. Tittle and Rowe found a significant sexual difference, with the decline in cheating being far greater for females. The decline was also far greater in the case of students with high grades and those who experienced no great discrepancy between expected grade and actual grade. The sexual difference is of interest because it is consistent with low official arrest rates for women, and the association of cheating with grades is indicative of an "instrumental" contingency in deterrence, one postulated by Chambliss (1967).

Tittle and Rowe's research is an excellent illustration of the problems and issues that are posed when interpreting the bearing of experimental findings (laboratory or field) on the deterrence doctrine. The problem is not just the contrast between the severity of experimental and

[11]Although not emphasized by Tittle and Rowe, their argument is consistent with the low initial level of cheating in the control group, where there were only 26 students.

Table 5-16. Cheating in Three Sociology Classes*

Sociology Classes or Groups	Examinations 1–3, with No Moral Appeal or Threat Col. 1	Examinations 4–6, with Moral Appeal Col. 2	Examinations 1–6 Combined Col. 3	Examination 7, with Threat of Spot Check Col. 4	Examination 8, with Sanction Threat Col. 5	Examinations 7 and 8 Combined Col. 6
			Mean Percentage of Cheating Opportunities Utilized			
Treatment Group A, a Total of 30 Students	31	41	34	13	11	12
Treatment Group B, a Total of 51 Students	41	43	42	32	22	31
Control Group, a Total of 26 Students	27	33†	30	24†	28†	24†

*From Tittle and Rowe (1973:491).
†No moral appeal or threat.

legal punishments. Additionally, it is commonly the case in experimental research that one cannot readily identify the property of punishment that has been manipulated or controlled. Thus, it *appears* that Tittle and Rowe attempted to manipulate the perceived certainty of punishment; but the investigators did not speak directly to that consideration. In any case, they did not attempt to measure changes in properties of punishment *independent* of the ostensible sanction threats or the postulated effect of the threat (reduction in cheating). Summarizing the matter briefly, it is not clear what property or properties of punishment were manipulated. On the other hand, if the property was perceived certainty, the experimental design was seemingly controlled for all other possibly relevant variables. To illustrate, there is no basis for supposing that cheating declined more in the treatment groups because cheating happened to be more socially or personally condemned in those groups than in the control group prior to the experiment. Observe then that there is no basis for assuming that the perceived severity of the sanction for cheating varied appreciably (if at all) from one group to the next.

Paradoxically, the controls ostensibly realized in Tittle and Rowe's experiment are not commendable when it comes to interpreting the bearing of the findings on the deterrence doctrine. In comparing jurisdictions or types of crime in the same jurisdiction, it is probably never the case that only one property of punishment varies (i.e., that all other relevant variables are constant). Viewed that way, in experimental deterrence research all properties of punishment and other relevant variables (e.g., social condemnation) should be manipulated rather than "held constant" by randomization. The point is not just that numerous properties of punishment and extralegal conditions vary in comparisons of actual crime rates; additionally, the relation between one particular property of punishment and the crime rate may depend on the magnitude or amount of variance in some of the other variables. To illustrate, consider two *universes* of jurisdictions, one in which the type of crime in question is socially condemned to a marked degree in all jurisdictions in that universe, and the other in which the type of crime is scarcely condemned in any of the jurisdictions. Even though the degree of social condemnation is more or less constant *within* each universe, the relation between the objective certainty of punishment and the crime rate may be much greater among the jurisdictions in one universe than among the jurisdictions in the other universe.

Tittle and Rowe's findings illustrate another consideration. The findings cannot be construed as demonstrating that the threat of punishment constrains individuals more than does social condemnation. Even assuming that the moral appeal intensified the social condemnation of cheating, there is no basis for knowing how much it was intensified. In any case, an even greater intensification might have resulted in a reversal of the findings (i.e., a greater reduction of cheating after a moral appeal), but that possibility cannot be examined without more manipulation of social condemnation than that achieved in Tittle and Rowe's experiment.

Far from being surprised by Tittle and Rowe's findings, laymen may wonder why it is necessary to demonstrate the "obvious," that is, the fact that individuals refrain from acts when threatened with punishment for doing otherwise. Such an assessment of Tittle and Rowe's study would reflect an ignorance of other findings that run contrary to the obvious. Stating the matter another way, laymen are unlikely to recognize that research findings support the deterrence doctrine only in experimental situations in which numerous variables are somehow controlled.

Lines of Work Slighted

A truly representative survey of deterrence studies would be difficult not only because of the sheer number of possibly relevant studies and divergent findings but also because the variety of research strategies or methodologies is seemingly infinite. Consequently, in a limited survey, such as the present one, certain lines of work on the deterrence question are bound to be slighted. Some of those works are referred to in this section, though only briefly. Their merits and shortcomings are considered without an analysis of particular studies, but the emphasis on their shortcomings is not a tacit suggestion that those kinds of research should be discontinued.

Enter the Economists

Shortly after the revival of interest in the deterrence question among sociologists, economists were drawn to the subject in large numbers. The entry of economists is a harbinger of progress in work on the deterrence question, for they come to the subject armed with an elegant conceptual scheme. Moreover, the principles of economics, particularly classical economics, are in keeping with the deterrence doctrine to a considerable degree. The congruence is hardly surprising, given the utilitarian, hedonistic, and rationalistic philosophy that Bentham shared with other prominent classical economists. Finally, economists commonly employ some very sophisticated statistical techniques in their deterrence research (see, especially, Ehrlich, 1972).

Stated in the briefest way possible, when employed in criminology the principles of classical economics reduce to one assertion: Individuals engage in criminal activity to the extent that it is profitable.[12] The assertion extends to include "individual" differences as well as variation in rates. Individuals who commit crimes are supposedly distinguished from those who do not by the fact that the commission of such crimes is more profitable for them; and the rate for a particular type of crime in a particular jurisdiction varies directly with the extent to which commission of the crime in that jurisdiction is profitable.

It would be a mistake to dismiss such generalizations out of hand as gross oversimplifications. One goal in formulating a theory about anything is parsimony, meaning the simplification of a seemingly complex matter. The validity or utility of the generalizations is, of course, another matter; but the more immediate concern is with relating those generalizations to the notion of deterrence.

Profit is the difference between cost and reward (or benefit). It may appear obvious that the cost of committing a crime includes punishment, but that relation is one of the most disputable aspects of the economists' treatment of deterrence. The problem stems from the conventional *conceptualization* of costs at the hand of economists, according to which the cost of any activity is the activities foregone. It is difficult to see how that conceptualization makes any sense in the case of committing a crime. The commission of an offense is an activity, but it is surely questionable to argue that the cost of, say, robbing a liquor store is the activity foregone, such as working during that time or attending a movie; and nothing is gained by speaking of the "value" of the activities foregone. So while the cost of committing a crime must be construed as somehow including punishment, it is by no means clear how including punishment is consistent with conventional conceptualization of cost. Moreover, no economist has specified how the cost of an actual punishment is to be expressed numerically, let alone in monetary units, and such expression would not even solve the problem. Surely one cannot use economic concepts to state the deterrence doctrine as a theory without speaking of "perceived costs of punishment," but it is not at all clear what that term means in an economic context, let alone how the phenomenon denoted by it can be expressed numerically.

[12]Consider two illustrative statements: "The basic thesis . . . is that offenders, as a group, respond to opportunities (costs and gains) available to them in legitimate and criminal activities in much the same way that those engaged in strictly legitimate activities as a group do" (Ehrlich, 1972:274). "Most economists who give serious thought to the problem of crime immediately come to the conclusion that punishment will indeed deter crime. The reason is perfectly simple: Demand curves slope downward. If you increase the cost of something, less will be consumed. Thus, if you increase the cost of committing a crime, there will be fewer crimes" (Tullock, 1974:104–105).

The term "perceived costs of punishment" can be treated as purely theoretical and somehow linked to properties of punishment; however, as shown in Chapter 4, there are at least nine possibly relevant properties of punishment.[13] Far from linking all those properties to cost, cost of punishment, or perceived cost of punishment, economists who work on the deterrence question do not even recognize most of those properties. Silver's survey (1974:3) indicates that studies of deterrence by economists are limited to seven variables in addition to the crime rate: (1) subjective probability of punishment, (2) subjective estimates of the severity of punishment, (3) proportion of the physiologically capable population who have been punished by imprisonment, (4) actual number of currently incarcerated persons per physiologically capable persons ever convicted of a crime, (5) expected legal earnings minus expected earnings from criminal activity, (6) availability of victims measured by population per unit space, and (7) a "portmanteau" variable (a catchall representing the tastes or the willingness of citizens to commit criminal acts). Of the seven variables, only the first four are properties of punishment, and even the identification of those four variables is disputable. In actual research, economists (like sociologists) work with data pertaining to the objective certainty and the presumptive severity of actual punishments, not with subjective estimates of certainty or severity (i.e., not with perceived certainty or perceived severity). Variables 1 and 2 have some bearing on objective certainty, but the presumptive severity of actual punishments is not listed. So, to summarize, economists really work with data pertaining to only two properties of punishment, and variables 5–7 actually relate to extralegal conditions conducive to crime.

Silver's list should not be construed as indicating that all studies of deterrence by economists have considered that range of variables or that all of those variables are interrelated in an explicit theory. To the contrary, economists leave their theory of deterrence largely implicit; and even if cost is the central notion, it is not clear (1) how that notion is linked with the seven variables in question or (2) how each variable (e.g., subjective severity of punishment, expected earnings from criminal activity) is to be expressed numerically. Some variables can be taken as immensurable (i.e., purely theoretical), but economists are not prone to speak to that question.

As for the properties of punishment that economists have not

[13]The nine are objective certainty, perceived certainty, objective celerity, perceived celerity, presumptive severity of prescribed punishments, presumptive severity of actual punishments, perceived severity of prescribed punishments, perceived severity of actual punishments, and public knowledge of prescribed punishments. Although treated in Chapter 4, cognition or identification of criminal acts is not a property of punishments in a strict sense.

treated in their deterrence research, they may deny that those properties are relevant; but, if so, one must surely wonder how relevance can be known at this stage in studies of deterrence. However, economists must do more than recognize the additional properties of punishment and speak to the problem of their numerical representation. They must relate those additional properties to cost if that is to be the central notion in their deterrence theory. It will not do for them to speak blithely of "letting C equal the cost of committing a crime" without stipulating what properties of punishment are subsumed under cost and indicating how the notion can be extended to that end. It may be that some properties of punishment are not to be treated as cost factors but rather as "assumed conditions." Yet economists say very little about the assumptions that enter into their version of the deterrence doctrine. In particular, it is not at all clear what assumptions they make about public knowledge of prescribed punishments. Finally, none of the foregoing problems can be solved by using some term other than "cost" in formulating a deterrence theory. Thus, Orsagh (1973) is content to speak only of "sanctions" as the independent variable in deterrence research, but that term scarcely identifies the relevant properties of punishment for a deterrence theory. Indeed, it is doubtful if any one term—be it "cost," "sanctions," or what have you—can designate all relevant properties of punishment as though they were somehow additive (i.e., as though all of them in principle or in practice could be expressed by adding up a series of values).

When it comes to recognizing complexities in testing the deterrence doctrine, economists have been no more sensitive than have sociologists. Only rarely do they recognize the possibility of any preventive mechanisms other than deterrence, and their awareness of the problem is restricted to the mechanism of incapacitation (see Silver's survey, 1974). As for extralegal conditions that are conducive to or inhibit crime, a portmanteau variable is little more than a tacit admission of ignorance.

As previously indicated, in deterrence research economists and sociologists have considered essentially the same properties of punishment, for the most part the objective certainty of punishment (imprisonment in particular) and the presumptive severity of actual punishments (length of imprisonment). The similarities even extend to the use of essentially the same kinds of data and the same method for the numerical representation of variables. Consequently, it is hardly surprising that the research findings of economists are consistent with conventional interpretations of the deterrence doctrine (see Silver, 1974), in the same sense that recent findings by sociologists (e.g., Logan, 1972b) are consistent with the doctrine. However, as emphasized by an economist (Tullock, 1974), the agreement in findings is significant even though economists and sociologists have used essentially the same data. It is significant if only because economists have used much more sophisticated statistical techniques and because standards of evidence are not necessarily the same in all disciplines.

All of the foregoing may appear to be another case in which an author in one discipline relishes sniping at another discipline; but the intent is not to deny that economists have made a contribution to work on deterrence. For that matter, their potential for making a greater contribution than that of sociologists is not questioned. Despite previous criticisms, the concepts of economics may prove to be appropriate for stating a deterrence theory, and the techniques of econometrics may be indispensable when it comes to tests of a sophisticated deterrence theory.

On the substantive side, economists have emphasized a consideration that sociologists have ignored—the potential benefit or gain from criminal activity. However, the relevance of that consideration for some types of crime (e.g., aggravated assault) is disputable, and economists have yet to devise a way to express the gain of some types of crime (e.g., rape). Even devising a defensible and feasible procedure for expressing gain through property crimes (e.g., robbery, burglary) will be a horrendous task (see Rottenberg, 1973:11–62), and the notion of expected gain complicates the problem even more. Nonetheless, a sophisticated deterrence theory will surely incorporate the notion of gain or benefit, and economists have rightly emphasized that notion.

All of the foregoing reduces to one major point. Economists appear to assume that the concepts and principles of their field are all that is needed for a theory of deterrence. In other words, the deterrence doctrine can be expressed by means of conventional economic terms and principles. But even ignoring the need to recognize preventive mechanisms other than deterrence and to control extralegal conditions, there is no basis to believe (1) that all of the relevant properties of punishment can be analyzed in terms of cost or (2) that economists have articulated the appropriate assumptions about perception and cognition as factors in deterrence.

Perceptual Studies

This survey has limited "conventional" deterrence research to analyses of the relation between properties of punishment and crime rates, and that limitation excludes several studies of the perception of punishment by members of two populations: (1) individuals classified by one criterion or another (e.g., record of a felony conviction) as criminal or delinquent and (2) individuals not classified in that way (so-called normals). Such studies may appear to be relevant in assessing the deterrence doctrine, especially those that have considered perceptions of the certainty or severity of punishment. Thus, so it could be argued, the deterrence doctrine leads to the prediction that members of a *criminal-delinquent* population perceive the punishment of crime (or at least the particular type of crime in question) as less certain than do members of a *normal* population. The same prediction may appear to extend to perceptions of the severity of punishment. In either case, the underlying argument is something like this: If individuals commit crimes because they have not been deterred and if individuals refrain from crimes because they have been deterred, then those who commit crimes tend to perceive punishment as less certain and/or less severe than do those who conform to laws. Another way to put the argument is that criminals tend to underestimate both the objective certainty of punishment and the magnitude (presumptive severity) of statutory penalties (e.g., length of imprisonment), while normals tend to overestimate both properties of punishment.

Whatever version of the argument one chooses, there is a fairly extensive body of evidence to assess it (e.g., California Assembly Committee, 1968; Claster, 1967; Jensen, 1969; Rettig and Rawson, 1963; Rettig, 1964; and Waldo and Chiricos, 1972); and that evidence is by no means consistent with the argument. The findings suggest that criminals or delinquents have more accurate knowledge of statutory penalties than do the so-called normals, and in that sense the former do not tend to underestimate the presumptive severity of prescribed punishments. As for perceptions of the certainty of punishment, contrasts between the two populations are not appreciable, and there is no convincing evidence that criminals or delinquents underestimate the objective certainty of punishment.

One may take the research findings on perception of punishment as a refutation of the deterrence doctrine, but the investigations have been methodologically defective and not only because of their failure to control for extralegal conditions that generate or inhibit crime. In most studies the individuals identified as criminal or delinquent had been taken into custody prior to the study and were incarcerated at the time of the study. As such, their perceptions of punishment might well have been altered by the experience of *actual* punishment, and there is surely no basis for knowing what their perceptions were *prior to* committing the crime for which they were apprehended. It may appear that the problem of "experiential impact" could be avoided by an analysis of individuals' perceptions of the punishment for a particular type of crime in two populations, one in which members have "self-reported" committing the crime but have not been interrogated or arrested. However, that data would not pertain to actual (official) crime rates, and even if all of the members of that population reported their past behavior truthfully and competently, there still would be no basis for knowing or defensibly inferring their perceptions of punishment prior to the alleged commission of the crime. The problem is illustrated by Jensen's finding (1969) of evidence of marked *decline* among boys in the perceived certainty of punishment from one school grade to a higher grade (i.e., perceived certainty evidently declines rapidly with age, at least up to a certain point). Since both official and self-reported delinquency rates increase rapidly with age (up to about 16 or 17), it may appear that juveniles commit more delinquencies as they grow older because they come more and more to perceive punishment as uncertain; but it could be that their delinquent experiences lead them to revise their estimates of the certainty of punishment.

All things considered, there is only one defensible strategy for assessing the relation in question. Given data on the perception of the certainty-severity of punishment by each individual among a large number of individuals, the appropriate question becomes: What is the association between those perceptions and the *subsequent* criminal or delinquent acts (official and self-reported) by those individuals? Even that research design would not be entirely satisfactory without controls for extralegal conditions, since Jensen (1969) found that boys who voice respect for the law tend to (1) perceive punishment for crime as certain, (2) report fewer criminal or delinquent acts, and (3) be less frequently officially reported as delinquent. The general point is that individuals who appear to subscribe the most to the social condemnation of crime are the ones who tend to view punishment as the most certain, and they may commit fewer criminal acts because of social condemnation rather than fear of punishment.

Traffic Offenses

Studies of deterrence in connection with traffic offenses are grossly underrepresented in this survey, and the findings of the one study considered in detail (Shoham, 1974) hardly supports the deterrence doctrine. Yet surveys of traffic studies (Cramton, 1969; European Committee on Crime Problems, 1967:189–257; Middendorff, 1968; and Zimring and Hawkins, 1973, especially 3) clearly suggest that the findings tend to support the deterrence doctrine, with two possible classes of exceptions. First, even in the case of traffic offenses the findings do not support the specific deterrence argument (see Cramton, 1969:453–454; European Committee on Crime Problems, 1967:228–230). And, second, it appears that some kinds of traffic offenses are much more deterrable than others, with parking violations being more so than moving violations (see Cramton, 1969:453; for a well-known study of parking violations, see Chambliss, 1966).

There are at least three studies of traffic offenses that are so sophisticated and complicated that only a full reading of the reports would do justice to them. Of those three, Ross's study (1973) provides impressive support for the deterrence doctrine, and it also illustrates the horrendous complexities in the interpretation of findings. The other two studies (Campbell and Ross, 1968; Glass, 1968) illustrate how what appears to be clear-cut evidence of deterrence in traffic studies may be misleading. The majority of other traffic studies suffer in comparison, which is the primary reason for their underrepresentation in this survey. However, the point is not just that the majority of other studies are methodologically defective. The appropriate methodology for deterrence studies of traffic offenses (or any type of offense, for that matter) is debatable; and truly rigorous criteria would eliminate far too many studies. Rather, the defect of traffic studies is that they are often little more than casual observations about change in the number of *officially* reported traffic violations after a change in prescribed punishment or enforcement procedures (usually the latter). Even if such observations can be taken as studies, they are not fully reported, and they are rarely published in professional journals, which would ensure scrutiny by a critical and informed audience.

Contingencies on the Impact of Punishment

Not even Beccaria or Bentham asserted that punishments (whatever their celerity, certainty, or severity) deter all individuals in all conditions from all types of crimes. Stating the matter even more abstractly, those who have attempted to explicate the deterrence doctrine accept the idea that the relation between punishment and crime is contingent. That idea is not altogether distinct from the belief that extralegal conditions have an impact on the crime rate that is independent of punishment. Nonetheless, one can rightly speak of the impact of punishment *itself* as contingent, meaning that (1) some individuals and perhaps even discernible classes of individuals are more deterrable than others and/or (2) some types of crimes are more deterrable than others. Both possibilities have received considerable attention in the literature (see, e.g., Chambliss, 1967; Zimring and Hawkins, 1973:97–141), but no illustrative study is included in this survey, and an explanation of the omission is in order.

It does not tax credulity to argue that individuals who have nothing to lose in a material sense (e.g., property, income) are the least likely to be deterred by the threat of a fine or imprisonment. A similar argument can be made in the case of corporal punishment; that is, individuals who have known only a hostile environment (e.g., hunger and harsh extralegal punishments) are the least likely to be deterred by the threat of a physically painful legal punishment, including the death penalty. Finally, there is the belief that the stigma of punishment (whatever the kind) holds little fear for those who have no reputation or prestige to lose.

Though not distinct, another argument is that some types of crimes are by their very nature less deterrable than others. To illustrate, since homicide is commonly committed by individuals in a state of rage or passion, the risk of punishment is rarely contemplated by killers (so the argument goes). Then there are types of crimes ostensibly committed to satisfy some seemingly uncontrollable physiological craving, such as when individuals either violate drug laws or commit a crime (e.g., robbery) to secure drugs. Finally, some types of crimes are indicative of a commitment to a social cause that compels individuals to risk punishment, "political crimes" being the most common instances.

None of the foregoing arguments are likely to be disputed; they are conventional wisdom when it comes to speculation about deterrence. Even in rare instances where someone has questioned one of the arguments (see, e.g., Tullock's commentary, 1974, on the deterrability of murder), no systematic evidence is presented in the refutation. However, the arguments themselves are scarcely supported by evidence. Consider the all too general observation that most murderers commit the crime in a rage or heat of passion. Even if that is so, just the opposite (most murderers kill after dispassionate contemplation of punishment) would be more compelling evidence against the deterrence doctrine. Then consider how readily the deterrence doctrine can be misconstrued when extended to include "crimes without victims" (see Schur, 1965). There is no reason to suppose, for example, that possession of marijuana in American jurisdictions is appreciably deterred, at least categorically, by fear of punishment (see Grupp and Lucas, 1970). However, since the objective certainty of punishment is probably negligible for that type of crime, its alleged frequency is hardly contrary to the deterrence doctrine. The real issue in the punishment of crimes without victims is the failure of legislators to recognize that criminal sanctions are effective only within limits (Kadish, 1967; Packer, 1968), some of which are identified by the deterrence doctrine itself.

The paucity of research on the "nondeterrability" arguments is a telling commentary on the arguments themselves. Briefly, the arguments are stated in such a way that systematic research is virtually precluded. Thus, Zimring and Hawkins (1968) suggest that some "marginal groups" are less deterred from crime, but it is not at all clear what they mean by that term, let alone exactly what kind of research findings would refute their argument. Similarly, Chambliss (1967) speaks of some types of crime as more deterrable than others, with the least deterrable being characterized as "high commitment and expressive," and the most deterrable being characterized as "low commitment and instrumental." The initial problem is that the meanings of "commitment," "expressive," and "instrumental" are very vague; and it appears that the related differences among *legal classes* of crimes (e.g., robbery and rape) are those of degree rather than kind. Indeed, it may well be that Chambliss's typological distinctions do not apply to *legal classes* of crimes at all but rather to individuals. Chambliss distinguishes four types of crime (combinations of high-commitment, low-commitment, expressive, and instrumental) but then recognizes that "some murderers" are instances of three types. In other words, he grants the types are not mutually exclusive; but that recognition does not make the assertions about "deterrability" any more testable, and the problems in that connection are formidable.

General observations can be made in support of Chambliss's argument and all other similar arguments, but general observations also cast doubts on them. If homicide is far less deterrable than certain other types of crime (e.g., burglary, robbery), then why is the homicide rate so much lower than the rates for other crimes? As for making inferences from the findings of systematic research on deterrence, the arguments about nondeterrability become even more suspect. As a case in point, none of Logans's findings (see Table 5-7) demonstrates that there is anything truly distinctive about homicide in terms of the relation between crime rates and the objective certainty or the presumptive severity of punishment.

All of the foregoing is not a tacit rejection of the argument that some types of crimes and/or some types of individuals are more deterrable than others. Intuitively, the argument makes sense, and it is difficult to imagine a sophisticated deterrence theory that does not recognize the argument one way or another. However, when it comes to systematic evidence, the argument is little more than an appeal to one's common sense; and it is likely to remain so until those who write on the subject commence formulating testable generalizations. Until such generalizations are formulated and supported in tests, theorists will be haunted by the awful possibility that the relevance of any property of punishment is contingent not only on kinds of crimes but also on largely unknown characteristics of potential offenders.

Experimentation with Punishment in a Laboratory Situation

The most questionable limitation of this survey is the exclusion of experimental studies of punishment (especially of human subjects). Exclusion of those studies is questionable if only because it may be that various methodological problems in deterrence research can be dealt with only through experimental designs (if at all). Three brief illustrations must suffice.

Attempts to express the amount of cognitive congruence (agreement between the public and officals in regard to the nature of crimes) is fraught with all manner of difficulties (practical and theoretical). But one can readily imagine an experimental situation designed so that the subjects ostensibly know what acts are subject to punishment. Even more elaborate experimental designs may enable investigators to control the amount of such knowledge, so that it varies from one experimental situation to the next and/or among individuals in the same experimental situation.

Another advantage of experimental studies is that factors analogous to extralegal conditions (those conducive to crimes or those that inhibit crimes) can be controlled. For example, to control social condemnation, investigators can either punish "socially neutral acts" (those neither socially approved nor disapproved) or select subjects at random for different experimental situations, thereby ensuring that the subjects in one situation are no more predisposed to commit or to refrain from the type of act in question than are subjects in the other situations.

Finally, experimental designs can be such that various possible preventive mechanisms of punishment other than deterrence are precluded. Considering two such mechanisms for illustrative purposes, mild electrical shocks are not incapacitating; and when punishments are mild, reformation is not a likely consequence.

Given the advantages of experimental work on punishment, the exclusion of such studies from this survey may appear most questionable. Rightly or wrongly, they are excluded because of doubts about generalizing experimental findings to penal systems. However, since critics of experimental research in the social sciences are all too prone to dismiss the findings as restricted to artificial situations and to do so uncritically, a defense of the present argument is in order.

As the first consideration, note that most experimental research on punishment has been limited to nonhuman subjects (rats or pigeons in particular). The point is not that the findings have no bearing whatever on human behavior; rather, it is simply questionable to generalize the findings to a penal system. No study of the reactions of rats or pigeons to punishment has incorporated a concept analogous to prescribed punishments, and it is hardly farfetched to argue that those animals cannot perceive a threat of punishment that is independent of their ever being punished or of their witnessing the punishment of others. Yet a statutory penalty can be perceived by humans as a threat of punishment that is independent of its actual administration.

Even the punishment of human subjects in experimental situations is extremely limited when compared to a penal system. Specifically, the bulk of the research is relevant *only* in contemplating specific deterrence. There have been few experimental studies of the responses of individuals to the punishment of others (so-called vicarious punishment), and even in those studies the subjects typically came to perceive a threat of punishment through direct and immediate experience rather than through indirect, or second-hand, experience (as is commonly the case in the interaction between the public and the penal system). So the vast majority of experimental studies of punishment (dealing with human subjects or otherwise) are of questionable relevance in contemplating general deterrence.

As for specific deterrence, the conditions of punishment of human subjects in experimental situations are radically different from the penal system. One obvious difference is that the punishments appear extremely mild in comparison to criminal sanctions (especially penalties for felonies). Less obvious, the objective certainty of punishment in the penal system does not remotely approach the objective certainty realized in virtually all experimental studies; and that is also true of objective celerity, which is commonly a matter of days, months, or years in the penal system but seconds or minutes in experimental work. Finally, modes of behavior that are punished in experimental situations are commonly not subject to social condemnation, nor are they a means to monetary gain comparable to crimes against property.

All of these differences are not inherent limitations of experimental work. With the possible exceptions of the severity of punishment and the nature of the types of behavior punished, experimental conditions can be designed to approximate features of the penal system, at least those features that appear relevant for specific deterrence. So there is an opportunity for a radically new course in deterrence research, and it may be that certain problems (e.g., selectivity in punishments) can be dealt with only in experimental situations.

Despite the marked difference between experimental situations and penal systems, the experimental work has influenced thinking on deterrence. Findings of some well-known experimental studies by psychologists in the 1930's and 1940's (see surveys by Johnston, 1972; Singer, 1970; and Solomon, 1964) indicated that punishment does not effectively eliminate or suppress established behavior patterns. Even though the experiments were restricted to nonhuman animals and employed seemingly mild punishments, behavioral scientists made unjustifiable generalizations with regard to their findings about punishment in general. That conclusion stood unchallenged for some 20 years, and as late as 1965 two authors (Appel and Peterson, 1965), writing in a criminological journal, invoked experimental studies of punishment in questioning the deterrence doctrine. However, in the 1960's there was a resurgence of experimental work on punishment, and the findings clearly indicated that previous conclusions were erroneous, largely because the earlier studies employed mild punishments (see Johnston, 1972; Singer, 1970; and Solomon, 1964).

The parallel between sociology and experimental psychology in beliefs about punishment is striking, even though the psychological research has not been directly concerned with deterrence. In both fields the punishment question was largely ignored throughout roughly the same period, and the resurgence of work on the subject altered conclusions in both fields. The major difference between them is that the major conclusion in experimental psychology (that punishment is ineffective) was based on findings pertaining to mild but certain punishments, whereas in sociology the concern was with a severe but uncertain punishment (i.e., the death penalty).

Recent experimental findings clearly indicate that severe punishments are effective in altering the behavior of some organisms under some conditions; but those findings should not be construed as suggesting support for the deterrence doctrine, the specific-deterrence argument in particular. The findings are largely restricted to nonhuman animals, and in any case the conditions in question differ sharply from a penal system. Nonetheless, the conditions are important in contemplating why specific deterrence is so seldom realized (ostensibly) in penal systems. Experimental findings indicate that the effectiveness of punishment in altering behavior depends on at least 12 conditions (see Solomon, 1964:251), and only one of the "conducive" conditions—seemingly intense punishment—is *clearly* realized in a penal system. To consider only one other conducive condition, punishment may be increasingly ineffective if delayed more than 5 seconds, and the effect may be negligible if punishment is delayed as much as 30 seconds (see Singer,

1970:418). The exact relation between the "timing" of a punishment and its effectiveness depends on several conditions (e.g., the kind of organism, the kind of behavior), but there is no doubt that the celerity of experimental punishments is very important even for human subjects. Consequently, when it is recognized that the celerity of penal sanctions (even procedural punishments) is reckoned in days if not months or years rather than in seconds, the meager evidence of specific deterrence is hardly surprising. Moreover, in regard to policy implications, it is difficult to imagine a penal system in which the celerity of punishment is a matter of seconds. The severity and certainty of punishment in a penal system may somehow counterbalance the delay in punishment, but experimental findings indicate that properties of punishment can be "substituted" only within fairly narrow limits.

Six

A Summary in Terms
of Theoretical Prospects

For reasons alluded to throughout the preceding chapters, it is not feasible at this stage to formulate a deterrence theory. Those reasons reduce to three major considerations, one being that the formulation of a theory should await answers provided by exploratory research to several empirical questions about the relevance of various properties of punishment and about alternative procedures for numerical representation of those properties. Those questions are set forth in preceding chapters, and only a few additional observations need be made.

It is not assumed that the empirical questions can be answered conclusively. The research will be restricted necessarily to certain types of crimes and particular jurisdictions, with no assurances that the findings can be generalized. Whatever the findings, the research will not lead automatically to a theory, and difficult problems of interpretation are inevitable. Nonetheless, attempts at a deterrence theory without exploratory research will be a study in conjectures, false starts, and failures.

An attempt could be made without awaiting exploratory research, but ignoring the distinctions introduced in Chapter 4 (e.g., severity of *prescribed* punishments and severity of *actual* punishments) virtually guarantees an untestable theory. A theorist could recognize the distinctions and exclude some properties on an intuitive basis (e.g., ignore the severity of prescribed punishments altogether). The sheer variety of properties virtually precludes treating all of them in one theory; yet it is difficult to imagine a defensible choice without exploratory research. In any case, a deterrence theory will be untestable unless the theorist stipulates a procedure for the numerical representation of each property of punishment, but at present there is scarcely a defensible basis for a choice among alternative procedures. So a theorist is not likely to "guess right" in formulating a testable deterrence theory without relying heavily on exploratory research findings; otherwise, attempts at a theory could fail to such an extent that the deterrence doctrine will be dismissed again.

Some problems in formulating a deterrence theory cannot be solved by exploratory research, and that is especially the case when it comes to identifying extralegal conditions that generate or inhibit criminal acts. Until such conditions are identified and somehow controlled in deterrence research, doubts will haunt the interpretation of tests of any deterrence theory.[1] However, as the matter now stands, relevant extralegal conditions cannot be identified in a defensible way; so a theorist has little choice but to ignore them. Even so, tests of a deterrence theory may facilitate the identification of relevant extralegal conditions through a focus on deviant cases (e.g., a jurisdiction with a much higher or much lower crime rate than that predicted from the properties of punishment). Alternatively, theories on criminality may develop to a point where relevant extralegal conditions are identified apart from the deterrence doctrine. Regardless of how the conditions come to be identified, the premises of a deterrence theory will not be altered; rather, instructions for tests of it will stipulate how extralegal conditions are to be controlled.

The situation is quite different when it comes to possible preventive consequences of punishment other than deterrence. Unlike extralegal conditions, some of those consequences can be identified (e.g., incapacitation), meaning that they are not purely conjectural. Accordingly, unless those other possible consequences are taken into account, any interpretation of tests of a deterrence theory will be debatable. To repeat a

---

[1]The rationale is stated in conventional terms, but disputes that center on the question of causation in the interpretation of tests are sterile. So observations throughout this book on controls, preventive consequences other than deterrence, extralegal conditions, etc., actually reflect a concern with predictive power, not causation. Briefly, one way to maximize the predictive power of a theory is to stipulate the conditions under which the asserted relations hold. Yet the concern with predictive power does not entail a denial of the fact that we commonly think in causal terms, nor is it inconsistent with the use of such terms as "consequences" and "prevention" in contemplating deterrence and making *general* observations. Indeed, thinking in causal terms may facilitate the creation or identification of order in the world of events; but the demonstration of order is not proof of causation, especially since both laymen and scientists differ in their conceptions of causation and criteria of relevant evidence. For that reason alone, the use of causal terms in the formulation of a theory makes the appropriate test procedure disputable and precludes consensus in the interpretation of tests. As for the idea that only causal theories have policy implications, reconsider the counterargument. Policy questions ultimately reduce to the following form: If such-and-such is done, what will happen? An answer to any instance of that question *is a prediction.*

previous illustration, an inverse relation between the objective certainty of imprisonment and the crime rate could reflect, *inter alia*, incapacitation rather than deterrence.

Isolated observations are made in preceding chapters on research strategies for taking into account possible preventive consequences of punishment other than deterrence. One strategy is to focus tests of a deterrence theory on homicide, the presumption being that the incapacitating consequences of punishment have a minimal influence on the crime rate. But such strategies are limited to particular preventive mechanisms, and all of them are debatable.

While a deterrence theory and test instructions can be formulated without regard to other possible consequences of punishment, the interpretation of tests will be confronted with imponderables. Yet is is not realistic to postpone theoretical work or research until ideal strategies are developed. They are not likely to be developed in one swoop, that is, without extensive exploratory research; but research has no sense of direction without some kind of theory.

Proposed Solution

Since there is no truly adequate way to control for possible preventive consequences of punishment other than deterrence, evidential problems in tests of a deterrence theory are currently insurmountable. But the situation does not preclude the formulation and test of a theory about the *general preventive consequences of punishment*, which is more inclusive than deterrence.

The proposal is an unconventional strategy—if evidential problems cannot be solved in analyzing some phenomenon, then circumvent those problems by analyzing an even more inclusive phenomenon. More specifically, granted that punishments may prevent crime through various mechanisms (e.g., incapacitation, deterrence), those distinctions are not directly relevant for a theory about general preventive consequences of punishment, since such a theory would pertain to any property of punishment that in *one way or another* prevents crimes. So the alternative to a deterrence theory is a more inclusive theory.

The proposal reflects an argument—that all past purported tests of the deterrence doctrine have been mislabeled. Since the findings do not distinguish between deterrence and other possible preventive consequences, those tests actually pertain to an idea that transcends deterrence.

Appearances to the contrary, the proposal is a step toward the formulation of a deterrence theory. Both theories, one on preventive consequences of punishment in general and one limited to deterrence, will share some variables in common, with the most inclusive list of possibilities being objective certainty of punishments, perceived certainty of punishments, objective celerity of punishments, perceived celerity of punishments, public knowledge of prescribed punishments, presumptive severity of prescribed punishments, presumptive severity of actual punishment, perceived severity of prescribed punishments, and perceived severity of actual punishments.

Exploratory research may indicate that certain properties are irrelevant for either theory (i.e., deterrence or preventive consequences), but some findings may be consistent with only one of them. Suppose it is found that the crime rate varies inversely with the objective certainty of imprisonment but not with the perceived certainty of imprisonment. Such a finding would be consistent with a theory of preventive consequences, but it would cast doubts on virtually any deterrence theory. The general point is that tests of a preventive theory are likely to throw light on the deterrence question.

Policy Implications

When it comes to penal policy, a theory of the preventive consequences is more strategic than a deterrence theory. Legislators and other policy makers are primarily interested in reducing the crime rate (see Crowther, 1969); therefore, for them the distinction between deterrence and other possible preventive consequences is unimportant. But that is the case only insofar as policy makers ignore the costs of alternative means.

A demand for more severe statutory penalties may reflect not only a belief in deterrence but also a desire for an inexpensive means to the reduction of crime. What could be less expensive than simply doubling statutory prison sentences for felonies? However, given evidence that long prison sentences have no impact on the crime rate unless actually imposed and then only through incapacitation, the pursuit of law and order would become an expensive undertaking. Then consider pleas for the death penalty, which commonly invoke the deterrence doctrine. Those pleas may reflect a yearning for retribution, but in any case there is a more general issue. The only seemingly irrefutable argument for the death penalty is that it incapacitates criminals, but its advocates should confront the following question: If superlative incapacitation is the only distinctive consequence of executions, is the penalty worth it? The question is especially relevant in light of the possibility that executions have no substantial impact on the incidence of capital crimes through incapacitation because the repetitive rates for those crimes are low. The conventional rejoinder is "Better that a thousand murderers be executed than one kill twice," but that dictum conveniently ignores the possibility of executing innocent persons.

Problems with the Proposal

The pursuit of a preventive theory will not circumvent all evidential problems. Interpretation of tests of a preventive theory will be haunted by doubts about extralegal conditions, inhibitory and generative. To illustrate, even a fairly close *inverse* relation between the length of imposed prison sentences and the crime rate would not be conclusive evidence of the preventive consequences of punishment, let alone of deterrence. The argument could be that the social condemnation of crime varies inversely with the crime rate but directly with the severity of punishment. Now contemplate a *direct* relation between length of imposed prison sentences and the crime rate. The finding might appear to be conclusive evidence that punishments do not prevent crimes, but consider an alternative interpretation. When extralegal generative conditions are especially prevalent, the crime rate is high, and officials react to that high rate with harsh punishments. If so, a direct relation between the crime rate and the severity of punishment is expected, and the argument can then include the claim that jurisdictions with harsh punishments would have even higher crime rates without those punishments.

Arguments pertaining to social condemnation or "official reaction" to high crime rates are not sheer conjecture; but unless the advocates present systematic comparative data on those phenomena, their arguments are hardly a defensible basis for interpreting research findings. The same is true when the arguments are invoked to refute purported evidence for or against the deterrence doctrine. However, in defending purported evidence of deterrence, one must dismiss not only arguments about extralegal conditions but also arguments about preventive consequences of punishment other than deterrence, and some of the latter arguments are less conjectural. (No one is likely to question that prison sentences for auto theft are incapacitating.) So a theory of preventive consequences of punishment could circumvent *some* of the evidential problems that haunt tests of a deterrence theory.

The Central Preventive Proposition

Given the foregoing rationale for ignoring the distinction between deterrence and other possible consequences of punishment, it is feasible to formulate a central proposition as the point of departure in pursuing a preventive theory: The greater the celerity, certainty, and severity of punishment, the less the crime rate.

Like all propositions previously considered, the foregoing applies to (1) variations in the rate for any particular type of crime among jurisdictional populations and (2) differences in the rates among types of crime in the same jurisdiction. However, the proposition must be understood as encompassing only four properties of punishment: (1) objective certainty, (2) objective celerity, (3) presumptive severity of prescribed punishments, and (4) presumptive severity of actual punishments. It may appear paradoxical that the central preventive proposition encompasses fewer properties of punishment than might be recognized in a deterrence theory, and the reason for the contrast cannot be stated readily or briefly. Preliminary to that consideration, a commentary on methods for testing the central preventive proposition is in order.

Appearances to the contrary, a test of the proposition would be a complicated matter, even assuming that a value can be computed so that it represents each of the four properties of punishment. In each test all of the values would pertain to some type of crime, and the question would be: What is the relation between those values and the crime rate? To answer that question it would be necessary to compare rates either for (1) the same type of crime in two or more jurisdictions or (2) several types of crimes in the same jurisdiction. The complexity stems from two considerations: first, values that represent *different* properties of a type of punishment cannot be added; and, second, values that represent the *same* property but different types of punishments cannot be added. To illustrate, suppose that a test of the central proposition pertains to variation in the felony theft rate among several jurisdictions. Now suppose that in *each* jurisdiction the alternative prescribed substantive punishments for that type of crime are imprisonment and probation. Taking just one of those jurisdictions and considering only two properties of imprisonment, objective certainty and presumptive severity of the prescribed term (minimum, maximum, or an average of the extremes), the value of one property cannot be added to that of the other property. The metrics of the two values would be different (a proportion in the case of certainty and a certain number of years in the case of presumptive severity). Not even the same metric would justify adding values that represent the same property but different types of punishment. Thus, even though the presumptive severity of actual imprisonment and the presumptive severity of actual instances of probation for felony theft may be expressed in years, the two values representing those two properties for felony theft in a particular jurisdiction cannot be construed as additive without assuming that the two properties are of equal importance in the prevention of crime (by one mechanism or another). There is no basis whatever for that assumption.

The complexity in question could not be avoided even if there were only one prescribed substantive punishment for felony theft in each jurisdiction. Again, the value that represents one property (e.g., objective certainty) of one type of punishment (e.g., imprisonment) cannot be added to the value of another property (e.g., objective celerity) of that type of punishment, not even if the two values have the same metric (as in the case of the presumptive severity of actual imprisonment and the presumptive severity of prescribed prison terms). Insofar as the test takes procedural punishments into account (as should be the case), there will be at least two different types of punishment in each jurisdiction, and that alone complicates matters, even if prescribed procedural and substantive punishments are the same for each jurisdiction.[2] Moreover, procedural punishments introduce a special complexity in that one cannot properly speak of the presumptive severity of such punishments (e.g., arrest, indictment) because unlike fines, incarceration, or probation there is no obvious metric for expressing the magnitude of procedural punishments. Finally, observe particularly that the complexities do not stem solely from a concern with *presumptive* severity rather than *perceived* severity. Values that represent the latter for different types of punishment can be additive, but the value that represents the perceived severity of one type of punishment cannot be added to the value that represents a nonperceptual property (e.g., objective certainty) of that punishment.

Fortunately, there are several conventional statistical techniques for examining the relation between one set of values (e.g., crime rates) and two or more sets of values (in this case, one set for each of the four properties of punishment), the most common technique being multiple correlation.[3] Of course, each test of the central preventive proposition should

[2]This argument and subsequent ones apply to differences among types of crimes in the same jurisdiction as well as to differences in the rate for the same type of crime among jurisdictions.

[3]Here and elsewhere observations about techniques for tests of a preventive theory also apply to tests of a deterrence theory. However, the treatment of the presumptive severity of prescribed or actual punishments poses a special problem in tests of a preventive theory. The notion scarcely applies to the death penalty or to procedural punishments, for those punishments have no obvious magnitude (unlike fines or imprisonment). So the appropriate units for tests of a preventive theory are jurisdictions in which the prescribed procedural punishments for the type of crime in question are the same and in which the death penalty is not one of the prescribed substantive punishments. If those conditions hold in the case of selected types of crimes in a particular jurisdiction, then those types would be appropriate units for tests of a preventive theory. The treatment of presumptive

include an examination of the relation between the crime rate and each of the four properties while controlling for the other properties; and to that end partial correlation would be the simplest technique. By that route, some of the properties of punishment may be eliminated as irrelevant (i.e., as having no relation to the crime rate when other properties are controlled statistically), and that would be a desirable step if only to simplify the central preventive proposition. In that connection, note that some of the properties incorporated in the proposition are of questionable relevance, and that is especially true of objective celerity. However, bear in mind that objective celerity can be irrelevant in regard to deterrence (general deterrence in particular) but relevant in regard to crime prevention (e.g., incapacitation may be a partial function of objective celerity).

The Exclusion of Other Properties of Punishment

Observe again that the terms of the central preventive proposition are defined so that they exclude five of the properties of punishment recognized in Chapter 4, those five being (1) perceived celerity, (2) perceived certainty, (3) perceived severity of prescribed punishments, (4) perceived severity of actual punishments, and (5) knowledge of prescribed punishments. Their exclusion may appear to border on the illogical and indefensible, so an extensive commentary on the subject is in order.

The four properties of punishment incorporated in the central preventive proposition are *primary* properties in that they pertain to the activities of legal officials that involve prescribing or administering punish' ments. Those properties excluded are *contingent* properties in that they depend in whole or in part on the reactions of the public to the activities of legal officials.[4] Insofar as a primary property (e.g., presumptive severity of actual punishments) is closely correlated with the corresponding contingent property (perceived severity of actual punishments), the lat-

---

severity is also a problem in testing a deterrence theory, but in that case the problem can be avoided if the theorist makes assertions only about the *perceived* severity of actual or prescribed punishments. That is so because (1) a perceived severity value can be computed for any kind of punishment, including the death penalty and procedural punishments; and (2) in principle at least, any two perceived severity values can be compared or treated as additive.

[4]The primary-contingent distinction is only another way of recognizing the difference between objective and perceptual properties of punishment. Such terminological redundancy is justified to emphasize the assumption that all preventive consequences of punishment follow from primary properties of punishment.

ter can be treated as a function of the former; hence it need not be recognized explicitly in the formulation of preventive propositions. Illustrating the point another way, assume (1) that there is a close direct relation between the objective certainty of punishment and the perceived certainty of punishment and (2) that objective certainty is related to the crime rate only through perceived certainty.[5] Even so, the validity of both assumptions would not preclude a preventive proposition that asserts an inverse relation between the objective certainty of punishment and the crime rate *without referring to perceived certainty*. Now consider the matter another way. Suppose there is no relation whatever between objective certainty and perceived certainty. Even so, there could be a close inverse relation between objective certainty and the crime rate. If that should prove to be the case, then the inverse relation between objective certainty and the crime rate could not be attributed readily to deterrence; but it could be attributed to incapacitation (especially if imprisonment is the type of punishment in question). The general point is that contingent properties of punishment (e.g., perceived certainty) need not be incorporated in preventive propositions.[6] Those properties become relevant only when an attempt is made to distinguish *particular* preventive mechanisms (e.g., deterrence as opposed to normative insulation).

Toward a Preventive Theory

The foregoing central preventive proposition is only illustrative, and even at this stage in research on crime and punishment there are doubts about recognizing the objective celerity and the presumptive severity of actual or prescribed substantive punishments as relevant. The more general point is that the formulation of a truly defensible preventive proposition may have to await much more exploratory work, especially on procedural punishments. For that matter, it may be proven that a preventive proposition cannot be stated in a simple way, whatever the properties of punishment. Given further evidence that the relation be-

[5]More specifically, in the absence of any variation in perceived certainty (among jurisdictions or among types of crime in the same jurisdiction), there will be no relation between the objective certainty of punishment and the crime rate. What is said about objective and perceived certainty applies to each pair of primary and contingent properties (e.g., objective celerity and perceived celerity).

[6]The argument extends even to public knowledge of the prescribed punishment. Such knowledge undoubtedly depends on the publicity of punishments, but applications of a prescribed punishment cannot be publicized frequently if objective certainty is negligible. However, bear in mind that public knowledge of prescribed punishments is assessed in terms of severity values and not in terms of the proportion of the jurisdictional population that knows the statutory penalty or penalties for the type of crime in question.

tween some properties of punishment and the crime rate is contingent in an interactive sense on other properties of punishment (see Erickson and Gibbs, 1973), it will not be feasible to state preventive propositions so that they can be tested by some multiple- or partial-correlation technique.

Whatever form preventive propositions may take, none of them will amount to a theory. Observe again that the central preventive proposition is only a point of departure in pursuit of a theory. In particular, it is not a *derived* statement, and its derivation would require recognition of deterrence and notions similar to those introduced in Chapter 3 (e.g., normative validation, enculturation). Such notions must somehow be incorporated in premises (axioms, postulates) that imply one or more testable theorems about the relation between properties of punishment and the crime rate. Those theorems will resemble the central proposition, but that central proposition does not even suggest any premises.

As indicated in Chapter 3, there are numerous *possible* ways in which punishment can prevent crimes. A theorist may ignore some possibilities; but a theory of the preventive consequences of punishment is likely to comprise several premises, and the statement of multiple premises will pose formidable problems. However, research on crime and punishment need not be delayed until a preventive theory is formulated. Tests of preventive propositions, such as the present one, can be and should be conducted, for those tests may provide theorists with a rationale for ignoring certain properties of punishment.

The only immediate problem in formulating and testing a preventive proposition stems from recognition that some possibly relevant features of punishment cannot be described in terms of celerity, certainty, or severity. Consider incapacitation in connection with two types of punishment for driving while intoxicated—a fine of $2,000 and a jail sentence of one month. Even if celerity, certainty, and perceived severity are the same for the two punishments, the jail sentence is more incapacitating. Similarly, all manner of punishments may be approximately the same in regard to celerity, certainty, and perceived severity, yet differ with respect to (*inter alia*) normative insulation and stigmatization. There is no systematic way to assess such differences, but research should include an examination of one possibility. Suppose that for *one list* of types of crimes, X, imprisonment is the only prescribed punishment (i.e., there are no alternative substantive punishments), while for another list, Y, fines are the only substantive punishments. In both lists, the presumptive severity of actual punishments would vary from one type of crime to the next, but in the case of list X the presumptive severity of actual punishments (sentences imposed) is likely to vary directly with incapacitation and normative insulation, at least much more than in the case of list Y. So the prediction would be that among list X crimes the relation between crime rates and presumptive severity of punishment is much more inverse, even when all other properties of punishment (e.g., objective certainty) are controlled. If so, the central proposition excludes relevant variables, and it would be necessary to consider measurements of the incapacitating and insulating effects of punishments in addition to their celerity, certainty, and severity.

Exploratory Research toward a Theory of Deterrence

Although a preventive theory of crime and punishment should be the immediate goal, tests of such a theory can and should extend to exploratory research, with the goal being the eventual formulation of a deterrence theory. While exploratory research will not lead directly to a deterrence theory, it could play a crucial role in preliminary steps. Certain lines of exploratory research beyond the test of a preventive theory (or isolated preventive propositions) would require data on contingent properties of punishment (e.g., perceived certainty) and/or the cognitive features of criminal acts. Gathering such data would be a costly undertaking. (Unlike primary properties, relevant data on contingent properties are not published by official agencies.) However, exploratory research would not require data on all contingent properties. Data on just one contingent property of punishment or cognitive feature of crime could provide answers to some questions about deterrence, questions that should be answered before even attempting the formulation of a deterrence theory. For that matter, some lines of exploratory research could be undertaken with no more data than those required for tests of the central preventive propositions. In any case, the lines of work described subsequently are only suggestive, and they are limited to some of the more feasible extensions of research on the central preventive proposition.

The Significance of Exploratory Work on Perception and Cognition.

All versions of the deterrence doctrine suggest that individuals cannot be deterred from an act unless they regard it as criminal and therefore subject to some kind of punishment. So the relation between general cognitive consensus and the crime rates takes on special significance. Specifically, suppose that investigators have computed a measure of general cognitive consensus for a particular type of crime in each of several jurisdictions, with the measure being the proportion of residents who agree with the police in regard to identifying particular instances of that type *as a crime* (i.e., even though the residents may not agree with the police in identification in regard to the type of crime). Now suppose there is virtually no relation (among the jurisdictions) between the measures of general cognitive consensus and the crime rate. That finding would be consistent with a putative assumption in the deterrence doctrine—that identification of a contemplated act as criminal is a necessary condition for deterrence. But it is not even a necessary condition for omission of a criminal act if individuals refrain from the act because of social condemnation or the dictates of their consciences, that is, for reasons independent of the perceived criminality of the act. That consideration is still another basis for not anticipating any relation between general cognitive consensus and the crime rate.

However, suppose there is a substantial inverse relation between general cognitive consensus and the crime rate. To the extent that such an inverse relation is close, doubts are cast on conventional interpretations of the deterrence doctrine. The relation would suggest that respect for the law governs conduct so much that the crime rate depends primarily on knowledge of the law; that is, variation in the crime rate from one jurisdiction to the next reflects greater knowledge of criminal law in some jurisdictions than in others.

The finding in question would not conclusively refute the deterrence doctrine, but the doctrine would have to be reinterpreted so that it would stress the relevance of general cognitive consensus. More specifically, the argument would be that when an individual identifies a contemplated act as criminal, he or she also recognizes the possibility of some kind of punishment and refrains because of that recognition. The crucial question would then be: Does the kind of punishment or the properties of that punishment make any difference? If not, the validity of the deterrence doctrine is clearly jeopardized.

The question could be answered by examining the relation between some type of crime rate and general cognitive consensus in *two universes* of jurisdictions. In the first universe the jurisdictions would be selected in such a way that they would *differ very little* in regard to the presumptive severity of prescribed punishments for the crime, and just the opposite would be true of jurisdictions in the second universe.[7] To the extent that the relation between general cognitive consensus and the rate for the particular type of crime in question is the same in *both* universes, then

---

[7]The same methodology could be and should be employed in treating the other properties of punishment incorporated in the central preventive proposition (i.e., objective celerity, objective certainty, and presumptive severity of actual punishments). So the presumptive severity of prescribed punishments is treated here only to illustrate the method.

conventional interpretations of the deterrence doctrine are dubious. The finding would suggest that even if cognition of criminality entails recognition of punishment, the primary properties of the punishment are irrelevant. That suggestion could have major policy implications, for there would be no reason to suppose that increasing the presumptive severity of prescribed punishments would increase cognitive consensus.

Now consider the opposite finding—that the relation between general cognitive consensus and the crime rate is much more inverse in the second universe, where the jurisdictions differ a great deal in regard to the presumptive severity of punishment for the type of crime in question. The findings would be much more consistent with the deterrence doctrine (or one might say the putative assumptions of the doctrine), for it would indicate that the primary properties of punishment (at least presumptive severity) do make a difference.

Exploratory research should not end with the comparison just described. The deterrence doctrine clearly asserts that individuals are deterred more from one type of crime than from another if the punishment for that type is perceived as more celeritous, certain, and severe. However, such differences are relevant only insofar as individuals distinguish types of crime, which is a matter of *specific* cognitive consensus rather than *general* cognitive consensus. To the extent that individuals perceive punishment as contingent on the type of crime and are deterred much more by some kinds of punishment than others, then among jurisdictions the rate for a *particular type of crime* should be more inversely related to a measure of specific cognitive consensus than to a measure of general cognitive consensus. The same expectation would hold in a comparison of the types of crime in the same jurisdiction, for each type of crime has two consensus values, specific cognition and general cognition.

Suppose that research findings are not consistent with any of the putative assumptions about the importance of specific cognitive consensus. That outcome would not justify the argument that perceptions of the celerity, certainty, and severity of punishment play no role in deterrence. Instead, the findings would suggest that individuals do not perceive properties of punishment in terms of particular types of crime. The idea is not that individuals are oblivious to types of crimes or totally unaware of different punishments for different types of crimes. Nonetheless, their judgments with regard to properties of punishment for a particular type of crime could reflect an unwitting "diffuse" perception of the punishment of crimes *in general*. So the perception of the celerity, certainty, and severity of the punishment for, say, robbery would be much greater in one jurisdiction than in another largely because the residents of that jurisdiction view the punishment of crimes in general as more celeritous, certain, and severe than do the residents of the other jurisdiction.

With that possibility in mind, exploratory research should examine the relation among jurisdictions between *general* properties of punishment (e.g., average objective certainty for all types of crimes) and the rate for particular types of crimes. If the relation is much more inverse than the relation between *specific* properties of punishment (e.g., objective certainty of imprisonment for robbery) and the rate for a particular type of crime (e.g., robbery), then any deterrence theory will have to incorporate *general* properties of punishment as principal variables. However, the specific properties of punishment would remain relevant in contemplating two kinds of comparisons: (1) a comparison of the rate for a particular type of crime among jurisdictions and (2) a comparison of the rates of different types of crimes in the same jurisdiction. The relation between specific properties of punishment and corresponding crime rates should be much more inverse in the second comparison, for in that comparison the general properties of punishment are constant from one type of crime to the next. The findings of one investigation (Erickson and Gibbs, 1974b) indicate that the relation between crime rates and primary properties of punishment is much closer among types of crimes in the same jurisdiction than among different jurisdictions.

Since the specific-general distinction applies both to primary properties of punishment and to contingent properties of punishment, the foregoing suggested lines of exploratory research can take two directions. Exploratory research on the contingent properties would be more desirable if only because those properties have received little attention in deterrence research. However, some light can be thrown on the significance of the specific-general distinction without gathering more data than are needed to test the central preventive proposition. Thus, to illustrate, if the general objective certainty of imprisonment (average for all types of crimes) is more inversely related to the robbery rate than is the specific objective certainty of imprisonment for robbery, theorists would be ill-advised to ignore diffuse perceptions of punishment in formulating a deterrence theory. The one study of the subject (Erickson and Gibbs, 1974a) indicates that the idea of diffuse perceptions of punishment could be important, but an isolated set of findings is not sufficient for a radical new direction in attempts to formulate a deterrence theory.

On the Relation between Primary and Contingent Properties

Though it is strategic, the simplest extension of research on the preventive proposition would be the inclusion of at least one contingent property of punishment. When that is feasible, two questions become crucial. First, what is the relation between the contingent property and the crime rate? Second, what is the relation between the contingent property and the corresponding primary property? To illustrate, suppose there is no relation between the perceived certainty of punishment and the crime rate. If so, it would be difficult for a theorist to include the certainty of punishment as a principal variable in a deterrence theory. However, the objective certainty of punishment could be inversely related to the crime rate even though there is no relation between the rate and the perceived certainty of punishment; but that would only serve to justify ignoring deterrence in formulating a preventive theory. Then suppose that just the reverse is true; that is, perceived certainty but not objective certainty is inversely related to the crime rate. A deterrence theory would still be feasible, but it would differ radically from all versions of the deterrence doctrine by virtue of having excluded any reference to the primary properties of punishment. Indeed, the theory would be paradoxical, for it would assert that the fear of punishment does deter crime even though it does so in a manner that is independent of prescribed or actual punishments.

The last possibility would have major implications for penal policy. If no primary property of punishment is even fairly closely related to the corresponding contingent property, it does not mean that legislators accomplish nothing by prescribing punishments. But it would mean that legislators must rely on preventive mechanisms other than deterrence. Once legislators abandon the notion of deterrence, they are likely to invoke incapacitation as the rationale for long prison sentences, if only because the notion of incapacitation is more comprehensible than other notions pertaining to preventive mechanisms (e.g., normative validation). Yet legislative enthusiasm for incapacitation may well be short-lived after it is realized that crime prevention through incapacitation is probably the most costly of all strategies.

Prospective Complexities

Findings from exploratory research will not lead automatically to a deterrence theory, but they could cast doubts on the feasibility of even attempting a theory. Even if the findings appear to substantiate the putative assumptions of the deterrence doctrine, the exact wording of the component statements of a deterrence theory is another matter. Judgments about wording will be a major difficulty, especially since all of the relevant principal variables cannot be thought of as linked in a simple causal chain.

All previous observations on exploratory research have ignored two very real possibilities: first, the findings may well be quite different for some types of crime; and, second, the findings are not likely to be approximately uniform in all jurisdictions. In either case, the strategy of theory formulation would have to be altered radically.

Suppose that (1) only in the case of robbery is there any relation between the perceived certainty of punishment and the crime rate, (2) only in the case of fraud is there a close inverse relationship between general cognitive consensus and the crime rate, and (3) only in the case of burglary is there no relation between public knowledge of punishment and the crime rate. It would be extremely difficult to formulate a deterrence theory so that it accounted for such divergent relations. To be sure, the ultimate goal is *one* deterrence theory, but for practical reasons alone the more immediate goal may have to be a series of "special" theories, each restricted to a particular type of crime.

The situation would be even more complicated if exploratory research findings differ markedly among jurisdictions. To illustrate, suppose that among British metropolitan areas there is a fairly close inverse relation between the perceived certainty of punishment for robbery and the robbery rate, but the relation does not hold among metropolitan areas of California. Now suppose that such divergent relations are not rare, that is, no relation between any property of punishment and the crime rate is even approximately uniform from one universe of jurisdictions to the next. Such findings would discourage attempts to formulate a deterrence theory (even for particular types of crimes) without identifying and controlling for extralegal conditions.

The prospect in question is not just a remote possibility, for it is difficult to believe that the relation between any property of punishment and crime rate is not contingent on sociocultural conditions. That contingent quality has received virtually no systematic attention; but once extensive exploratory research is undertaken, it may become obvious that a defensible deterrence theory cannot be formulated without qualifying it, that is, without stipulating something about sociocultural conditions.

Up to this point it has been tacitly assumed that exploratory research will find at least one relation between properties of punishment and crime rates that is fairly consistent with the putative assumptions of the deterrence doctrine. However, the findings may appear to refute the doctrine at all points. If so, conventional interpretations of the doctrine and strategies for bringing evidence to bear on it will have to be abandoned entirely.

All versions of the deterrence doctrine make some assumptions about *public* perception of punishments, and the conventional crime rate is based on the total population. But in some populations a small number of individuals may account for most crimes (especially for certain types of crime). Such individuals are variously described as career, professional, or hard-core criminals. The argument is not that career criminals are insensitive to the threat of punishment; indeed, they may be more sensitive than is the public at large. However, when data on the contingent properties of punishment pertain to a random sample of the total population, career criminals may be excluded entirely, and even if included their statements might not be given special weight. For that matter, the activities of career criminals are not adequately reflected by the conventional crime rate (e.g., the conventional robbery rate for a metropolitan area may be relatively low even though the repetitive rate is relatively high). So even if deterrence research is extended to the contingent properties of punishment, the data can be inadequate because they are not restricted to the truly *relevant* division of each population (career criminals).

The idea of focusing deterrence research on career criminals rests on two questionable presuppositions: (1) that the vast majority of the citizenry conform to *all* laws and (2) that such conformity has nothing to do with the threat of punishment. Moreover, even granting that deterrence research should be refocused, it is difficult to imagine a criterion for identifying a career criminal that would not be arbitrary, and identifying career criminals is one thing but securing their disinterested cooperation in surveys of self-reported crimes is quite another.

The only viable alternative is to abandon conventional crime rates and attempt to compute categorical rates (the proportion of the population that has committed a type of crime at least once) on the basis of self-reported crimes. Categorical rates would be more consistent with data on the contingent properties of punishment that pertain to the total population, for categorical rates are less influenced by career criminals than are conventional crime rates (which also reflect repetitive and recidival rates). However, since an attempt to restrict deterrence research to categorical crime rates would be a radical departure and would pose major practical problems, the decision should be postponed until more exploratory research with conventional rates has been attempted.

The Amorphous Character of the Strategy

The suggested lines of exploratory research do not constitute a truly systematic program for arriving at a deterrence theory, and the argument is that a systematic program would not be feasible. For one thing, the immediate concern should be tests of the central preventive proposition, and the findings that are particularly strategic in contemplating a deterrence theory would stem from ancillary research in the course of those tests. Tests of the preventive proposition are far less difficult to interpret than any purported test of the deterrence doctrine, and research to that immediate end is the most feasible way to pursue a deterrence theory.

The danger with the alternative—a direct and immediate pursuit of a deterrence theory—is that theorists will fail prematurely or become immobilized in a swamp of imponderables. Of course, in order to answer all empirical questions that need to be answered before formulating a deterrence theory, it would be desirable to plan a series of research projects, with the design of each project contingent on the conclusion reached in the previous one. But the empirical questions cannot be arranged in a neat sequence, and it is most unlikely that any of them can be answered conclusively by one research project alone, if only because the findings of one project cannot be generalized readily with regard to all types of crimes and all jurisdictions. No less important, limited resources preclude the planning and execution of numerous research projects in some prearranged sequence. So the long and short of the matter is that social scientists must grope in an unorganized way toward a deterrence theory, with strategic findings coming only in a piecemeal fashion (if at all).

Investigators will be able to consider only certain types of crimes, punishments, and jurisdictions; but each type could be significant in light of the notions introduced in preceding chapters. Thus, to illustrate, imprisonment is significant because of its possible incapacitating effect, while criminal homicide is significant because the rate may scarcely be influenced by the incapacitating effects of imprisonment. Finally, the choice of jurisdictions for comparison and the analysis of deviant cases could further the identification of sociocultural conditions that generate or inhibit criminal acts. Such concerns are strategic in the pursuit of both a deterrence theory and a theory of the preventative consequences of punishment, but they cannot be directed by any systematic plan. All that investigators can do is select jurisdictions that differ sharply with regard to sociocultural conditions (e.g., urbanization, unemployment) and pay particular attention to deviant cases (jurisdictions that have much higher crime rates than those predicted from properties of punishment).

Prospects for Work on Specific Deterrence

Exploratory research along the line just described would differ in several respects from past studies of the deterrence question. However, jurisdictions would continue to be the basic units of comparison, and for that reason alone the concern would continue to be with general deterrence. When it comes to specific deterrence, an even more radical departure from convention is needed.

There is virtually no systematic evidence to support the deterrence doctrine when it is extended to include an assertion about the effects of punishment on those punished. To be sure, none of the purported tests of the assertion have even recognized the *absolute* specific deterrent efficacy of punishment. As observed in Chapter 5, virtually all research has been limited to a comparison of official recidival rates of groups that have been subject to different types of punishment (e.g., imprisonment versus probation). As such, the findings are at best indicative of the *marginal* specific deterrent efficacy of particular punishments, but it would be a mistake of the first order to presume that research on absolute efficacy can be conducted without abandoning conventional methods entirely. There is no alternative to a comparison of *repetitive* rates and *recidival* rates for the same type of crime, which is to say a comparison of the relative number of criminal acts in two divisions of the members of a jurisdictional population: (1) individuals who have committed the act at least once without being punished and (2) individuals who have been punished for the act. Data on self-reported crimes must be used in that comparison because not even arrest or conviction records can be used as the basis for estimating the incidence of crimes among those who have never been apprehended.

Of course, it could be maintained that official recidival data are satisfactory for assessing the marginal specific deterrent efficacy of particular punishments, even though they throw no light on absolute efficacy. The strategy has been employed frequently in the past, but it is questionable on at least two counts. First, as indicated in Chapter 2, the relation between rearrest, reconviction, or reincarceration rates and true recidival rates is most debatable. Second, as indicated in Chapter 5, there is so much selectivity in sentences received and imposed for the same type of crime that one can scarcely attribute contrasts in the recidival rates to types of punishment.

Observe that the first objection might be somewhat blunted by the use of self-reported crimes to compute recidival rates, but those data would in no way solve the problem of selectivity in the imposition of punishments (e.g., individuals with previous conviction records are likely to receive and serve more severe sentences). The problem of selectivity in punishment could be eliminated if it were possible to impose different sentences for the same type of crime on a purely random basis.[8] For ex-

---

[8]The alternative is, of course, a statistical control (e.g., partial correlation) of all relevant prepunishment variables (e.g., number of previous convictions) or a "matching" of

ample, of all the individuals convicted of the same type of theft in a jurisdiction, some would be fined, others imprisoned, and still others placed
on probation, with the sentence in each case determined by chance. But
no imagination is required to anticipate the issues that "random punishments" would raise. It would fairly reek with injustice, and no magistrate
is likely to cooperate unless the alternative punishments are all mild and
the type of crime does not inflame public opinion. Even so, the recidival
rates would be most questionable if based on official data (e.g., records
of arrest after punishment); but the alternative, data on self-reported
crimes after punishment, poses practical problems and is questionable
apart from feasibility.

So it appears that attempts to assess assertions about punishment
and specific deterrence have reached an impasse. Until a new research
strategy (a comparative methodology) is developed, further debate on
the subject is pointless. The development of a research strategy will not
be a purely technical matter divorced from theory, and it should be recognized that currently there is no "theory" of specific deterrence. The
specific deterrence argument is vague, and virtually all purported tests
of it have considered only the severity of punishment. Yet there is no
basis whatever for assuming that other properties of punishment are irrelevant. Considering just one property for illustrative purposes, it is difficult to imagine the impact of punishment on those punished as not
being contingent on perceived certainty (both before and after punishment). However, the role that each of the various properties of punishment plays in specific deterrence has never been stipulated systematically.
But no amount of concern with properties of punishment will solve the
problems that are inherent in the use of official recidival rates and in
the selectivity of sentences imposed for the same type of crime. Until a
methodology is developed to deal with those problems, further research,
even with regard to the eventual formulation of a theory of specific deterrence, is not advisable.

There are at least two conspicuous possibilities for new strategies in
research on specific deterrence. One of them is radical alteration of the
conventional designs in social psychology for experimental research on
the relation between punishment and conformity. The aim should be

subjects with regard to those variables (see Kraus, 1974). Either strategy is disputable because (1) some relevant variables may go unrecognized and/or (2) the statistical techniques
employed may not detect interaction effects. Stating the matter more generally, the variety
of variables that could condition the outcome of punishment or any correctional measure
is so vast and complicated that only a randomization methodology will be satisfactory (see
Bailey, 1971; Davis, 1964; Glaser, 1971; Hood, 1971; Kassebaum et al., 1971; Levin, 1971;
Logan, 1972a; Uusitalo, 1972; Wilkins, 1969; and Zeisel, 1969).

the creation of experimental situations that (1) permit control of properties of punishment and (2) resemble penal systems much more than do
conventional designs for experimental work on punishment. The creation of such situations will be a costly, time-consuming endeavor; and the
ethical or legal limit on the severity of punishments will make generalizations hazardous. However, some complexities and problems can be
avoided by limiting experimental work to specific deterrence.

The other possibility lies in more elaborate field studies of traffic
violations, speeding in particular. The major advantage would be that
investigators could compute violation rates by direct but unobtrusive observations, that is, in a manner independent of official violation rates.
Those observations could include the compilation of driving records for
particular drivers on particular roads, with violations before and after
punishment distinguished. In brief, field studies of traffic violations
would permit the computation of categorical, repetitive, and recidival
rates for special groups of drivers (distinguished by place of residence
and/or routes regularly traveled). While such field studies could throw
light on questions about absolute and restrictive deterrence, they would
be the most advantageous in contemplating specific deterrence. That is
the case because magistrates are much more likely to be willing to random-
ize punishments for traffic offenses than for felonies (see Mecham,
1968), and such randomization is essential in order to overcome the
problem of selectivity in sentences imposed. Of course, the field studies
would treat a very limited range of phenomena; but defensible conclusions, however limited, are better than the inconclusive, disputable character of past research on specific deterrence.

Summary and Conclusions

It would be questionable to call for more conventional research on
the deterrence question. A sophisticated theory will not be realized
without exploratory research to answer several empirical questions
about the relation between properties of punishment and crime rates,
but the research and the interpretation of findings will have to be quite
different from those in the past.

Past studies of crime rates and the deterrence question were limited
to three properties of punishment: (1) presumptive severity of prescribed punishments, the death penalty in particular; (2) objective
certainty of punishment, imprisonment in particular; and (3) the
presumptive severity of actual punishments, length of prison sentences
in particular. Deterrence research cannot be strategic until it is extended
to include public knowledge of punishments, cognition of criminal acts,

perceived certainty of punishment, perceived severity of actual punishments, objective celerity of punishments, perceived celerity of punishments, and perceived severity of prescribed punishments. Yet consideration of those additional variables is at most only a necessary condition for more conclusive results in deterrence research. Truly strategic findings cannot be realized without recognition that the relation between crime rates and properties of punishment may reflect preventive consequences of punishment other than deterrence (e.g., incapacitation). Attempts to take those other consequences into account can be postponed but only insofar as investigators are content to test a theory about the preventive consequences of punishment in general, meaning a theory that is more inclusive than the deterrence doctrine. But even tests of a preventive theory cannot be interpreted readily without identifying and controlling for extralegal conditions that inhibit criminality (one possibility being social condemnation) or generate crimes (one possibility being unemployment). Speculation about those conditions is not sheer conjecture, but criminological theory does not identify them in a defensible way (see Radzinowicz and Wolfgang, 1971I).

Whatever strategy is eventually adopted to take into account extralegal conditions and preventive consequences of punishment other than deterrence, defensible tests of the deterrence doctrine are precluded until that doctrine is stated as a systematic theory. Such a statement is not feasible without extensive exploratory research and the assessment of alternative methods. The methodological problems are not limited to numerical representations of properties of punishment; additionally, special crime rates are needed because there is every reason to believe that conventional crime rates are unsatisfactory for deterrence research.

For reasons just suggested, there is no immediate prospect of deterrence research having an impact on penal policy. All social scientists can do at present is emphasize the difficulties in assessing evidence for or against the deterrence doctrine. Legislators undoubtedly want more than a litany of difficulties, but the only alternative to recognizing the difficulties is a penal policy based on comfortable ignorance or a concealed yearning for retribution.

REFERENCES

Action, H. B., ed. 1969. *The Philosophy of Punishment* (London: Macmillan).

Adams, Reed and Harold J. Vetter. 1971. "Probation Caseload Size and Recidivism Rate," *British Journal of Criminology,* 11 (October) 390–393.

Alexander, Franz and Hugo Staub. 1956. *The Criminal, the Judge, and the Public* (New York: Free Press).

Allen, Francis A. 1964. *The Borderland of Criminal Justice* (Chicago: University of Chicago Press).

Ancel, Marc. 1965. *Social Defense: A Modern Approach to Criminal Problems* (New York: Schocken Books).

Andenaes, Johannes. 1952. "General Prevention—Illusion or Reality?" *Journal of Criminal Law, Criminology and Police Science,* 43 (July–August) 176–198.

Andenaes, Johannes. 1956. "Determinism and Criminal Law," *Journal of Criminal Law, Criminology and Police Science,* 47 (November–December) 406–413.

Andenaes, Johannes. 1966. "The General Preventive Effects of Punishment," *University of Pennsylvania Law Review,* 114 (May) 949–983.

Andenaes, Johannes. 1968. "Does Punishment Deter Crime?" *Criminal Law Quarterly,* 11(November)76–93.

Andenaes, Johannes. 1970. "The Morality of Deterrence," *University of Chicago Law Review,* 37(Summer)649–664.

Andenaes, Johannes. 1971. "The Moral or Educative Influence of Criminal Law," *Journal of Social Issues,* 27(2)17–31.

Antunes, George and A. Lee Hunt. 1973. "The Impact of Certainty and Severity of Punishment on Levels of Crime in American States: An Extended Analysis," *Journal of Criminal Law and Criminology,* 64(December)486–493.

Appel, James B. and Neil J. Peterson. 1965. "What's Wrong with Punishment?" *Journal of Criminal Law, Criminology and Police Science,* 56(December)450–453.

Armstrong, K. G. 1971. "The Retributivist Hits Back," in Grupp, 1971:19–40.

Baier, Kurt. 1972. "Is Punishment Retributive," in Ezorsky, 1972a:16–24.

Bailey, Walter C. 1971. "Correctional Outcome: An Evaluation of 100 Reports," in Radzinowicz and Wolfgang, 1971III:187–195.

Bailey, William C. and Ronald W. Smith. 1972. "Punishment: Its Severity and Certainty," *Journal of Criminal Law, Criminology and Police Science,* 63(December)530–539.

Bailey, William C. et al. 1974. "Crime and Deterrence: A Correlational Analysis." *Journal of Research in Crime and Delinquency,* 11(July)124–143.

Balbus, Isaac D. 1973. *The Dialectics of Legal Repression: Black Rebels before the American Criminal Courts* (New York: Russell Sage Foundation).

Ball, John C. 1955. "The Deterrence Concept in Criminology and Law," *Journal of Criminal Law, Criminology and Police Science,* 46(September–October)347–354.

Bandura, Albert. 1969. *Principles of Behavior Modification* (New York: Holt, Rinehart and Winston).

Barnes, Harry E. and Negley K. Teeters. 1959. *New Horizons in Criminology* (Englewood Cliffs, N.J.: Prentice–Hall).

Beattie, Ronald H. 1960. "Criminal Statistics in the United States—1960," *Journal of Criminal Law, Criminolgy and Police Science*, 51(May–June)49–65.

Beccaria, Cesare. 1963. *On Crimes and Punishments* (Indianapolis, Ind.:Bobbs-Merrill).

Bedau, Hugo A., ed. 1967. *The Death Penalty in America: An Anthology* (Garden City, N.Y.: Anchor Books).

X Bedau, Hugo A. 1970. "Deterrence and the Death Penalty: A Reconsideration," *Journal of Criminal Law, Criminology and Police Science*, 61(December)539–548.

Bean, Frank D. and Robert G. Cushing. 1971. "Criminal Homicide, Punishment, and Deterrence: Methodological and Substantive Reconsiderations," *Social Science Quarterly*, 52(September)277–289.

Benn, Stanley I. 1973. "Punishment," in Murphy, 1973a:18–34.

Bentham, Jeremy. 1962. *The Works of Jeremy Bentham*, Bowring ed., vol. I(New York:Russell and Russell).

Berkowitz, Leonard and Nigel Walker. 1967. "Laws and Moral Judgments," *Sociometry*, 30(December)410–422.

Berndt, R. M. 1962. *Excess and Restraint* (Chicago: University of Chicago Press).

Beutel, Frederick K. 1957. *Some Potentialities of Experimental Jurisprudence as a New Branch of Social Science* (Lincoln, Neb.: University of Nebraska Press).

Biddle, W. Craig. 1969. "A Legislative Study of the Effectiveness of Criminal Penalties," *Crime and Delinquency*, 15(July)354–358.

Biderman, Albert D. 1967. "Surveys of Population Samples for Estimating Crime Incidence," *Annals of the American Academy of Political and Social Science*, 374(November)16–33.

Bittner, Egon and Anthony M. Platt. 1966. "The Meaning of Punishment," *Issues in Criminology*, 2(Spring)79–99.

Blumberg, Abraham S. 1967. *Criminal Justice* (Chicago: Quadrangle Books).

Bolin, Wesley. 1972. *Arizona Revised Statutes, Title 13: Criminal Code* (Phoenix, Ariz.: State of Arizona, Secretary of State).

Bonger, Willem. 1916. *Criminality and Economic Conditions* (Boston:Little, Brown).

Bonjean, Charles M. and Reece McGee. 1965. "Scholastic Dishonesty among Undergraduates in Differing Systems of Social Control," *Sociology of Education*, 38(Winter)127–137.

Bowers, William J. and Richard G. Salem, 1972. "Severity of Formal Sanctions as a Repressive Response to Deviant Behavior," *Law and Society Review*, 6(February)427–441.

Brooker, Frank. 1972. "The Deterrent Effect of Punishment," *Criminology*, 9(February)469–490.

Bucher, Bradley and O. Ivar Lovaas. 1968. "Use of Aversive Stimulation in Behavior Modification," in Marshall R. Jones, ed., *Miami Symposium on the Prediction of Behavior, 1967: Aversive Stimulation* (Coral Gables, Fla.: University of Miami Press), pp. 77–145.

Caldwell, Robert G. 1944. "The Deterrent Influence of Corporal Punishment upon Prisoners Who Have Been Whipped," *American Sociological Review*, 9(April)171–177.

California Assembly Committee on Criminal Procedure. 1968. *Deterrent Effects of Criminal Sanctions* (Sacramento, Calif.: Assembly of the State of California).

Cameron, Mary Owen. 1964. *The Booster and the Snitch* (New York: Free Press).

Campbell, Byron A. and Russell M. Church. 1969. *Punishment and Aversive Behavior* (New York: Appleton-Century-Crofts).

Campbell, Donald T. and H. Laurence Ross. 1968. "The Connecticut Crackdown on Speeding: Time Series Data in Quasi-experimental Analysis," *Law and Society Review*, 3(August)33–53.

Campbell, Ernest Q. 1964. "The Internalization of Moral Norms," *Sociometry*, 27(December)391–412.

Carter, Robert M. and Leslie T. Wilkins. 1967. "Some Factors in Sentencing Policy," *Journal of Criminal Law, Criminology and Police Science*, 58(December)503–514.

Carter, Robert M. and Leslie T. Wilkins, eds. 1970. *Probation and Parole: Selected Readings* (New York: Wiley).

Chambliss, William J. 1966. "The Deterrent Influence of Punishment," *Crime and Delinquency*, 12(January)70–75.

Chambliss, William J. 1967. "Types of Deviance and the Effectiveness of Legal Sanctions," *Wisconsin Law Review*, 1967(Summer)703–719.

Chiricos, Theodore G. et al. 1972. "Inequalities in the Imposition of a Criminal Label," *Social Problems*, 19(Spring)553–572.

Chiricos, Theodore G. and Gordon P. Waldo. 1970. "Punishment and Crime: An Examination of Some Empirical Evidence," *Social Problems*, 18(Fall)200–217.

Clarke, R. V. G. 1966. "Approved School Boy Absconders and Corporal Punishment," *British Journal of Criminology*, 6(October)364–375.

Claster, Daniel S. 1967. "Comparison of Risk Perception between Delinquents and Non-Delinquents," *Journal of Criminal Law, Criminology and Police Science*, 58(March)80–86.

Clinard, Marshall B. and Richard Quinney. 1973. *Criminal Behavior Systems: A Typology*, 2nd ed. (New York: Holt, Rinehart and Winston).

Cloward, Richard A. and Lloyd E. Ohlin. 1960. *Delinquency and Opportunity: A Theory of Delinquent Gangs* (New York: Free Press).

Cohen, Bernard L. 1970. *Law without Order: Capital Punishment and the Liberals* (New Rochelle, New York: Arlington House).

Cohen, Morris R. 1971. "Moral Aspects of Punishment," in Radzinowicz and Wolfgang:1971II,27–42.

Conklin, John E. 1972. *Robbery and the Criminal Justice System* (Philadelphia: Lippincott).

Conrad, John P. 1965. *Crime and Its Correction* (Berkeley, Calif.: University of California Press).

Cooper, H. H. A. 1973. "Crime Control and the Deterrence Perspective," *Criminology*, 11(August)161–182.

Costner, Herbert L. and Hubert M. Blalock, Jr. 1972. "Scientific Fundamentalism and Scientific Utility: A Reply to Gibbs," *Social Science Quarterly*, 52(March)827–844.

Cramton, Roger C. 1969. "Driver Behavior and Legal Sanctions: A Study of Deterrence," *Michigan Law Review,* 67(January)421–454.
Cressey, Donald. 1962. "Limitations of Treatment," in Johnston et al., 1962: 181–187.
Crowther, Carol. 1969. "Crime, Penalties, and Legislatures," *Annals of the American Academy of Political and Social Science,* 381(January)147–158.
Czajkoski, Eugene H. 1969. "Functional Specialization in Probation and Parole," *Crime and Delinquency,* 15(April)238–246.
Damaska, Mirjan R. 1968a. "Adverse Legal Consequences of Conviction and Their Removal: A Comparative Study, Part I," *Journal of Criminal Law, Criminology and Police Science,* 59(September)347–360.
Damaska, Mirjan R. 1968b. "Adverse Legal Consequences of Conviction and Their Removal: A Comparative Study, Part II," *Journal of Criminal Law, Criminology and Police Science,*59(December)542–568.
Davis, George F. 1964. "A Study of Adult Probation Violation Rates by Means of the Cohort Approach," *Journal of Criminal Law, Criminology and Police Science,* 55(March)70–85.
Davis, Kenneth C. 1969. *Discretionary Justice: A Preliminary Inquiry* (Baton Rouge, La.: Louisiana State University Press).
D'Esposito, Julian C., Jr. 1969. "Sentencing Disparity: Causes and Cures," *Journal of Criminal Law, Criminology and Police Science,* 60(June)182–195.
Devlin, Patrick. 1965. *The Enforcement of Morals* (London: Oxford University Press).
Dikijian, Armine. 1969. "Capital Punishment: A Selected Bibliography," *Crime and Delinquency,* 15(January)162–164.
Doleschal, Eugene. 1969. "The Deterrent Effect of Legal Punishment: A Review of the Literature," *Information Review on Crime and Delinquency,* 1(June)1–16.
Doleschal, Eugene. 1970. "Hidden Crime," *Crime and Delinquency Literature,* 2(October)546–572.
Durkheim, Emile. 1949. *The Division of Labor in Society* (New York: Free Press).
Ehrlich, Isaac. 1972. "The Deterrent Effect of Criminal Law Enforcement," *Journal of Legal Studies.* 1(June)259–276.
Ehrmann, Herbert B. 1952. "The Death Penalty and the Administration of Justice," in Sellin, 1952:73–84.
England, Ralph W. 1957. "What is Responsible for Satisfactory Probation and Postprobation Outcome," *Journal of Criminal Law, Criminology and Police Science,* 47(March–April)667–676.
England, Ralph W. 1962. "A Study of Postprobation Recidivism among Five Hundred Federal Offenders," in Johnston et al., 1962:239–246.
Ennis, Philip H. 1967. *Criminal Victimization in the United States: A Report of a National Survey* (Chicago: National Opinion Research Center, University of Chicago).
Erickson, Maynard L. and Jack P. Gibbs. 1973. "Deterrence Questions: Some Alternative Methods of Analysis," *Social Science Quarterly,* 54(December)534–551.
Erickson, Maynard L. and Jack P. Gibbs. 1974a. "Certainty and Severity of Legal

Punishment: Two Alternative Conceptions," unpublished manuscript.

Erickson, Maynard L. and Jack P. Gibbs. 1974b. "Another Strategy in Deterrence Research," unpublished manuscript.

Erickson, Maynard L. 1972. "The Changing Relationship between Official and Self-Reported Measures of Delinquency: An Exploratory-Predictive Study," *Journal of Criminal Law, Criminology and Police Science*, 63(September)388–395.

European Committee on Crime Problems. 1967. *The Effectiveness of Punishment and Other Measures of Treatment* (Strasbourg: Council of Europe).

Ewing, Alfred C. 1929. *Morality of Punishment* (London: Routledge).

Eysenck, H. J. 1964. *Crime and Personality* (Boston: Houghton Mifflin).

Ezorsky, Gertrude, ed. 1972a. *Philosophical Perspectives on Punishment* (Albany, N.Y.: State University of New York Press).

Ezorsky, Gertrude. 1972b. "The Ethics of Punishment," in Ezorsky, 1972a:xi–xxvii.

Federal Bureau of Investigation. 1969. *Uniform Crime Reports, 1968* (Washington, D.C.: Department of Justice).

Federal Bureau of Investigation. 1972. *Uniform Crime Reports, 1971* (Washington, D.C.: Department of Justice).

Feest, Johannes. 1968. "Compliance with Legal Regulations: Observations of Stop Sign Behavior," *Law and Society Review*, 2(May)447–461.

Feinberg, Joel. 1972. "The Expressive Function of Punishment," in Ezorsky, 1972a: 25–34.

Ferracuti, Franco et al. 1962. "A Study of Police Errors in Crime Classification," *Journal of Criminal Law, Criminology and Police Science*, 53(March)113–119.

Fleisher, Belton M. 1966. *The Economics of Delinquency*, (Chicago: Quadrangle Books).

Forslund, Morris A. 1970. "A Comparison of Negro and White Crime Rates," *Journal of Criminal Law, Criminology and Police Science*, 61(June)214–217.

Frankel, Marvin E. 1972. *Criminal Sentences* (New York: Hill and Wang).

Friday, Paul C. and David M. Petersen. 1973. "Shock of Imprisonment: Short-term Incarceration as a Treatment Technique," *International Journal of Criminology and Penology*, 1(November)319–326.

Fuller, Lon L. 1964. *The Morality of Law* (New Haven, Conn.: Yale University Press).

Gerber, Rudolph J. and Patrick D. McAnany, eds. 1972. *Contemporary Punishment: Views, Explanations, and Justifications* (Notre Dame, Ind.: University of Notre Dame Press).

Gerstein, Robert S. 1970. "The Practice of Fidelity to Law," *Law and Society Review*, 4(May)479–493.

Gibbons, Don C. 1965. *Changing the Law Breaker* (Englewood Cliffs, N.J.: Prentice-Hall).

Gibbs, Carole. 1971. "The Effect of the Imprisonment of Women upon Their Children," *British Journal of Criminology*, 11(April)113–130.

Gibbs, Jack P. 1968. "Crime, Punishment, and Deterrence," *Social Science Quarterly*, 48(March)515–530.

Gibbs, Jack P. 1972a. "Causation and Theory Construction," *Social Science Quarterly*, 52(March)815–826.

Gibbs, Jack P. 1972b. "A Fundamentalistic Rejoinder," *Social Science Quarterly*, 52(March)845–851.

Gibbs, Jack P. 1972c. "Issues in Defining Deviant Behavior," in Robert A. Scott and Jack D. Douglas, eds., *Theoretical Perspectives on Deviance* (New York: Basic Books) pp. 39–68.

Glaser, Daniel. 1964. *The Effectiveness of a Prison and Parole System* (Indianapolis, Indiana: Bobbs-Merrill).

Glaser, Daniel. 1971. "Correctional Research: An Elusive Paradise," in Radzinowicz and Wolfgang, 1971III:182–187.

Glass, Gene V. 1968. "Analysis of Data on the Connecticut Speeding Crackdown as a Time-Series Quasi-experiment," *Law and Society Review*, 3(August)55–76.

Gould, Leroy C. 1969. "Who Defines Delinquency: A Comparison of Self-Reported and Officially-Reported Indices of Delinquency for Three Racial Groups," *Social Problems*, 16(Winter)325–336.

Gould, Leroy C. and Zvi Namenwirth. 1971. "Contrary Objectives: Crime Control and Rehabilitation of Criminals," in Jack D. Douglas, ed., *Crime and Justice in American Society* (Indianapolis, Ind.: Bobbs-Merrill) pp.237–267.

Graves, William F. 1967. "The Deterrent Effect of Capital Punishment in California," in Bedau, 1967:322–332.

Gray, Louis N. and J. David Martin. 1969. "Punishment and Deterrence: Another Analysis," *Social Science Quarterly*, 50(September)389–395.

Green, Edward. 1961. *Judicial Attitudes in Sentencing* (New York: St. Martin's Press).

Grupp, Stanley E., ed. 1971. *Theories of Punishment* (Bloomington, Ind.: Indiana University Press).

Grupp, Stanley E. and Warren C. Lucas. 1970. "The 'Marihuana Muddle' as Reflected in California Arrest Statistics and Dispositions," *Law and Society Review*, 5(November)251–269.

Hagan, John. 1973. "Labelling and Deviance: A Case Study in the Sociology of the Interesting;" *Social Problems*, 20(Spring)447–458.

Harris, Richard. 1969. *The Fear of Crime* (New York: Praeger).

Hart, H. L. A. 1957. "Murder and the Principles of Punishment: England and the United States," *Northwestern University Law Review*, 52 (September –October) 433–461.

Hart, H. L. A. 1963. *Law, Liberty and Morality* (Stanford, Calif.: Stanford University Press).

Hart, H. L. A. 1968. *Punishment and Responsibility* (Oxford, England: Oxford University Press).

Hauge, Ragnar. 1968. "Institutional Dilemmas in Probation and Parole," *Scandinavian Studies in Criminology*, 2:41–52.

Hawkins, D. J. B. 1971. "Punishment and Moral Responsibility," in Grupp, 1971:13–18.

Hills, Stuart L. 1971. *Crime, Power, and Morality* (Scranton, Pa.: Chandler)

Hindelang, Michael J. 1974. "Moral Evaluations of Illegal Behaviors," *Social Problems,* 21(Winter)370–385.

Hoebel, E. Adamson. 1954. *The Law of Primitive Man* (Cambridge, Mass.: Harvard University Press).

Honderich, Ted. 1969. *Punishment: The Supposed Justifications* (London: Hutchinson).

Hood, R. G. 1971. "Some Research Results and Problems," in Radzinowicz and Wolfgang, 1971III:159–182.

Hood, Roger. 1962. *Sentencing in Magistrates' Courts* (London: Stevens and Sons).

Hood, Roger and Richard Sparks. 1970. *Key Issues in Criminology* (New York: McGraw-Hill).

Ingraham, Barton L. and Gerald W. Smith. 1972. "The Use of Electronics in the Observation and Control of Human Behavior and Its Possible Use in Rehabilitation and Parole," *Issues in Criminology,* 7(Fall)35–53.

Irwin, John. 1970. *The Felon* (Englewood Cliffs, N.J.: Prentice-Hall).

Jeffery, C. R. 1965. "Criminal Behavior and Learning Theory," *Journal of Criminal Law, Criminology and Police Science,* 56(September)294–300.

Jeffery, C. R. 1971. *Crime Prevention through Environmental Design* (Beverly Hills, Calif.: Sage Publications).

Jensen, Gary F. 1969. " 'Crime Doesn't Pay': Correlates of Shared Misunderstandings," *Social Problems,* 17(Fall)189–201.

Johnston, James M. 1972. "Punishment of Human Behavior," *American Psychologist,* 27(November)1033–1054.

Johnston, Norman et al., eds. 1962. *The Sociology of Punishment and Correction* (New York: Wiley).

Kadish, Sanford H. 1967. "The Crisis of Overcriminalization," *Annals of the American Academy of Political and Social Science,* 374(November)157–170.

Kassebaum, Gene et al. 1971. *Prison Treatment and Parole Survival: An Empirical Assessment* (New York: Wiley).

Kelsen, Hans. 1945. *General Theory of Law and State* (Cambridge, Mass.: Harvard University Press).

Kittrie, Nicholas N. 1971. *The Right to be Different* (Baltimore: The Johns Hopkins University Press).

Knudten, Richard D., ed. 1968. *Criminological Controversies* (New York: Appleton-Century-Crofts).

Kobrin, Solomon et al. 1972. *The Deterrent Effectiveness of Criminal Justice Sanction Strategies* (Los Angeles: Public Systems Research Institute, University of Southern California).

Kraus, J. 1974. "A Comparison of Corrective Effects of Probation and Detention on Male Juvenile Offenders," *British Journal of Criminology,* 14(January)49–62.

LaPiere, Richard T. 1954. *A Theory of Social Control* (New York: McGraw-Hill).

Lefcourt, Robert, ed. 1971. *Law against the People* (New York: Vintage Books).

Lemert, Edwin M. 1967. *Human Deviance, Social Problems, and Social Control* (Englewood Cliffs, N.J.: Prentice-Hall).

Levin, Martin A. 1971. "Policy Evaluation and Recidivism," *Law and Society Review*, 6(August)17–46.

Lewis, C. S. 1971. "The Humanitarian Theory of Punishment," in Radzinowicz and Wolfgang, 1971II:43–48.

Logan, Charles H. 1971. "On Punishment and Crime (Chiricos and Waldo, 1970): Some Methodological Commentary," *Social Problems*, 19(Fall)280–284.

Logan, Charles H. 1972a. "Evaluation Research in Crime and Delinquency: A Reappraisal." *Journal of Criminal Law, Criminology and Police Science*, 63(September)378–387.

Logan, Charles H. 1972b. "General Deterrent Effects of Imprisonment," *Social Forces*, 51(September)64–73.

Lovald, Keith and Holger R. Stub. 1968. "The Revolving Door: Reactions of Chronic Drunkenness Offenders to Court Sanctions," *Journal of Criminal Law, Criminology and Police Science*, 59(December)525–530.

Lunden, Walter A. 1961. *Facts on Crime and Criminals* (Ames, Iowa: Art Press).

Mabbott, J. D. 1972. "Punishment," in Ezorsky, 1972a:165–181.

MacDonald, Arthur. 1910. "Death Penalty and Homicide," *American Journal of Sociology*, 16(July)88–116.

McTaggert, J. E. 1972. "Hegel's Theory of Punishment," in Ezorsky, 1972a:40–55.

Madden, Edward H. et al., eds. 1968. *Philosophical Perspectives on Punishment* (Springfield, Ill.: Charles C Thomas).

Martinson, Robert. 1974. "What Works?—Questions and Answers about Prison Reform," *Public Interest*, 35(Spring)22–54.

Mecham, Garth D. 1968. "Proceed With Caution: Which Penalties Slow Down the Juvenile Traffic Violator?" *Crime and Delinquency*, 14(April)142–150.

Menninger, Karl. 1966. *The Crime of Punishment* (New York: Viking Press).

Menninger, Karl. 1973. "Therapy, Not Punishment," in Murphy, 1973a:132–141.

Merton, Robert K. 1957. *Social Theory and Social Structure* (New York: Free Press).

Middendorff, Wolf. 1968. *The Effectiveness of Punishment, Especially in Relation to Traffic Offenses* (South Hackensack, N.J.: Fred B. Rothman).

Miller, Martin B. 1972. "The Indeterminate Sentence Paradigm: Resocialization or Social Control," *Issues in Criminology*, 7(Fall)101–124.

Miller, Walter B. 1973. "Ideology and Criminal Justice Policy: Some Current Issues," *Journal of Criminal Law and Criminology*, 64(June)141–162.

Mitford, Jessica. 1973. *Kind and Usual Punishment* (New York: Knopf).

Moberly, Walter. 1968. *The Ethics of Punishment* (London: Faber and Faber).

Morris, Norval. 1966. "Impediments to Penal Reform," *University of Chicago Law Review*, 33(Summer)627–656.

Morris, Norval. 1973. *The Habitual Criminal* (Westport, Conn.: Greenwood Press).

Morris, Norval and Gordon Hawkins. 1970. *The Honest Politician's Guide to Crime Control* (Chicago: University of Chicago Press).

Morris, Norval and Frank Zimring. 1969. "Deterrence and Corrections,"*Annals of the American Academy of Political and Social Science*, 381(January) 137–146.

Morris, William N. et al. 1973. "The Effect of Vicarious Punishments on Prosocial Behavior in Children," *Journal of Experimental Child Psychology*, 15(April)222–236.

Murphy, Jeffrie G., ed. 1973a. *Punishment and Rehabilitation* (Belmont, Calif.: Wadsworth).

Murphy, Jeffrie G. 1973b. "Introduction," in Murphy, 1973a:1–12.

Murphy, Jeffrie G. 1973c. "Criminal Punishment and Psychiatric Fallacies," in Murphy, 1973a:197–210.

Neithercutt, M. G. 1969. "Consequences of 'Guilty,'" *Crime and Delinquency*, 15(October)459–462.

Northrop, F. S. C. 1947. *The Logic of the Sciences and the Humanities* (New York: Macmillan).

Orsagh, Thomas. 1973. "Crime, Sanctions and Scientific Explanation," *Journal of Criminal Law and Criminology*, 64(September)354–361.

Orwell, George. 1949. *1984* (New York: Harcourt, Brace).

Osborne, Harold. 1968. "On Crime, Punishment, and Deterrence," *Social Science Quarterly*, 49(June)157–160.

Packer, Herbert L. 1968. *The Limits of the Criminal Sanction* (Stanford, Calif: Stanford University Press).

Pincoffs, Edmund L. 1966. *The Rationale of Legal Punishment* (New York: Humanities Press).

Playfair, Giles and Derrick Sington. 1957. *The Offenders: The Case against Legal Vengeance* (New York: Simon and Schuster).

President's Commission on Law Enforcement and Administration of Justice. 1967. *The Challenge of Crime in a Free Society* (Washington, D.C.: Government Printing Office).

Quinney, Richard. 1970a. *The Problem of Crime* (New York: Dodd, Mead).

Quinney, Richard. 1970b. *The Social Reality of Crime* (Boston: Little, Brown).

Quinney, Richard. 1972. "From Repression to Liberation: Social Theory in a Radical Age," in Robert A. Scott and Jack D. Douglas, eds., *Theoretical Perspectives on Deviance* (New York: Basic Books), pp. 317–341.

Quinney, Richard. 1973. "Crime Control in Capitalist Society," *Issues in Criminology*, 8(Spring)75–99.

Quinton, A. M. 1972. "On Punishment," in Ezorsky, 1972a:6–15.

Radzinowicz, Leon. 1948. *A History of English Criminal Law and Its Administration from 1750,* vol. I (London: Stevens and Sons).

Radzinowicz, Leon and Marvin E. Wolfgang, eds. 1971I. *Crime and Justice,* vol. I, *The Criminal in Society* (New York: Basic Books).

Radzinowicz, Leon and Marvin E. Wolfgang, eds. 1971II. *Crime and Justice,* vol. II, *The Criminal in the Arms of the Law* (New York: Basic Books).

Radzinowicz, Leon and Marvin E. Wolfgang, eds. 1971III. *Crime and Justice,* vol. III, *The Criminal in Confinement* (New York: Basic Books).

Rashdall, Hastings. 1948. *The Theory of Good and Evil,* vol. I (London: Oxford University Press).

Reiss, Albert J., Jr. 1973. "Surveys of Self-reported Delicts," unpublished paper for the Symposium on Studies of Public Experience, Knowledge, and Opinion of Crime and Justice (Washington, D.C., March 17–18, 1972). Revised July, 1973.

Reitzes, Deitrich Ĉ. 1955. "The Effect of Social Environment upon Former Felons," *Journal of Criminal Law, Criminology and Police Science,* 46(July–August) 226–231.

Rettig, Salomon. 1964. "Ethical Risk Sensitivity in Male Prisoners," *British Journal of Criminology,* 4(October)582–590.

Rettig, Salomon and Harvey E. Rawson. 1963. "The Risk Hypothesis in Predictive Judgments of Unethical Behavior," *Journal of Abnormal and Social Psychology,* 66(March)243–248.

Ross, Alf. 1970. "The Campaign against Punishment," *Scandinavian Studies in Law,* 14:109–148.

Ross, H. Laurence. 1973. "Law, Science, and Accidents: The British Road Safety Act of 1967," *Journal of Legal Studies,* 2(January)1–78.

Rottenberg, Simon, ed. 1973. *The Economics of Crime and Punishment* (Washington, D.C.: American Enterprise Institute for Public Policy Research).

Royal Commission on Capital Punishment [1949–1953]. 1953. *Report* (London: Her Majesty's Stationery Office).

Rusche, Georg and Otto Kirchheimer. 1939. *Punishment and Social Structure* (New York: Russell and Russell).

Salem, Richard G. and William J. Bowers. 1970. "Severity of Formal Sanctions as a Deterrent to Deviant Behavior," *Law and Society Review,* 5(August)21–40.

Samuels, Alec. 1970. "The Fine: The Principles," *Criminal Law Review* (May)268–272.

Samuelson, Glenn W. 1969. "Why Was Capital Punishment Restored in Delaware?" *Journal of Criminal Law, Criminology and Police Science,* 60(June)148–151.

Sartorius, Rolf E. 1972. "The Enforcement of Morality," *Yale Law Journal,* 81(April)891–910.

Savitz, Leonard D. 1967. "The Deterrent Effect of Capital Punishment in Philadelphia," in Bedau, 1967:315–322.

Schrag, Clarence. 1971. *Crime and Justice: American Style* (Rockville, Md.: National Institute of Mental Health, Center for Studies of Crime and Delinquency).

Schuessler, Karl F. 1952. "The Deterrent Influence of the Death Penalty," *Annals of the American Academy of Political and Social Science,* 284(November)54–62.

Schur, Edwin M. 1965. *Crimes without Victims: Deviant Behavior and Public Policy* (Englewood Cliffs, N.J.: Prentice-Hall).

Schur, Edwin M. 1969. "Reactions to Deviance: A Critical Assessment," *American Journal of Sociology,* 75(November)309–322.

Schur, Edwin M. 1971. *Labeling Deviant Behavior: Its Sociological Implications* (New York: Harper and Row).

Schwartz, Barry. 1968. "The Effect in Philadelphia of Pennsylvania's Increased Penalties for Rape," *Journal of Criminal Law, Criminology and Police Science,* 59(December)509–515.

Schwartz, Richard D. and Sonya Orleans, 1967. "On Legal Sanctions," *University of Chicago Law Review,* 34(Winter)274–300.

Schwartz, Richard D. and Jerome H. Skolnick. 1962. "Two Studies of Legal Stigma," *Social Problems,* 10(Fall)133–142.

Sellin, Thorsten, ed. 1952. Murder and the Penalty of Death, *Annals of the American Academy of Political and Social Science,* 284(November).

Sellin, Thorsten, ed. 1967a. *Capital Punishment* (New York: Harper and Row.)

Sellin, Thorsten. 1967b. "Experiments with Abolition," in Sellin, 1967a: 122–124.

Sellin, Thorsten. 1967c. "Homicides in Retentionist and Abolitionist States," in Sellin, 1967a:135–138.

Sellin, Thorsten, ed. 1967d. Combating Crime, *Annals of the American Academy of Political and Social Science,* 374(November).

Sellin, Thorsten and Marvin E. Wolfgang. 1964. *The Measurement of Delinquency* (New York: Wiley).

Shapiro, Michael H. 1972. "The Use of Behavior Control Technologies: A Response," *Issues in Criminology,* 7(Fall)55–93.

Shapiro, Michael H. 1973. "Legislating the Control of Behavior Control: Autonomy and the Coercive Use of Organic Therapies," *Southern California Law Review,* 47(November)237–356.

Shoham, S. Giora. 1974. "Punishment and Traffic Offenses," *Traffic Quarterly,* 28(January)61–73.

Silver, Morris. 1974. "Punishment, Deterrence and Police Effectiveness: A Survey and Critical Interpretation of the Present Econometric Literature," unpublished manuscript in the form of a report prepared for the Crime Deterrence and Offender Career Project (135 West 78th Street, New York, N.Y.).

Silverman, Edgar. 1956. "Surveillance, Treatment, and Casework Supervision," *National Probation and Parole Association Journal,* 1(January)22–26.

Singer, Barry F. 1970. "Psychological Studies of Punishment," *California Law Review,* 58(March)405–443.

Sington, Derrick and Giles Playfair. 1965. *Crime, Punishment and Cure* (London: Secker and Warburg).

Skogan, Wesley G. 1974. "The Validity of Official Crime Statistics: An Empirical Investigation," *Social Science Quarterly,* 55(June)25–38.

Solomon Richard L. 1964. "Punishment," *American Psychologist,* 19 (April) 239–253.

Sparks, R. F. 1971. "The Effectiveness of Probation," in Radzinowicz and Wolfgang, 1971III:211–218.

Sudnow, David. 1965. "Normal Crimes: Sociological Features of the Penal Code in a Public Defender Office," *Social Problems,* 12(Winter)255–276.

Sutherland, Edwin H., annotator and interpreter. 1937. *The Professional Thief: By a Professional Thief* (Chicago: University of Chicago Press).

Sutherland, Edwin H. and Donald R. Cressey. 1970. *Criminology* (Philadelphia: J. B. Lippincott).

Szasz, Thomas S. 1963. *Law, Liberty, and Psychiatry* (New York: Macmillan).

Szasz, Thomas S. 1965. *Psychiatric Justice* (New York: Macmillan).

Tapp, June L. 1971. "Reflections," *Journal of Social Issues,* 27(2):1–16.

Tapp, June L. and Lawrence Kohlberg. 1971. "Developing Senses of Law and Legal Justice," *Journal of Social Issues,* 27(2):65–91.

Tappan, Paul W. 1960. *Crime, Justice and Correction* (New York: McGraw-Hill).

Thorsell, Bernard A. and Lloyd M. Klemke. 1972. "The Labeling Process: Reinforcement and Deterrent," *Law and Society Review,* 6(February)393–403.

Tittle, Charles R. 1969. "Crime Rates and Legal Sanctions," *Social Problems,* 16(Spring)408–423.

Tittle, Charles R. 1974. "Prisons and Rehabilitation: The Inevitability of Disfavor," *Social Problems,* 21(Winter)385–395.

Tittle, Charles R. and Charles H. Logan. 1973. "Sanctions and Deviance: Evidence and Remaining Questions," *Law and Society Review,* 7(Spring)371–392.

Tittle, Charles R. and Allan R. Rowe. 1973. "Moral Appeal, Sanction Threat, and Deviance: An Experimental Test," *Social Problems,* 20(Spring)488–498.

Tittle, Charles R. and Allan R. Rowe. 1974. "Certainty of Arrest and Crime Rates: A Further Test of the Deterrence Hypothesis," *Social Forces,* 52(June)455–462.

Toby, Jackson. 1964. "Is Punishment Necessary?" *Journal of Criminal Law, Criminology and Police Science,* 55(September)332–337.

Tornudd, Patrick. 1968. "The Preventive Effect of Fines for Drunkenness," *Scandinavian Studies in Criminology,* 2:109–124.

Toulmin, Stephen. 1960. *The Philosophy of Science* (New York: Harper and Row).

Tullock, Gordon. 1974. "Does Punishment Deter Crime?" *Public Interest,* 36(Summer)103–111.

Turk, Austin T. 1969. *Criminality and Legal Order* (Chicago: Rand McNally).

United Nations. 1968. *Capital Punishment* (New York: United Nations).

Uusitalo, Paavo. 1972. "Recidivism after Release from Closed and Open Penal Institutions," *British Journal of Criminology,* 12(July)211–229.

Van den Haag, Ernest. 1969. "On Deterrence and the Death Penalty," *Journal of Criminal Law, Criminology and Police Science,* 60(June)141–147.

Vold, George B. 1952. "Extent and Trend of Capital Crimes in the United States," *Annals of the American Academy of Political and Social Science,* 284(November)1–7.

Vold, George B. 1958. *Theoretical Criminology* (New York: Oxford University Press).

Waldo, Gordon P. 1970. "The 'Criminality Level' Of Incarcerated Murderers and Non-Murderers," *Journal of Criminal Law, Criminology and Police Science,* 61(March)60–70.

Waldo, Gordon P. and Theodore G. Chiricos. 1972. "Perceived Penal Sanction and Self-reported Criminality: A Neglected Approach to Deterrence Research," *Social Problems,* 19(Spring)522–540.

Walker, Nigel. 1968. *Crime and Punishment in Britain* (Edinburgh: University Press).

Walker, Nigel. 1969. *Sentencing in a Rational Society* (New York: Basic Books).

Walker, Nigel. 1971. "Aims of Punishment," in Radzinowicz and Wolfgang, 1971II:48–65.

Walker, Nigel and Michael Argyle. 1964. "Does the Law Affect Moral Judgments?" *British Journal of Criminology*, 4(October)570–581.

Wallerstein, James S. and Clement J. Wyle. 1947. "Our Law-abiding Law-breakers," *Probation*, 25(March–April)107–112.

Ward, Paul. 1970. "Careers in Crime: The F.B.I. Story," *Journal of Research in Crime and Delinquency*, 7(July)207–218.

Weihofen, Henry. 1956. *The Urge to Punish* (New York: Farrar, Straus, and Cudahy).

Wilkins, Leslie T. 1963. "The Measurement of Crime," *British Journal of Criminology*, 3(April)321–341.

Wilkins, Leslie T. 1969. *Evaluation of Penal Measures* (New York: Random House).

Wilson, James Q. 1974. "Crime and the Criminologists," *Commentary*, 58(July)47–53.

Wolfgang, Marvin E. 1963. "Uniform Crime Reports: A Critical Appraisal," *University of Pennsylvania Law Review*, 111(April)708–738.

Wolfgang, Marvin E. et al. 1972. *Delinquency in a Birth Cohort* (Chicago: University of Chicago Press).

Wootton, Barbara. 1963. *Crime and the Criminal Law* (London: Stevens and Sons).

Zeisel, Hans. 1969. "Methodological Problems in Studies of Sentencing," *Law and Society Review*, 3(May)621–631.

Zimring, Franklin E. and Gordon Hawkins. 1968. "Deterrence and Marginal Groups," *Journal of Research in Crime and Delinquency*, 5(July)100–114.

Zimring, Franklin E. and Gordon Hawkins. 1971. "The Legal Threat as an Instrument of Social Change," *Journal of Social Issues*, 27(2)33–48.

Zimring, Franklin E. and Gordon Hawkins. 1973. *Deterrence: The Legal Threat in Crime Control* (Chicago: University of Chicago Press).

Name Index

Subject Index